DELUSIONS OF NORMALITY

DELUSIONS OF NORMALITY

Sanity, Drugs, Sex, Money and Beliefs in America

BY J.P. HARPIGNIES

Coolgrovepress with Ruthless Reality Institute, Brooklyn, New York

ISBN 10: 1-887276-50-5

ISBN 13: 978-1-887276-50-4

Acknowledgments
My profound thanks to: my publisher, Tej Hazarika, for
his trust and energy; the San Francisco-based international private investigator extraordinaire and different
drummer, Adam Raskin, for his support, generosity and
investigative prowess; my friends Anne Hemenway,
Glenn Macura, Donald Nicholson-Smith, André
Spears, Amelia Amon and Elizabeth Thompson for
their encouragement and help (and for listening to my
rants for all these years); the always brilliant Jeremy
Narby, for serving as the *porte-parole* of the snake goddess of the *selva* and answering a crucial question at a
critical moment; and Barbara Moulton for her valuable
feedback.

— J. P. Harpignies

Printed in the United States of America

Contents:

INTRODUCTION

What do we mean when we say someone or something is normal? My goal in this book is to explore a few central aspects of contemporary life-specifically our: mental health, drug use, sexual behavior, relationship to money, and core beliefs-and to challenge some of the basic assumptions that color how we view these topics. In a nutshell, my hypothesis is that we are collectively far less sane, far more corrupt, and far druggier, kinkier and zanier than we generally assume or admit, and that we should therefore recalibrate our ideas about normality, in these domains at least. I try to marshal sufficient evidence to make this case in the pages ahead.

In all societies, besides formal legal codes, there are, obviously and inevitably, wide-ranging assumptions about behavioral and attitudinal norms. In some cultures and during some historical periods norms can be narrow and strictly enforced; in other times and places they can be far less rigid. They can be constraining in one sphere and fluid in another domain of life-a society may tolerate many forms of religion but not a whiff of political opposition, for example (or vice versa). Norms obviously vary from culture to culture, class to class, region to region, and they change over time, sometimes rapidly, sometimes at a glacial pace. Some norms are virtually universal and constant (e.g. the incest taboo); others are highly culture-specific (e.g. the banning of many artifacts of technology by the Amish).

By and large, Western societies have slowly become more tolerant and fluid since the late Renaissance, with, of course, many notable exceptions (witch burnings, colonialism, slavery, the 3rd Reich, Stalinist Russia...). Recent decades have certainly seen a broadening of attitudes regarding race, gender roles, sexuality, and artistic expression, though even today strong socio-political forces strive to return us to less tolerant and freewheeling customs, and reactive periods invariably follow more Dionysian ones. And clearly history is not at all a linear affair. It would, for example, take a couple of thousand years (till the pre-HIV 1970s) for some moderns to even come close to the level of wild sexual behavior engaged in by some ancient Etruscan and Roman elites. Still, there is no question that by recent historical standards (the last millennium, say), and without at all denying the continued existence of many grievous social injustices and forms of intolerance, this is a fairly tolerant time in terms of social mores in the urban industrialized world at least.

Why then, if we indeed live in a fairly loose, by and large less restrictive era, devote a whole book to analyzing the fallacies surrounding certain current norms? Seeking to expose hypocrisies in the Victorian era, or even the 1950s might perhaps have made some sense, one might argue, but what is there to reveal now in a culture that seems shameless about publicly exposing even its most grotesque features?

The answer is that while we have indeed made strides in tolerance and openness in many areas, we still live with unspoken assumptions and unexamined, or weakly examined, attitudes in a wide range of key spheres of life, and I have long felt driven to scrutinize more closely at least some of them. I have no precise overall prescriptive goal in mind, and I have to admit that I embark upon this project with some ambivalence. I realize that the human condition dictates that every individual, every society, and every subculture inevitably has to operate with a range of unconscious assumptions and implicit norms, and I can't say I'm absolutely sure that digging into everything is invariably a good idea. Just as most individuals seem to require an inflated sense of their own self-worth to carry on without getting demoralized, perhaps societies too require the sanitized, exaggerated, mythologized sense of their virtues they all seem to insist on projecting, and some of the things I am choosing to examine may be disturbing to look at, and probing them may not necessarily help us in any tangible way. After all, the truth is not always productive in personal life or in politics. People who insist on telling the truth at all times are the stuff of silly comedy (or, in real life, are not infrequently murdered or executed).

Nonetheless, one of the most important missions of the social sciences and of cultural analysis (and of art and literature in their own ways) is to seek to present as accurate a picture of societies as possible, warts and all. Whether they ultimately turn out to be productive or subversive should not deter attempts to arrive at more honest appraisals of our psychosocial reality. I have to believe that, ultimately, the more penetrating analyses of a broad gamut of our attitudes and institutions there are, the better. And anyway, in this case I feel drawn to the topic and can't resist the urge to stir up some of these murky waters.

Starting in adolescence I began to get a strong sense that many assumptions made in the "official" media of "reputable" newspapers and TV and radio news and in the discourse I was subjected to in school and in my family were often seriously at odds with what I saw in the streets and in my own and others' psyches and behaviors. Adolescence is of course a period during which we are hyper-sensitized to adult hypocrisy, not realizing till much later that there are at least on occasion excellent reasons for masking the harsh truth, and that, in fact, societies can't run without healthy doses of denial and hypocrisy. Still, while my adolescent rebelliousness inevitably mellowed a bit with age's hormonal decline, and our culture certainly made substantial progress addressing at least some of the most blatant outrages that roiled the social order during my youth, my sense of a chasm between quite a few of our society's implicit norms and the reality of people's lives never faded. In fact it only grew over the decades as life experience, reading, research and travel permitted me to ponder the question with more sophistication.

Let me offer a quick example. Scandals, be they political, financial, sexual, or other, are a common staple of journalism. Many of us become fascinated by the lurid details of these episodes, especially if the people involved are major figures. The problem is that in most of these cases, what is portrayed as an aberration-the breaking of laws or societal codes by individuals-is in fact part of a much deeper, systemic problem. Until just recently, when a famous athlete was caught taking performance-enhancing drugs, for example, the story focused on that individual's fall from grace, but knowledgeable insiders knew full well that a wide range of sports had been almost completely permeated by drug use for decades. This finally came home to roost in baseball in the U.S. and cycling in Europe, and now in international track and field (and even in horse racing) but whether it's football or weightlifting or wrestling or swimming, drug use has long been rampant. In quite a few sports it's the norm, not the exception. This is finally being widely acknowledged because so much incontrovertible evidence emerged, but it was completely obvious for decades.

Even beyond professional sports, the use of substances such as steroids or Human Growth Hormone has long been widespread within specific groups in our society: high school and college athletes, the body building subculture, policemen, actors, performers and entertainers, and well-to-do people trying to slow down the aging process. It long flew under the radar of public awareness, but millions of people around the world continue to take these substances. It's a multi-billion dollar global business. Several notorious instances of serious, violent incidents involving police over-reactions and of other cop misbehavior have been at least partially attributed to "roid rage." Cops in at least 10 U.S. states (as of 2005) had been charged with steroid related offenses (from possession to dealing to murder). In 2007 the largest ever national crackdown on home-made illegal steroid manufacturers (with Chinese-made chemicals as raw ingredients) and sales operations resulted in 124 arrests nationwide, and the seizure of 2.5 million doses in New York City's eastern suburbs on Long Island alone, an area notorious for its "juiced" bodybuilding gyms and high school athlete steroid use. The scope of the operations surprised even drug crime specialists and the authorities. So, clearly, the famous athletes exposed and humiliated for using performance-enhancing drugs are only the small tip of a very big iceberg. The deeper problem is structural: the temptations and rewards are simply too great in a society that places such a premium on celebrity, wealth, athletic prowess and physical appearance, and moral strictures don't carry much weight when none of our other public spheres exhibit a very high standard of ethics either.

Scandals involving spiritual organizations are another case in point. Finally the Catholic Church was exposed and forced to at least timidly begin to address its widespread enabling of pedophilia, but for decades before a critical mass of evidence made further denials impossible, each case of an exposed wayward priest was treated as an isolated incident rather than as a systemic pattern. The same is true when a guru or other spiritual figure is accused of sexual or fiscal shenanigans (or worse, e.g. Jim Jones). The deeper truth is that spiritual authority figures embody for dedicated followers of their respective traditions (quite a few of whom are naïve and vulnerable to begin with) a unique form of numinous power. Abuses are inevitable, and my own study of the question has led me to the conclusion that scandals in spiritual groups are, if not universal, at least exceedingly common.

And anyone who has a modicum of experience in high finance or politics or business involving government contracts at any level in most places will surely appreciate this next point. The implicit assumption in a newspaper article or other journalistic account when corruption or

improper business practices of some kind are exposed is that this is newsworthy because, again, it's an aberration. But (and yes, I'm being flippant to make
a point) rather than headlines reading "Scandal Rocks City Hall" more realistic headlines might rather read "Impeccable, Absolutely Honest Politician
Discovered in Western Samoa" or "Stock Market Free of High-Level,
Routine Insider Trading Found in Outer Hebrides." German leaders purported to be shocked to discover the extent of income tax evasion among
that country's capitalist elites in the recent Lichtenstein banking scandal, but
their claims of surprise elicited widespread snickers and wry smiles-it's a classic example of a completely pervasive behavior among global elites that has
long been common knowledge to all but the most naïve.

Yes, of course some financial scandals are indeed newsworthy if they are
particularly blatant or on a grand scale, as the current, massive global financial panic certainly is, but the fact remains that nearly all of our problems surrounding power and money are not isolated episodes but deeply rooted in
profound, long-standing contradictions about our very complex, uneasy and
usually unexamined attitudes toward wealth and morality. Many aspects of
our relationship to money are deeply uncomfortable, virtually taboo topics
for most of us. They are rarely honestly tackled in either private conversation or in public media. And our legal standards of propriety are wildly irrational: a government figure might be forced to resign for accepting a gift of
tickets to a sporting event or some other bits of "chump change," while
another awards dubious contracts worth billions to CEO golf buddies, who
then hire him (or her) at an insanely high salary a year or two later after he
has left government "service," and that's often perfectly legal if no blatant
"smoking gun" proving bribery beyond the shadow of a doubt emerges. But
what should we expect in a society in which many of our sharpest legal and
accounting minds are handsomely remunerated for devising incredibly convoluted strategies to help the richest among us pay the lowest possible taxes?
Even the current market collapse that has revealed the deep rot and madness
in our global financial architecture seems unlikely to push us into deeper
examinations of our core relationship to money.

It's not as though a lot of this isn't common knowledge. Occasional articles and other exposés discuss a number of the main points I will touch upon
in this book, and there are still quite a few good investigative journalists and
serious researchers around, so penetrating socio-political and cultural analyses of many aspects of contemporary life certainly are published and broad-

cast, but of course they usually don't get an iota of the attention that the juicy scandals and celebrity dramas do. The fascination with anecdotes and personalities continuously overshadows sustained looks at deeper social patterns, though this is obviously deeply ingrained in human beings' perennial attraction to exciting stories about larger-than-life figures, so nothing new. When scandals seize the public imagination, the media shine a spotlight on the misbehavior in question, be it sexual or financial or other, and some public discussions about how widespread these behaviors might be invariably ensue. In fact, at the very moment I was working on the chapter on sex in this text the governor of my state was forced to resign for consorting with prostitutes, and his successor confessed to past infidelity and drug use within weeks. And then, just as I was putting the finishing touches on this book, the world's financial markets began to swoon en masse and the deep rot on Wall Street was on all lips. But after the dust settles, we seem, each time, no matter how common and routine or dramatic these incidents are, to collectively drift back to our previous sets of assumptions about how rare and aberrant the behavior is. It's akin to someone who refuses to believe he falls asleep frequently because every time it's pointed out to him, he wakes up for a few moments to deny having been asleep.

While we may seem at first blush to be living in a fairly transparent society with few secrets, the truth is far more nuanced. Quite a few aspects of modern life are surprisingly opaque and understudied. In those domains that have been intelligently studied in some depth, revelatory information is indeed available, if we make a concerted effort to seek it out, but it barely penetrates into collective awareness compared to the flood of superficial narratives and unspoken suppositions we swim in daily, an incessant bath in insidious illusions even the most astute among us are bound to be unconsciously affected by.

As a lifelong New Yorker, The New York Times, the most respected and influential newspaper in the U.S., has encapsulated for me throughout my life the norms of America's urban elites and well-heeled intelligentsia. It embodies their unspoken assumptions in both its content and its tone (which have of course shifted as social mores have evolved-in my youth, in a notorious incident, the paper wouldn't even accept an ad for an off-Broadway play that had the word "whore' in its title), so it provides an ideal lens in that regard. I also have to admit that the Times is an invaluable news resource, one that I consult frequently and cite often in the notes in this book because the

facts presented in many of its articles consistently offer evidence that undermines the paper's overseers' underlying presuppositions. I became fascinated
with exploring to what extent the archetypal, assumed readers of the nation's
"journal of record" measured up to its actual flesh and blood readers (and to
the larger population described in its pages). This work is in many ways a
result of decades of my daily, internal running monologues of annoyed
responses to many of the unspoken suppositions embedded between the
lines in "All the news that's fit to print." I understand that the norms
expressed in the Times are not invariably those of a majority of Americans,
but I believe that the core values and cultural assumptions of our educated
elites are the ones that are most politically consequential in the long term,
and for that reason it is those I am especially interested in examining and
challenging.

It is obviously impossible to begin to do justice to even a tiny fragment
of a society's norms. It's an immensely vast topic. There are norms and unexamined attitudes in every nook and cranny of life, from foreign policy to religion to sports to hygiene. Assumptions even vary within one newspaper
depending on which section one is reading (or nowadays which website or
cable news channel one is scanning). The business pages tend to be far more
brutally honest about how savvy investors profit when workers are paid less
and have fewer rights or when corporations can set up shop where environmental monitoring is feeble, for example, because it is assumed only investors
are reading those articles. Our still largely unconscious attitudes about race,
class, gender and American exceptionalism are some of the most important,
thorny domains it would behoove many of us to probe into far more deeply
than we normally do, but I leave those weighty topics to more credentialed
analysts, and there are plenty doing good work on these topics. I have instead
chosen to look at a few more shadowy, less frequently deeply probed areas.

This book is mostly focused on data from the U.S. because that is the
society I live in and know best, and some of the social phenomena I explore
are uniquely American, but I suspect a number of my overarching points
should also be at least partially relevant to other industrialized societies. My
goals are fairly modest. This is merely an exploratory exercise, an attempt to
tentatively shed a little more light on a few zones of our lives and psyches
that I think most of us don't normally look at dispassionately enough. I make
absolutely no pretense to being systematic or exhaustive, and I am not (for
the most part) attempting the Herculean task of delving into the root caus-

es of the social realities I describe or offering cures for our problems. This text only seeks to help us arrive at a somewhat more realistic, less idealized collective self-image in a few very visceral domains of our existence. As I said, I don't know if this effort will be invariably helpful, but I can't help but feel that an honest quest for a more accurate picture of our psyches and lives is likely to have at least a little bit of a salutary effect.

We live in an age in which rapidly evolving electronic media and global capital flows have contributed to fragmenting the cultural commons and speeding up the pace of communication (and of life) so that even when a serious, revelatory book or article or TV exposé is noticed and discussed, attention spans are short. News can travel blindingly quickly and "virally," but widespread, consequential, sustained, in-depth debates about profound questions that go to the root of our civilization's paradoxes seem few and far between these days.

In that context, I have absolutely no illusions about the impact a modest essay such as this could have. I have written it to explore a few hunches I have long entertained about "normality" in our culture, to see if my initial notions stand up after closer scrutiny. I didn't begin this project with any certainty of the conclusions I might reach, but I did start with a hypothesis, or at least a strong suspicion. My initial hunch was that if one were to take a few major categories of life (and I wanted ones that were as intimate and emotionally-charged as possible, hence, as I mentioned, I picked mental health, drug use, sexual behavior, relationship to money, and core beliefs) and found a way to interview thousands of people in a truly random sample and gotten them to be rigorously honest (as we'll see, close to impossible!), one would discover that very few individuals would rank (according to the current dominant attitudes implicit in our media and public discourse) as "normal" across the board.

In other words, person "A" might be centered, drug-free, sexually conventional and fairly fiscally honest, but she happens to believe that aliens have abducted her on multiple occasions. Person "B" may be basically sane, sexually more or less run-of-the-mill with no offbeat worldviews, but make a living committing acts of fraud and enjoy smoking weed. Person "C" may be honest, conventionally religious and well adjusted but be into a kinky erotic subculture of one kind or another. You get the idea.

My hypothesis, then, is that if one explores the matter, it is likely one will arrive at the following conclusions:

a) Very few people are "normal" across the board, so, in the words of Professor Kenji Yoshino: "It's not normal to be normal." Or, as an old therapist joke puts it: "The clinical definition of a normal person is someone you don't know very well."

b) The illusion of a preponderant majority of people being "normal" persists because in most domains of life, taken one at a time, a majority or at least a sizeable plurality probably are, by society's current standards, more or less within the boundaries of normality at a given point in time (and many who aren't hide it pretty well).

c) Cumulatively, however, when a fuller gamut of key categories is examined, that illusion of widespread, society-wide normality is seriously undermined.

To many observant people with some life experience under their belts this notion will seem fairly self-evident and barely worth mentioning, but it seems to me to be a far more radical idea than it may appear at first glance. One of the key, foundational sets of assumptions made by The New York Times or any other reasonably upscale media organ when it communicates with its audience is this: Our audience is composed of eminently sane, impeccably ethical, drug-free, law-abiding folks with post-Enlightenment rational attitudes toward science and religious tolerance, who are largely free of sexual kinks and flaky cultural or spiritual worldviews.

This hypothetical audience may be a necessary fiction, but if we probe the matter, I predict, as I stated at the onset, that we will discover that there are far, far more people who have at least some degree of mental health issues, who use (or at least have used) some illegal drugs, who lead unconventional sex lives, whose ethics are shaky or whose relationship to money is deeply problematic, and who have very offbeat worldviews than is usually acknowledged in our society's public discourse. If this is true we're either pretending we don't know the painful truth, or we're lying to ourselves about who we are. As I said earlier, there may be some understandable reasons for such self-deception. Maybe individuals and societies require idealized self-images to function and the social order would collapse without them, but how warped that self-image really is seems to me an interesting question I for one can't help but want to explore.

At least some evidence for some of my hypotheses is not that hard to find. It's in official statistics and professional publications and openly debated by specialists in various fields, whose views, reports and surveys are even at times covered in serious mainstream publications (including the Times). However, it is also true that in many of the domains I'm exploring incontrovertibly reliable statistics simply don't exist and a lot of the available information is just white noise/pseudo-data. Many of the behaviors I am looking at are illegal or socially frowned upon, so solid data is in some cases almost impossible to come by (e.g. sales figures for the porn industry; the actual number of men who have frequented prostitutes; the real numbers of drug users; the extent of bribery and corruption).

An additional problem is that the quality and quantity of research almost invariably decline during conservative administrations, which tend to cut funding for nearly all serious studies and surveys of social issues, from the census to poverty to sexuality. They tend to see this sort of rigorous data as potentially politically dangerous, and usually, the government funds the largest scale studies. So, because we've had conservatives in the executive branch of the federal government for 20 of the last 28 years, this has exacerbated the paucity of good data in many domains. Quite a few of the best studies are decades old, with no large-scale follow-up since. Finally, as in most fields of inquiry, one finds that various specialists often vehemently disagree with each other's figures. I've tried to avoid selecting only those sources of data that most favor whatever argument I'm making and to present a range of statistics I have found on a topic. I am writing a polemic, but I hope it's not an intellectually dishonest one. I don't want to draw a conclusion when a legitimate case can't be made, and I admit it when the evidence for one of my arguments isn't conclusive.

So, there are sources of data out there for some of the topics I've chosen to focus on, but not always reliably. Some information is easy to find, clear, uncontroversial and extensively discussed. More often it's harder to find and to decipher, highly contentious, and far from definitive. However, if one digs a bit, even in those domains where facts and figures are lacking, or vigorously disputed and hopelessly confusing, one can generally (with a few notable exceptions) piece together enough partial sources of information, solid clues, and strong bits of anecdotal evidence to at least begin to get some rough sense of the scope of a phenomenon.

The unflattering aspects of social reality are not being completely ignored. Serious people do study a number of them, but these people are most often specialists looking at these matters field by field, in isolation (and generally far from front pages and in very technical language). And a few of these topics are almost terra incognita, mysterious domains of collective life characterized by an almost complete lack of credible hard data. So I was able to marshal convincing facts in some cases and could only come up with suggestive circumstantial evidence in others, but I did ultimately come away with a sense that my initial hunch was correct and that our holistic, cumulative societal self-portrait is grossly distorted and sanitized. I try to at least begin to make a case for this hypothesis and to offer a bit of a corrective lens to our rose-colored myopia in the pages that follow.

Notes:

On steroid use see:
- "Police Officers in Many Areas Face Charges of Steroid Involvement" in NY Times; Feb. 5th, 2005
- "Long Island Steroid Labs Found to Be Big Business" by Corey Kilgannon in the NY Times, September 26th, 2007
- "Prominent Entertainers Cited in Steroids Inquiry" in NY Times, by Bruce Lambert, January 14th, 2008
- "Jeepers, Rappers, Where'd You Get Those Arms and Torsos?' in NY Times, by Ben Sisario, January 15th, 2008

- *The Day the Whores Came Out to Play Tennis* was a 1965 play by Arthur Kopit that the NY Times refused to run an ad for.

-Kenji Yoshino, Law professor and gay Asian American, is the author of
Covering: The Hidden Assault on Our Civil Rights, (Random House, 2006) a part memoir/part treatise that deals with identity politics, the psychological harm of pretending to be other that one is, and how civil rights law relates to those issues.

MENTAL HEALTH

"Onward, through the fog." —Oat Willie

Perhaps the first automatic assumption we take for granted in our public discourse is that most of us are what we would consider "sane." This seems to be a reasonable deduction. Our complex, highly technological societies do, by and large, function. Most people seem to get up, go to work or school and get through the day. I would agree that, clearly, most people are, at the very least, functional much of the time. But I also think far more of us than we suspect are at least a tad dysfunctional and somewhat, or more than somewhat, troubled. Several members of my close family and friends and acquaintances have committed suicide, and quite a few people I have known over the decades also have people close to them who have died that way, so I have long suspected that suicide and despair, pain and depression were more common than most of us realize. Also, among the people I've gotten to know at least fairly well in my life, nearly all (including me) have regularly exhibited some forms or other of self-defeating, irrational behaviors in one aspect of life or another. I realize this is purely subjective and anecdotal, but my impression, to be blunt, is that most of us are at least a bit unhinged some of the time.

I absolutely don't want to trivialize mental illness. Obviously one has to distinguish between very serious conditions that make people incapable of living effectively in the world, that make them too terrified or depressed or anxious or manic to function or dangerous to themselves or others, and less serious symptoms. Those with these most serious illnesses need whatever best treatments are available (alas, also a highly contentious topic), and they couldn't be a majority at any given moment or our social order would most likely break down. Most studies I've looked at put the percentage of people with active "Serious Mental Illness" (SMI) somewhere between 6% and 10%

at any given moment, which is certainly not a majority but is far from an insignificant number. However, more to the point, there is a lot of room between "normality" and serious mental illness, and I tend to think a lot more of us are somewhere along that line than totally ensconced at one end.

We tend to think of mental illnesses or neurological conditions as specific conditions with names, say "Obsessive Compulsive Disorder" or "Tourette's Syndrome." However, just to take those two random examples, many (perhaps most) of us exhibit obsessive behaviors at various times, and many of us have mild tics. Think of children who make a ritual behavior of desperately trying not to walk on cracks in the sidewalk, or nearly all baseball batters (or tennis players before serving or receiving) who go through a complex, elaborate, compulsively repetitive, nearly always identical, ritualized set of tic-like motions and gestures before taking a pitch. Those people who are diagnosed as suffering from one of those named conditions are simply those whose symptoms are too extreme to be missed or ignored. But the difference, I would argue, is one of degree. Latently we probably all have some predispositions to many of these types of mental or neurological behaviors, but their manifestation is not disruptive enough for most of us to seek treatment.

This very issue: how to decide the level of severity that would constitute a mental illness, is, in fact, currently a major bone of contention in the world of psychiatry and psychology. One camp of specialists feels that only really serious cases should be counted as true mental illnesses, while another asserts this would miss far too many people who genuinely suffer and whose symptoms might get far worse if early warnings are not heeded. The field of mental health care is very far from a hard science. The next issue of the uniquely influential DSM (*Diagnostic and Statistical Manual of Mental Disorders*) is due out in 2010 or '11, and conditions that make it into that manual are far more likely to receive insurance coverage and research dollars, so the stakes are high. Borderline Personality Disorder (BPD), for example, is a very fashionable diagnosis these days, even, in very recent years, astonishingly, among children under 4, something unimaginable till very recently. Well, BPD only made into the DSM in 1980. And now a number of specialists would like to rename it. "Emotional Regulation Disorder", "Impulse Disorder" and "Mercurial Syndrome" are among the candidates.

Also, a group of more psychoanalytically inclined therapists has created if not a competitor, at least a complement/corrective to the DSM, the

Psychodynamic Diagnostic Manual, because they feel the DSM is too focused on disease categories and not holistic enough in treating patients as holders of whole personalities. So clearly there are different views and movements among mental health practitioners, and therefore finding reliable, universally agreed upon statistics about the frequency of mental health problems is next to impossible when the profession can't even agree on names for some conditions, let alone what actually constitutes a diagnosable illness. It was only fairly recently that homosexuality was taken out of the DSM, for example: it's now, finally, no longer considered a disorder by the profession. It's also a bit hard to be absolutely clear about mental illness categories when we don't really have a solid definition of what mental health actually is.

To make things worse, highly dubious, sordid episodes have tainted psychiatry from the 19th Century on, from widespread diagnoses of "hysteria," to thousands of lobotomies in the 1940s and 50s, to the locking away of many "overly" assertive women in asylums until far into the 20th Century, to the enthusiastic embrace of completely unproven Freudian ideas, to the fad for "multiple personalities" and then "repressed memories" of supposed ritual sex abuse in the 1980s, and now to the shocking extent of psychiatric drug prescribing in our society, even in children. So, we have to take any data (or worldviews) from the world of psychiatry with many grains of salt.

All that said, there is a lot of data out there, and if we look at the range of estimates in a few key areas, we can begin to develop at least somewhat of a sense of a picture of the relative mental health of the population. According to Patricia Pearson's *A Brief History of Anxiety*, 40 million Americans suffer from anxiety. A 2002 World Mental Health Survey found that nearly 29% of U.S. residents suffered from anxiety, the highest rate in the world (Mexicans, by comparison, had a rate of 6.6%). A very recent research paper by specialists led by Dr. Ronald Kessler, a professor of health care policy at Harvard, estimates that more than half of all Americans will develop some form of mental disorder at some point in their lives. Granted, those in the camp that feels that only more extreme mental conditions should be the focus of diagnosis and treatment think that figure is too high. Still, the difference between the two camps, while substantial, is not always big enough to change a clear conclusion: a whole lot of people suffer from mental problems.

For example, a large 1994 survey estimated that 30% of adult (over 18) Americans had had some form of mental illness in the previous year. Dr. Darrel Regier, Director of Research at the American Psychiatric

Association, felt that that estimate was too high, so he led a second study using much stricter criteria (i.e. people who had actually gotten treatment and received diagnoses) to go over the figures, and they came up with a figure of around 19%. Yes, that's lower than 30%, but it's still, counting only those who were troubled enough to go seek some sort of help, close to one fifth of the adult population in one year! If we split the difference between the two camps' estimates, we get around 25%, one quarter of the population, with fairly serious mental health concerns per annum. I suspect that's still a tad on the low end. My personal experience makes me lean toward the camp that argues we are undercounting because, anecdotally, quite a few of the people I have known who suffered from at least moderately serious mental issues never sought treatment. In any case, it turns out the National Institute of Mental Health (NIMH) comes up with an estimate very close to our "compromise" above-26.2% of Americans ages 18 and older, it asserts, suffer from a diagnosable mental disorder in a given year, and mental disorders are the leading cause of disability in the U.S. and Canada for ages 15-44.

Now even if we grant that many of those seeking treatment do so for several years running, there are still bound to be a good proportion of new people experiencing mental health problems each year in that 25% (or 26.2%), so 50% of the population over a whole lifetime, as dramatic a figure as it is, may very well be, if anything, an undercount. Figures from Canada seem to indicate the higher estimates are probably the more realistic. A Canadian study, for instance, estimated 20% of adult Canadians suffer from clinical depression. That's 20% for just depressives, not counting the slews of other mental illness categories (all the various anxieties, phobias, mood disorders, and bipolar conditions)! And my experience of Canadians has always been that they seemed, if anything, at least a tad saner than Americans. Draw your own conclusions.

There are other less obvious places to look to begin to flesh out a fuller picture, and they also suggest that the level of mental health of our population may be even worse than the figures I cited above would suggest. It is well known that the U.S. currently incarcerates a higher proportion of its citizens than any nation on earth, somewhere around 2.3 million people as of now (early 2008). Roughly 1 in 100 of adults are in prison, 1 in 15 for African American men. The rate was 738 per 100,000 in 2005. Some studies conclude that 25% of the world's prisoners are in the U.S. In 2006 over 7.2 million people were actively in the criminal justice system, i.e. on probation, in jail or prison or on parole. That was 3.2% of all U.S. adult residents, 1 in every 31 adults.

What is less well known is how many of these prisoners suffer from mental illness. According to a September 2007 U.S. Justice Department report, 64% of all U.S. inmates reported mental health problems in the previous year! Our prisons have become, among other things, the new warehouses for many people with the most serious mental health conditions. It's also true prison life is often dehumanizing and conducive to causing vulnerable people to snap, so it is likely jails are as much a cause of such illnesses as warehouses for people with pre-existing conditions.

This prison warehousing turns out to be a new wrinkle in an old pattern. According to Bernard Harcourt, a professor of law and criminology at the University of Chicago who rigorously studied old records, the U.S. consistently institutionalized somewhere between 700 to 800 people per 100,000 per annum in the years between 1935 and 1963 in a wide range of mental hospitals and asylums. With the advent of new drugs and some exposés that revealed the dehumanizing scale of those institutions and the neglect and discredited treatment modalities that characterized a lot of them, many of these giant facilities were closed down starting in the 1960s and 1970s, but we now seem to be incarcerating many of the mentally ill in, arguably, even more punitive, brutal institutions that don't even pretend to be rehabilitative.

Harcourt also points out that the population in those mental hospitals was nearly half women and older and whiter than today's prisoners who are 95% male and largely young men of color. Clearly, while we expressed revulsion at the Soviet practice of sending political dissidents to mental hospitals, there is no doubt that many women who rebelled against patriarchal norms as best they could or who had emotional problems as a result of the constrained possibilities for women in that pre-feminist era, wound up being locked away and medicated and electro-shocked (Lisa Appignanesi's recent *Mad, Bad and Sad: Women and the Mind Doctors* offers a revelatory history of this abuse of women by psychiatry). Today we deal with the rage of many poor youths by locking as many of them away as we can fit in our enormous prison-industrial complex. In any case, for the purposes of this text, we can see that adding prisons to our analysis reveals on the one hand that the total figures of people with mental health issues may be a small tad higher than even the dramatic figures we looked at earlier indicated, but above all they reveal that there are more people with very serious such conditions that we may keep out of sight/out of mind because they're incarcerated.

Another data set worth looking at is for suicides and suicide attempts. There are slightly above 30,000 suicides each year in the U.S. but as many as 400,000 emergency room visits for self-inflicted injury, some half of which were counted as full-fledged suicide attempts (roughly 195,000 in '04). Some studies say there are perhaps as many as 750,000 suicide attempts annually. A figure oft cited is that some 5 million Americans have attempted suicide at least once. One could argue that, while that is a lot of people, out of a population of over 300 million, it's perhaps not an enormously high percentage. Still, one has to assume that for every person who attempts it, many others have been in enough pain to at least think about it.

What I find most interesting is that the suicide-prone are a radically different group than the prison population. While suicide is only the 11th leading cause of death overall, it is the second among college students, but the highest rate, not surprisingly, has historically been among the elderly, and whites of all ages are far more likely than minority members to kill themselves, as are men in general (roughly 80%) compared to women (actually women attempt suicide far more, but men succeed at a much higher rate). However, a very recently released Centers for Disease Control and Prevention five-year study of suicide rates between 1999 and 2004 has shocked researchers because the rate for 45 to 54 year olds inexplicably spiked some 20% in just those few years, and for women in that demographic it shot up by 31%, just as rates among the elderly have been in decline. There are as of yet no solid explanations, but one theory is that the astonishing increase in prescription drug use in the whole population may be partially to blame. In any case, we see serious mental suffering among incarcerated, predominantly poor and minority youth, and very different, but no less serious such conditions among elderly whites, and now spiking suicide rates among the middle aged middle classes (and now war veterans as well). This paints a picture of a fairly high level of mental misery well cross-culturally and cross-generationally distributed.

Women exhibit some distinctive patterns in their mental health disruptions. Eating disorders (anorexia, bulimia and binge eating) are a major issue for young women 12 to 25 (who constitute perhaps 85 to 90% of cases, though figures for males are reportedly on the rise-a recent Harvard study cited that 25% of new cases are now males, some of them athletes with food and weight issues related to sports). These sometimes tragically lethal conditions constitute an often hidden epidemic, because their scope is very hard to determine. Doctors are not required to report such patients to any medical agency, and most of those with such a problem hide it and often deny its existence (including to themselves). Once again, we're faced with a range of numbers. In 2003, the journal Clinician Reviews estimated that 5 million Americans had eating disorders, but the National Association of Anorexia Nervosa and Associated Disorders (ANAD) comes up with 8 million or roughly 3% of the population. The Alliance for Eating Disorders Awareness, citing NIMH (National Institutes of Mental Health) studies, has much higher figures: 1 in 5 women, it says, struggle with an eating disorder of some kind, including 11% of high school students. These last figures may be higher because they may also include some "sub-clinical" eating disorders that disrupt people's lives to some extent but don't reliably show up on the medical profession's radar, probably a very large group. But it seems that no one has a definitive idea about the real numbers of the "eating disordered" though it's clearly a widespread and devastating problem, and most of its victims are covert and therefore very hard to heal. Another problem plaguing teenagers and young adults of both sexes that's very hard to measure the scope of because it's usually a secretive behavior is self-injury. The most credible figures I've seen estimate that some 15 to 17% of the adolescent and college-aged populations self-injure and that it's a growing problem.

Another group worth looking at is the very young. As I alluded to earlier, the use of psychiatric drugs among children and adolescents has been skyrocketing in recent years. It has among adults as well, but the rate of increase is more dramatic for kids because the widespread use of such drugs in that age group is a relatively new phenomenon. It is hard to know whether we are witnessing a fad of over-diagnosing and over-medicating that will eventually seem as horrific as lobotomies do in hindsight, or whether there has been, for some societal or environmental reasons, a dramatic upsurge in mental disorders among the very young (toxic chemicals? far less in the way of free playtime and outdoor experiences than in generations past?), or, as the drug companies argue, that these problems were there all along but that they now have the pharmaceutical tools to address them (which, forgive my cynicism, just happen to be hugely profitable, and which psychiatrists who receive money from manufacturers happen to prescribe to kids three times more often than those who don't).

Whatever we think about all that, the statistics are shocking. From 1994 to 2002, the use of stimulants such as Ritalin among children doubled. The exact figures vary depending on the source. Some go as low as 3 to 4 % of all children on such medications, other studies claim 10% of young boys (and roughly half as many girls, and over 4% of adults) are diagnosed with ADHD (Attention Deficit Hyperactivity Disorder) and are on prescribed stimulants. Yet others cite higher numbers, up to 1 in 7 boys. According to the "American Family Physician" website, primary care pediatricians and family physicians recognized behavior problems that might affect academic achievement in some 18 percent of the school-aged children seen in their offices and clinics, and hyperactivity/inattention was diagnosed in 9 percent in 1999. What is not in dispute is that the U.S. has the highest rate of childhood ADHD diagnosis in the world. In 2005, 1.9 million U.S. prescriptions were written for Ritalin, 8.7 million for Adderall-XR and 8.2 million for Concerta, the three main amphetamine-type drugs prescribed for ADHD.

Autism is another condition that seems to have radically spiked among children in recent years, though its prevalence and causes are very contentious topics, and reliable data on the various "Autism Spectrum Disorders" (ASDs), which range from more mild variants such as Asperger Syndrome to full-blown autism, is very hard to pin down. The Autism Society of America's estimates that autism affects roughly 1 in 150 births, and says that it's the fastest-growing developmental disability (10-17% annual growth, 172% increase in the 1990s alone), costing the economy $90 billion annually, projected to rise to $200 to 400 billion within a decade.

And now, most recently, more and more kids of both genders are being diagnosed with other conditions, especially "bipolar" disorders. The issue of children and anti-psychotic and antidepressant drug use is controversial, but what is not in dispute is the rapid increase of children taking such drugs. Between 1996 and 2002, the annual number of doctor visits by children between 5 and 17 at which an antidepressant was prescribed nearly tripled (from 1.1 to 3.1 million), according to a 2004 National Center for Health Statistics report. In 2000-02, that report says, 8.8 percent of adolescents 12 to 17 were prescribed antidepressants, most of them "off -label"-only Prozac has been approved by the FDA for use in children. Many of the other drugs they are prescribed have barely been tested in children, so their doctors often have to experiment to see which ones will "work" with specific kids, who often develop serious mental and physical "side effects."

The diagnosis of bipolar disorder in children's most famous advocate, Dr. Joseph Biederman, a Harvard-based child psychiatrist, was recently investigated for failing to report to Harvard or to medical journals he wrote for $1.4 million dollars in income from companies that manufacture anti-psychotic medications. And just as I was doing the final edit of this text (November '08) a panel of drug experts reporting to the federal government for a supposed routine review of the anti-psychotic drugs Risperidal and Zyprexa in pediatric medicine shocked the FDA by condemning the cavalier over-prescription of such anti-psychotics to children. The newest figures reveal that nearly 390,000 children, 240,000 of them 12 or under, were "treated" with Risperidal last year, a drug with substantial "side effects" in kids-over 1200 well documented cases of serious health problems among kids taking it have emerged in the last 15 years, including 31 deaths. Risperidal is only one of five of the most popular such drugs used on children (Zyprexa, Seroquel, Geodon and Abilify are the four others), and their collective sales for use in children have quintupled in fifteen years. Often these drugs are prescribed for ADHD though that is an "off label" use.

It's really hard to come up with exact figures for the total amount of children on medication, as for some drug categories different studies cite different numbers, but it's quite possible that, combining these estimates of youthful stimulant, anti-psychotic, and anti-depressant prescriptions, over 20% of U.S. children and teenagers are on some sort of serious, strong psychotropic drugs at some point, and their numbers are, by and large, expanding. And this does not count illicit drug and alcohol use among kids. College students are apparently faring no better. A 2003 study published in the journal *Professional Psychology: Research and Practice* found that the number of college students treated for depression and for suicidal tendencies doubled between 1989 and 2001, that students visiting counseling facilities on campuses had far more complex and severe issues than previous generations, and that psychiatric hospitalizations of students had dramatically spiked at many colleges.

Another interesting indicator of mental health is the overall rate of consumption of mood altering prescription pharmaceuticals in the whole population. A key category here is, again, anti-depressants, now the most prescribed type of drug in the country. The CDC (Centers for Disease Control) says that 25% of all American adults will have a major depressive episode at some point; that the use of anti-depressants tripled between 1994 and 2004;

that 118 million prescriptions for anti-depressants were counted in 2005; and that at least 10% of adult women (and 4% of men) are currently on anti-depressant medication (and this is just legally obtained, prescribed drugs). These medications have been raising a lot of controversy recently because there is a growing body of anecdotal evidence linking their side-effects to hundreds of young people's suicides and a few acts of extreme violence (including just three days ago as I write this, the inexplicable gunning down at Northern Illinois University of five students and himself by a young man with no previous troubled history but who had stopped taking his Prozac). The defenders of these drugs argue that they prevent far more suicides than they cause, but even if that were true (and it's very far from established), one has to wonder why such large swaths of our population are suddenly getting so depressed.

Meanwhile a whole lot of folks are on other frequently prescribed drug categories-stimulants ("mother's little helper"), barbiturates, and, more and more, sleeping aids (some 42 million prescriptions in the U.S. in 2005, up 60% from 2000 and growing, as ads for Lunesta, Ambien, and their ilk are incessant on TV, with hundreds of millions spent on promoting them). Some of these sleeping aids have attracted much attention recently, as there have been a slew of incidents of individuals on such medications who have had truly bizarre, terrifying episodes of sleepwalking behavior, even getting into their cars and driving great distances, sometimes on the wrong side of the road, occasionally having accidents, and often not remembering any of it later on.

There is no doubt that the major drug companies have waged an extraordinarily successful, massive propaganda and advertising campaign, aimed at both doctors and the general public, to get Americans to consume ever greater quantities of prescription drugs, some for novel illnesses such as "restless leg syndrome" or "overactive bladder." In books such as Marcia Angell's *The Truth About the Drug Companies* and Melody Petersen's *Our Daily Meds*, a very compelling case is made that many drugs are over-prescribed and misused, and that thousands of people are dying annually as a result. The massive, soaring prescribing of anti-psychotic drugs to elderly dementia sufferers, especially in nursing homes, despite convincing evidence these drugs are largely ineffective in such patients, is a good example of such abuse. Spending on prescription drugs by U.S. citizens increased seventeen-fold between 1980 and 2003. And quite a few people consume dizzying daily drug cocktails for a slew of conditions, some most likely caused by the very drugs they are taking.

In any case, when we look at all these statistics, behaviors and patterns of prescription drug consumption, what we see is that mental misery seems to affect nearly every wedge of the population, but that different groups express their dysfunction differently: poor youth are more likely to lash out at others; middle class white boys and elderly white men more likely to (successfully) take their own lives; women more likely to have eating disorders, and more likely to seek out medication for depression, anxiety, and insomnia; and children just have to do whatever they're forced to do by adults...

My view is that the reality of our collective mental health is actually far more problematic than all these already alarming statistics indicate. For one thing, some 40 to 50 million Americans are uninsured (more if one counts undocumented immigrants), many others very badly insured (with high deductibles or no mental health coverage for example), so a substantial portion of those people wind up being un or under-represented in our health statistics, since they only seek medical help for the most glaringly serious health emergencies. And many people in our culture self-medicate by abusing a wide range of illicitly obtained drugs and/or alcohol. A great many of those also don't make it into the mental health statistics.

Another million and a half suffer from some form of brain trauma from accidents each year, and quite a few of them suffer serious, long-term cognitive impairment as a result (far more since the inception of the Iraqi and Afghani military operations, which have also obviously created a spike in the rates of Post Traumatic Stress Disorder-according to a recent RAND study, one in five returning Iraqi War veterans suffer from war related mental health impairments and/or brain trauma but only half of them seek help). Another far from small group with extremely serious cognitive problems is composed of dementia/Alzheimer's patients (who have doubled since 1980 to some 5 million and whose numbers are growing rapidly as the population ages). These last two categories are not, of course, classical mental illnesses, but they certainly result in less than optimal mental functioning.

I could pile on and dig further and find other groups to add to the list, but I think I've made my point. However, there is another powerful secondary effect that is rarely discussed and that doesn't make it into medical statistics that is important to consider. Imagine that you are the parent or guardian of a child on anti-depressants, or a close family member or intimate friend of someone who attempted suicide (or worse, succeeded), or the relative of someone in prison with serious mental problems, or the significant other of someone suffering from depression or bipolar disorder, or the child of a parent with Alzheimer's. How would your own level of stress and mental equilibrium be affected? I think we have to realize that the impacts of the large scale of mental suffering in our society reach far beyond the people actually counted (or undercounted) in published figures.

So, I think we can conclude, after just this cursory look at some basic statistics and a bit of deduction, that, at the very least: fairly hefty segments of our population are deeply troubled at any moment; that their numbers seem to be increasing rapidly (or at least the medical-pharmaceutical establishment is busily diagnosing and medicating more and more of them); and that in all likelihood more than half of us will suffer at least some form of fairly disruptive mental health crisis during our lives. So, in light of that, how would one define "normality" in the context of mental health? At the very least, it certainly seems that it's every bit as statistically normal to have a mental health problem at some point as not to, and that one would be exceedingly hard-pressed to claim that contemporary American society is characterized by the mental soundness of its inhabitants.

Notes

-The quote that opens the chapter was the signature expression of "Oat Willie," a character in Austin, Texas-based underground comic books in the 60s and 70s.

-the *Diagnostic and Statistical Manual of Mental Disorders,* fourth edition (DSM-IV) (Washington, DC: American Psychiatric Press, 2000)

-the PDM-*Psychodynamic Diagnostic Manual* (Alliance of Psychoanalytic Organizations, 2006)
 about the PDM, see:
-"For Therapy, A New Guide With a Touch Of Personality" by Benedict Carey, in NY Times, January 24th, 2006

on Borderline Personality Disorder naming debate, see:
-"Personality, interrupted: Clinicians Consider Rebranding Borderline Personality Disorder" by Aina Hunter in the Village Voice, January 17th, 2006

-*A Brief History of Anxiety* by Patricia Pearson (Bloomsbury, 2008)

For a discussion of the debate within the profession about the real number of those with mental illness, see:
-"Snake Phobias, Moodiness, And a Battle in Psychiatry" by Benedict Carey, in the NY Times, June 14th, 2005

On basic mental health stats, see:
-National Institutes of Mental Health: Mental Disorders in America, at www.nimh.nih.gov

on Kessler's estimates of the numbers of those with mental illnesses, see:
-Kessler RC, Chiu WT, Demler O, Walters EE: "Prevalence, severity and comorbidity of twelve-month DSM-IV disorders in the National Comorbidity Survey Replication," in Archives of General Psychiatry, June 2005
-Kessler RC, Berglund P, Demler O, Jin R, Koretz D, Merikangas KR, Rush AJ, Walters EE, Wang PS: "The epidemiology of major depressive disorder: results from the National Comorbidity Survey Replication," in the Journal of the American Medical Association, June, 2003

on a smaller estimate of the numbers of the mentally ill, see:
-Robins LN, Regier DA, eds: *Psychiatric disorders in America: the Epidemiologic Catchment Area Study* (New York: The Free Press, 1991)

on the incarceration of the mentally ill, see:
- "The Mentally Ill, Behind Bars" by Bernard E. Harcourt, NY Times Op-Ed, January 15, 2007, and Harcourt's book: *Against Prediction: Profiling, Policing and Punishing in an Actuarial Age*
-*Mad, Bad and Sad: Women and the Mind Doctors* by Lisa Appignanesi (W.W. Norton, 2008)

on suicide statistics, see:
-Suicide Prevention Resource Center (SPRC: www.sprc.org)
-Centers for Disease Control and Prevention, National Center for Injury Prevention and Control Web-based Injury Statistics Query and Reporting System (WISQARS: www.cdc.gov/ncipc/wisqars/default.htm)
-Conwell Y, Brent D: "Suicide and aging I: patterns of psychiatric diagnosis" in International Psychogeriatrics, 1995
-Kochanek KD, Murphy SL, Anderson RN, Scott C: "Deaths: final data for 2002" in National Vital Statistics Reports, 2004
-Weissman MM, Bland RC, Canino GJ, et al: "Prevalence of suicide ideation and suicide attempts in nine countries" in Psychological Medicine, 1999
-on mid-life suicide statistics, see: "Midlife Suicide Rises, Puzzling Researchers" by Patricia Cohen in NY Times, February 19th, 2008

on anorexia/bulimia:

-Andersen AE. "Eating disorders in males," in: Brownell KD, Fairburn CG, eds: *Eating disorders and obesity: a comprehensive handbook* (New York, Guilford Press, 1995)

-Spitzer RL, Yanovski S, Wadden T, Wing R, Marcus MD, Stunkard A, Devlin M, Mitchell J, Hasin D, Horne RL: "Binge eating disorder: its further validation in a multi-site study" in International Journal of Eating Disorders, March 1993

-American Psychiatric Association Work Group on Eating Disorders: "Practice guideline for the treatment of patients with eating disorders (revision)" in the American Journal of Psychiatry, Jan. 2000

-Bruce B, Agras WS: "Binge eating in females: a population-based investigation" in the International Journal of Eating Disorders, 1992

-Sullivan PF: "Mortality in anorexia nervosa" in the American Journal of Psychiatry, July 1995

-ANAD Ten Year Study/National Association of Anorexia Nervosa and Associated Disorders (www.anad.org)

-National Institute of Mental Health's (NIMH) guide: Eating Disorders: Facts About Eating Disorders and the Search for Solutions

-The Renfrew Center Foundation for Eating Disorders: Eating Disorders 101 Guide: A Summary of Issues, Statistics and Resources, September 2002, revised October 2003 (www.renfrew.org)

on self-injury, see:
-The Cornell Research Program on Self-injurious Behavior in Adolescents and Young Adults: www.crpsib.com/

for some figures on children on psychiatric drugs, see:
-The American Association of Family Physicians website, at:
www.aafp.org/online/en/home.html
-National Center for Health Statistics reports at: www.cdc.gov/nchs/hus.htm
- "Use of Antipsychotics In Children Is Criticized" by Gardiner Harris in the NY Times, November 19th, 2008

on autism figures:
-Yeargin-Allsopp M, Rice C, Karapurkar T, Doernberg N, Boyle C, Murphy C: "Prevalence of Autism in a US Metropolitan Area" in The Journal of the American Medical Association, Jan. 2003.
-the Autism Society of America at: www.autism-society.org/

for U.S. government statistics on mental health data, see:
-The CDC (Centers for Disease Control) at: www.cdc.gov/mentalhealth/data.htm

on the Northern Illinois University shootings, see:
- "Reports of Gunman's Use of Antidepressant Renew Debate Over Side Effects" by Benedict Carey in NY Times, February 19th, 2008.

on sleeping aid use, see:
-"Some Sleeping Pill Users Range Far Beyond Bed" by Stephanie Saul in the NY Times,

March 8th, 2006.
-"Record Sales of Sleeping Pills Are Causing Worries" by Stephanie Saul in the NY Times, February 7, 2006

- *The Truth About the Drug Companies* by Marcia Angell (Random House, 2004)

- *Our Daily Meds: How the Pharmaceutical Companies Transformed Themselves Into Slick Marketing Machines and Hooked the Nation on Prescription Drugs*, by Melody Petersen (Sarah Crichton Books/Farrar, Strauss & Giroux, 2008)

on antidepressant statistics, see:
-the Health, United States report from the Centers for Disease Control (CDC)at: www.cdc.gov/nchs

on college student mental health, see:
-"More in College Seek Help For Psychological Problems" by Erica Goode in NY Times, February 3, 2003

on college students' depression and suicidal tendencies, see:
-"Changes in Counseling Center Client Problems Across 13 Years" by Sherry A. Benton, Ph.D., John M. Robertson, Ph.D., Wen-Chih Tseng, M.Ed., Fred B. Newton, Ph.D., and Stephen L. Benton, Ph.D., Kansas State University; in the American Psychological Association's journal: Professional Psychology: Research and Practice, Vol. 34, No. 1., Feb. 2003, available at: www.apa.org/journals/releases/pro34166.pdf

on Alzheimer's statistics:
-Hebert LE, Scherr PA, Bienias JL, Bennett DA, Evans DA: "Alzheimer disease in the US population: prevalence estimates using the 2000 census" in Archives of Neurology, August 2003

on veterans' and PTSD, see:
-"Nearly a Fifth of War Veterans Report Mental Disorders, a Private Study Finds" by Lizette Alvarez in NY Times, April 8th, 2008

ILLEGAL DRUG USE

"Everybody must get stoned." —Bob Dylan

"The other day they asked me about mandatory drug testing.
I said I believed in drug testing a long time ago.
All through the sixties I tested everything."
Attributed to former Red Sox pitcher, —Bill "Spaceman" Lee

A s we touched on in the previous chapter, Americans consume a lot
of mood-altering prescription drugs. If one adds our society's main
legally available staple drugs-alcohol, nicotine, caffeine and the theo-
bromine in chocolate-it is pretty obvious we are already dealing with an
overwhelming majority of the population who regularly consume some fairly powerful consciousness modifying substances. For a variety of social, cultural and political reasons, we encourage or at least tolerate the advertisement
and use of these aforementioned drugs but severely proscribe a whole range
of others. This is especially baffling because in the case of alcohol and nicotine at least, the costs to society are astronomically higher than for all illegal
drugs. One credible estimate is that alcohol kills 6 times more young people
than all other drugs combined. And the health damage caused by the growing misuse of prescription drugs is now also becoming greater than that
caused by all illegal drugs.

If we add illicit substances (including the unapproved use of prescription
drugs) to the picture, it is hard to avoid the conclusion that we are a very,
very druggy society (which is nothing new since rates of (completely legal
at the time) opiate and cocaine use were most likely much higher in the late
19th Century). Finding reliable numbers on current illegal drug use turns
out to be a very tricky affair, however, because most of the large-scale statistical studies on the topic are based on a few surveys that ask people about
their own use. Given the social stigma attached to drug use, one would

expect quite a few people to be less than fully truthful. The main data gathering techniques are: household surveys conducted in people's homes; phone surveys to people's residences; surveys administered in schools; prisoner and jail questionnaires (the main one is administered by "ADAM"-The Arrestee Drug Abuse Monitoring program); and medical and law-enforcement data. None of these are likely to make all respondents feel totally safe in responding honestly.

There are many methodological problems with nearly all these data sources. The main ones are that they are next to impossible to corroborate and that they invariably fail to capture data from "difficult-to-survey" groups, i.e. those with no permanent address, or who don't answer the phone, or who refuse to participate, absentee/truant students, dropouts, and so on. These are all groups more likely to include a higher than average proportion of drug users, therefore, it is widely understood that these main surveys tend to under-report drug use.

Just how iffy these estimates can be is illustrated by the example of cocaine use. The main U.S. government survey estimated that there were some 450,000 frequent users in the U.S. in 2000, but several other credible studies came up with figures of over three million for the same period. Again, we're far from hard science here, but we have to use some sort of data if we want to try and flush out a picture of drug use frequency, so we have no choice but to look at the most accepted data sets with a critical, analytic eye to try to at least get an approximate sense of what the truth is.

The Substance Abuse and Mental Health Services Administration (SAMHSA), part of the Department of Health and Human Services, conducts the biggest of these data collections on a random sample of U.S. households to determine the prevalence of the illicit use of all types of drugs. SAMHSA also runs the Drug Abuse Warning Network (DAWN), which surveys a sample of hospital emergency rooms around the country on their records of substance misuse and abuse, and the Treatment Episode Data Set (TEDS), which collects data on admissions to federally funded drug and alcohol addiction treatment programs.

According to SAMHSA in its aforementioned "National Household Survey on Drug Abuse" (recently rechristened the National Survey on Drug Use and Health-NSDUH), in 2001 15.9 million Americans 12 and older (7.1%) admitted having used an illicit drug in the previous month, 12% during the past year and 41.7% at least once during their lifetimes. Also, more telling, among those 18 to 34 years old, roughly 55% admitted to some drug use during their lives. Some 32% of those 18 to 25 admitted to some use in the past year. Approximately 37% of those over 12 reported some lifetime use of marijuana, 12.3% some use of cocaine, and 12.5% some use of hallucinogens. Another major government survey from a different agency found that in 2002 53% of high school seniors reported using an illegal drug at least once in their lives, 41% within the past year, and 25.4% within the past month.

If these figures are more or less accurate, these 18 to 34 year olds would still be people who when they become 50 or 60 would be part of a generation some 55% of whom once took illegal drugs. But an interesting form of amnesia seems to occur: it turns out there are discrepancies between the numbers of younger people reporting some lifelong drug use and their answers later in life. And it turns out that a more rigorous look at the data reveals that, in fact, the lifelong drug-use numbers stated above are most likely highly understated.

The second biggest government sponsored survey is the National Institute on Drug Abuse's "Monitoring the Future" (MTF) study, which mostly focuses on school-age youth 14-18. It's been conducted annually since 1975 by the Survey Research Center in the Institute for Social Research at the University of Michigan and has a reputation as perhaps the most sophisticated survey of its type. It has a fairly low refusal rate among respondents, and its experts work hard to correct for potential sources of error in the numbers. One very interesting aspect to MTF's work is that it has conducted a series of follow-up interviews with some of its respondents over a thirty-year period, a treasure-trove of drug-use data, because a cohort of 50 year olds has now been tracked for three decades. One of the most fascinating aspects of the findings is that, as I alluded to above, a pronounced "recanting" effect takes hold as people age, i.e. they now deny ever having used drugs even though they admitted to it previously. This is a piece of information the NSDUH does not factor in and that ultimately probably seriously skews its data.

According to the 2003 data, there was already a 3.1% recanting rate by age 21. By 30, nearly 11% of those who had admitted to the use of an illegal drug at least twice before changed their story and now claimed they never had. The rate of recanting varied by substance, lowest for alcohol, higher for cannabis, higher still for tranquilizers and amphetamine, and over

50% for inhalants. Clearly, older people realize they have way more to lose and are therefore far more likely to lie about illegal behavior, especially for substances that are most frowned upon.

When MTF's statisticians adjust their numbers to correct for this recanting effect, they come up with a staggering estimate: 88% of 45-year-olds in the U.S. they say, have tried an illegal drug at some time in their lives. 81% have tried cannabis. And, according to MTF's own account, these are still likely understatements of actual use. Now, even I have trouble believing these numbers. If these figures were generated by a cabal of extreme libertarian statisticians, I would view them as ridiculously inflated, but they're produced by the most rigorous of all the government's drug-use monitoring initiatives, so I have to assume that, whatever the ultimately unknowable exact figures, the truth is most likely somewhere in the ballpark they describe, and that the overwhelming majority of middle-aged Americans have at some point consumed at least one illicit drug.

So, for that population cohort, it is far more "normal" (i.e. majority behavior) to have consumed an illicit, black market drug at some point than not to have. If 81% have at least tried cannabis, then if marijuana is a "gateway" drug, it is above all a gateway to conformity. In other words, the overwhelmingly normal behavior in numerical terms has been defined as criminal. That should strike us as a truly bizarre situation, especially since this cultural behavior has been fairly stable and seems well established in the population for nearly a half-century.

Illegal drug use has become a de facto right of passage for many adolescents and young people of college age. The numbers have gone up or down a bit, with youthful drug consumption higher in the 70s, mostly trending lower in the 80s, then rising again in the 90s, and now slightly declining again in the first few years of the new millennium after 2002, but by and large, drug use among the young has remained broadly constant since the emergence of the "counterculture" in its widespread modern form in the 1960s. Some of the substances have been perennials for many decades (marijuana, the main psychedelics, cocaine, heroin, amphetamines, alcohol), a few have faded away or become far less prevalent ("ludes," "angel dust," ketamine), while others have been added to the repertoire over the years, some widely (ecstasy, meth, and most recently ecstasy-meth combos) and more and more powerful prescription drugs, especially opiates such as Oxycontin and the even more powerful Opana (oxymorphone hydrochloride), and some whose use is restricted to subcultures or regional scenes (e.g. promethazine-codeine cough syrup in the Houston rap world; chemist Sasha Shulgin's countless exotic phenethylamine molecular concoctions for West Coast super hipsters; ayahuasca and hoasca analogs and Salvia divinorum, and even iboga for the shamanic revival crowd, steroids for the muscle heads, etc.). Whatever fad drugs are "in" at any one time, youthful drug use seems to be a well-established feature of contemporary life that has resisted all the efforts of the "War on Drugs" over the decades, and quite a few people continue some use of illegal drugs well past youth of course, perhaps not in the same numbers as the young, but for heroin and "speed" and illicit pharmaceuticals quite a few users are far from young. The urges to experience altered states of consciousness and to numb pain are powerful human instincts, it seems, that no laws can ever extirpate.

Our government devotes enormous amounts of money and manpower on a global level to eradicating these substances, even when this obviously un-winnable "war" alienates Central Asian and South American peasant populations whose political rage can generate far worse outcomes than mere drug production; even when it involves poisoning whole ecosystems with toxic herbicides; and even when it has helped generate billions of dollars for multinational crime cartels, corrupting entire regions and even whole countries, replicating the pattern in the U.S. when alcohol Prohibition helped birth the modern Mafia, except this time around the business mirrors the larger, rapidly globalizing economy. The recent discovery of over 200 million dollars in cash in the Mexico City home of a Chinese/Mexican importer of tons of precursor chemicals (from China, of course) for the manufacture of methamphetamine for the U.S. market offers a dramatic illustration of just how profitable, large and international new branches of the drug trade have become. If the patterns of the past hold up, perhaps the grandchildren of the richest drug dealers will become the political leaders and respectable elites of the future, just as the progeny of some of the biggest bootlegging families of the 1920s are now viewed as the crème de la crème of our society.

The lucrative nature of the street drug trade, a result of prohibition, contributes to making some of our inner cities and southern border towns (and now rural areas with the "meth" epidemic) war zones. The last two years have seen extraordinary levels of drug-gang related violence in many parts of Mexico and on the U.S.-Mexican border, claiming not just the lives of criminals but many high ranking civilian and police officials and slews of innocent bystanders, in what is widely being described as an ongoing "wild west bloodbath." In the first three months of 2008 210 people were killed in such violence in the border town of Ciudad Juarez alone. And in the last few days, as I was writing this, the chief of Mexico's federal police was gunned down by a drug cartel hit-man in Mexico City, the 11th major, high-level law enforcement official to die in such a manner in the last 2 months, and if one adds all the bodyguards and ordinary police staff and cartel gunmen and civilians (including dozens of famous singers and musicians!) killed in those incidents, around 450 Mexican rank and file cops and some 4000 other people have died in this mini civil war since President Felipe Calderon came to power 18 months ago. Never has Porfirio Diaz's famous quip about his country seemed more apt: *"Pobre México! Tan lejos de Dios y tan cerca de los Estados Unidos"* ("Poor Mexico, so far from God and so close to the United States").

One could go on and on with a long litany of the disastrous "side-effects" of the "war on drugs"-one of the most poorly conceived long-term policies in human history. The epiphenomena associated with the way our government tries to suppress these drugs are far more costly and socially damaging than the social costs of drug use itself. *In Wages of Crime: Black Markets, Illegal Finance, and the Underworld Economy*, R.T. Naylor, Professor of Economics at McGill, hits the nail on the head: "Never in history has there been a black market tamed from the supply side. From prohibition to prostitution, from gambling to recreational drugs, the story is the same. Supply-side controls act to encourage production and increase profits. At best a few intermediaries get knocked out of business. But as long as demand persists, the market is served more or less as before. In the meantime, failure to "win the war" (against crime) becomes a pretext for increasing police budgets, expanding law enforcement powers, and pouring more money into the voracious maw of the prison-industrial complex."

This is not to deny that "hard" drugs such as heroin, cocaine and meth can be extremely harmful to individual users, but the cost of the drugs is what leads to the high crime rates and violence that are even more harmful to the larger society. And marijuana can perhaps be problematic for some heavy, chronic smokers, but it's certainly far less injurious to the national health than, say, artery clogging fast food. A list of drug related deaths supposedly arrived at by studying a range of actuarial tables for 1990 has been widely circulated in countercultural circles. It lists estimates of substance-induced deaths for that year as follows: Tobacco-360 000; Alcohol-130 000; Prescribed drugs-18,675; Caffeine-5800; Cocaine-2390; Heroin-2147; Aspirin-986; Marijuana-0. Now I doubt these figures are even remotely rigorous, but neither is a lot of the data bandied about by the war on drug enthusiasts. In fact no one really knows the exact figures, but the list I just gave is at least poetically accurate in capturing the absurdity of making the consumption of "soft" drugs such a proscribed criminal act.

Law enforcement priorities and public perceptions are certainly skewed. Those who are most gung-ho about the war on drugs remained focused on iconic drugs such as marijuana and psychedelics and cocaine because of their cultural associations and were very late in recognizing the far more harmful use of methamphetamine sweeping rural America. Now the largest health threat (even more than methamphetamine use) in this realm is from the exploding use of ultimately even more dangerous pharmaceutical drugs. One can't help but wonder how so many of these drugs wind up being diverted to the black market without the extraordinarily lucrative and powerful "big pharma" firms being able to better track their wares. Certainly, prescription forgeries, thefts, teens raiding their parents' medicine cabinets, and internet sales of knockoff versions of these drugs are major factors in their illicit use, but the major tobacco companies knew full well a large amount of their products were being illegally smuggled for decades and closed their eyes to it (or worse, colluded through intermediaries), and one would have to be naïve not to at least suspect something similar could be occurring in this case.

According to the United Nations' International Narcotics Control Board, the abuse and trafficking of prescription drugs, including painkillers such as Oxycontin (oxycodone) and Vicodin (hydrocodone) and Fentanyl (80 times as potent as heroin), and stimulants and appetite suppressants (anorectics), have globally overtaken the use of nearly all illegal drugs with the sole exception of cannabis. Some of these drugs are far more potent than traditional street drugs, so the risk of overdosing is much higher. In 2000, nearly half the U.S. emergency room drug overdose admittances were due to misused prescription drugs. In just two years, from 1998 to 2000, such visits due to hydrocodone rose 48%, those due to oxycodone 108%. Then in just one year, 2000 to 2001, oxycodone-induced emergency room visits went up another 44%. Even as most other illicit drug use among teens began to dip a bit in 2002, abuse of prescription drugs soared. The number of 12 to 25 year olds who newly, illegally used prescription painkillers grew five-fold in just a few years. And at the other end of the age spectrum, according to government estimates, more than 17 percent of adults over 60 abuse prescription drugs.

And more people are even admitting that they have abused prescription drugs in surveys. One study found a 94% increase in such people between 1992 and 2002 (seven times the rate of demographic growth in the same period). The U.S. population grew 13% in that decade, but prescriptions for controlled drugs grew by 154% (to about 234 million individual prescriptions, mostly for opioids). In 2003, more people in surveys admitted illegally using pharmaceutical drugs than those who used cocaine, heroin, inhalants and all hallucinogens combined. In 2001, The National Community Pharmacists Association estimated prescription drug misuse costs the U.S. healthcare system more than $100 billion annually.

The National Center on Addiction and Substance Abuse (CASA) at Columbia University (not always the most reliable source on drug data as they have a clear pro drug war agenda, but they seem to be less biased on this topic) published *Under the Counter: The Diversion and Abuse of Controlled Prescription Drugs in the U.S.* in 2005. It documents the enormous increase in the manufacture and distribution of controlled prescription drugs. Between 1992 and 2003, this report says, the number of people abusing controlled prescription drugs indeed jumped 94 percent, twice the increase in the number of people using marijuana, five times the number using cocaine, and 60 times the increase in the number using heroin. And, in more and more jurisdictions, law enforcement agencies are reporting that pharmaceuticals are beginning to supplant other illegal drugs as the main contributors to violent and property crime.

So, the drug warriors, still rabidly fighting the last war against the remnants of the counterculture that is their bête noire, are missing the boat once again. The public perception of the nature of what our nation's "drug problem" really is and who the biggest and most dangerous drug "pushers" and cartels really are, has also lagged. One can't help but wonder if the enormous power and clout of the pharmaceutical firms (and their copious campaign contributions to politicians and gigantic advertising budgets) contribute to our societal failure to grasp the real nature of our national drug addiction. Public opinion does not fully take in that the most dangerous substances are not the ones we are collectively focused on.

Despite these chasms of logic in our national drug policies, efforts to challenge them are anemic at best and, despite occasional tactical successes-a few victorious medical marijuana initiatives at the state level, free needle exchanges to cut HIV transmission in some cities, treatment alternatives to prison in some legal jurisdictions, and some legal victories surrounding religious/sacramental use of peyote and ayahuasca-they never gain any real political traction. Though I obviously strenuously object to current drug policies, the purpose of this particular text is not to rail against them (others, especially Ethan Nadelmann of the Drug Policy Alliance, do that eloquently and exhaustively), but to examine inconsistencies and strange paradoxes in some of our societal norms. And what is especially baffling about the continued relentlessness of our failed approach to illegal drug use, is that, first, so many people (as we saw, almost certainly a large majority) have at one point or another violated drug laws, yet we cruelly punish a lot of nonviolent drug offenders for either using or trafficking in substances most of us have at some point consumed but have been lucky enough not to get caught imbibing, and almost no one seems too actively agitated by the hypocrisy of the situation.

Not only have most people been guilty of criminal behavior in this domain, but among them one finds very high proportions of our ruling elites, including the last two and the (just elected as I did the final edit of this) new president. Obviously drug use couldn't have been all that severely harmful for many of these folks, or they wouldn't have had the successful career trajectories they did. And yet, all the politicians, judges, doctors, lawyers, engineers, radio personalities, and athletes who dabbled in drug use in high school or college or beyond are perfectly willing to allow hundreds of thousands of mostly poor, young people of color to be incarcerated, sometimes for long stretches, for doing what they had done (or for taking jobs in one of the only growth industries in their communities), without lifting a finger to change the laws.

The current mayor of New York City, for example, Michael Bloomberg, widely viewed as a "liberal" on social issues, once admitted to having used marijuana and to having enjoyed it, but during his administration's first six years, 214,300 people were arrested and often jailed for misdemeanor marijuana possession, 83% of them black and Hispanic youths (even though it is well known that a higher percentage of young whites smoke weed)-the most of any city in the world and far more than under previous administrations, including that of the notoriously racially insensitive and authoritarian previous mayor, Rudy Giuliani. Yet Bloomberg is totally unconcerned about jailing young people of color for doing what he once enjoyed doing. Bill Clinton, who also admitted smoking grass (without inhaling!), saw federal drug incarcerations, including for marijuana, skyrocket during his administration, without the slightest shame or remorse for his hypocrisy. And the racism of the war on drugs is glaringly obvious. In 2003, over 53% of those entering prison on a drug charge were black, though African Americans are under 13% of the nation's population, and most serious studies find that drug use per capita is about the same among all racial groups.

A substantial percentage of our prison population is now incarcerated on drug charges. The Department of Justice reported that as of September 30th, 2006, federal prisons held 176,268 inmates, of whom 93,751 (53%) were drug offenders, up from 74,276 in 2000. In state prisons, the 2006 percentage of drug offenders was 19.6% of all adults, some 249,400 inmates. Drug crimes are the main driver of the rising number of inmates: 80% of the increase in the federal prison population from 1985 to 1995 was due to drug convictions. In 1980 there were about 40,000 people across the U.S. jailed on drug charges at all jurisdictional levels; now it's upward of half a million, and 82% of the 1.9 million annual drug arrests are for simple possession of a substance, 40% of them for marijuana. According to a 2002 Office of National Drug Control Policy (ONDCP) report, federal spending to incarcerate drug offenders totaled nearly 3 billion dollars that year. U.S. sentences for drug crimes are often longer than for violent crimes and certainly much longer than in Europe or Canada. According to the U.S. Department of Justice's Bureau of Statistics, in 2001, federal mean drug felony sentences were 75.6 months, compared to 63 months for violent felonies.

Craig Haney and Philip Zimbardo point out the obvious: "Department of Corrections data show that about a fourth of those initially imprisoned for nonviolent crimes are sentenced for a second time for committing a violent offense. Whatever else it reflects, this pattern highlights the possibility that prison serves to transmit violent habits and values rather than to reduce them." And no less a gung-ho drug war crusader than retired general and former Director of the Office of National Drug Control Policy, Barry McCaffrey, admitted in 1996, that: "I...believe that we have created an

American gulag."

There may be no domain of life toward which our society has as bizarre, convoluted and paradoxical an attitude as the widespread use of drugs, one that highlights the battle between puritanical and hedonistic strains of DNA in the American soul. Late night comedians routinely joke about the use of pot or psychedelics, usually mocking it, but in such a way that makes clear that they know from past experience what they're talking about, and that they know most members of the audience will laugh along knowingly, and that no one takes it too seriously. These late-night comedy show monologues are an interesting barometer because they try to appeal to a broad common cultural denominator, so their writers seek to craft jokes most people will understand and find amusing. "Stoner" film comedies in the Cheech and Chong lineage from "Up in Smoke" to "Harold and Kumar Go to White Castle" (and now to Guantanamo Bay!) have also become a genre unto themselves. They are viewed as slight (if idiotic) entertainments with harmless, lovable imbecile protagonists. It seems a bit surreal that almost no one finds it unusual that our entertainment industry produces druggy slapstick comedies for the young, but that some of these kids (the unluckiest and/or poorest) will wind up incarcerated if they are caught behaving like the characters in those silly, lighthearted films.

A study by a team from the University of Pittsburgh School of Medicine led by Doctor Brian Primack, which was published in early 2008, calculated that 15 to 18 year olds who listen to 2.4 hours of popular music a day, will, on average, hear 84 references to alcohol or drugs a day, 30,000 a year, nearly all portraying these substances in a positive or at least a somewhat glamorous light. And they weren't just listening to Rap. The researchers based their study on the 279 most popular songs of 2005 from the Billboard charts in R+B, Pop, Rap, Rock, and Country (which is almost a bit unfair to use since that entire genre is so intimately linked to drinking). A spokesman for the Recording Industry Association, when confronted with this study, said: "It's important to note that music is generally a reflection of society." This may be a cop-out on the part of the industry, but based on the statistics we've been looking at, it's certainly also true.

When a political figure is confronted with rumors of youthful drug use, it can be a big story in the media, but something is generally considered newsworthy if it stands apart from humdrum, run-of-the-mill daily reality. Obviously, if the government's own figures are correct (whether one uses the more conservative NSDUH or the probably more accurate MTF estimates), a majority of us have tried illegal drugs, so it should be absolutely normal and totally un-newsworthy that a politician would have as well. In fact, a more relevant line of questioning should be posed to those political figures claiming never to have consumed any such drugs. First, since most people have: "Are you lying (as mere probability would suggest)?" "If you are indeed telling the truth, what makes you different than the rest of us? Do you think you're morally or intellectually superior to those of us (the majority) who have dabbled in drug use?" "Do you attribute your deviant behavior (absence of drug experimentation) to your rectitude and strength of personality or to a rigid temperament or perhaps even cowardice when faced with novelty?" "Or were you so pathologically politically ambitious and such a control freak even in your youth that you avoided any behavior that could reflect poorly on you later on when you planned to run for office?"

I realize this series of questions sounds flippant, but if there is to be an onus of justification on politicians (or anyone else in the public eye), shouldn't it be upon those whose behavior is outside the norm, not those whose behavior conforms to that of the majority? I'm not at all arguing that majority behavior or attitudes are invariably correct, but in this case, the perceived, widely accepted social belief, implicit in nearly all media discourse on the subject, is that taking illegal drugs is deviant behavior. I think we have established just how erroneous that perception is: in today's U.S.A., to paraphrase H. Rap Brown, taking drugs is as American as apple pie.

Notes:

-The 2nd chapter-opening quote is from Bill "Spaceman" Lee (William Francis Lee III) who pitched for the Boston Red Sox from 1969 to 1978 and the Montreal Expos from 1979 to 1982. A very colorful, countercultural character, Lee has written several books and a documentary film about him, Spaceman in Cuba, came out in 2006.

-The National Household Survey, renamed the National Survey on Drug Use and Health (NHS or NSDUH), is the largest regular survey covering psychoactive drug use, conducted since 1971 by the Substance Abuse and Mental Health Services Administration (part of the Department of Health and Human Services): www.oas.samhsa.gov/nsduh.htm

-Drug Abuse Warning Network: dawninfo.samhsa.gov/
(DAWN tracks reports from U.S. hospital emergency rooms)
-The National Institute on Drug Abuse's "Monitoring the Future" (MTF) study, conducted annually since 1975 by the Survey Research Center in the Institute for Social Research
at the University of Michigan: www.monitoringthefuture.org/

-Alexander "Sasha" Shulgin is a pharmacologist and chemist who "rediscovered" MDMA
("Ecstasy") in the late 1970s and early 1980s, and later discovered and synthesized well over
200 new psychoactive drugs, especially in the phenethylamine family. These include the
whole "2C" group of drugs. He and his wife co-wrote two odd books about their relationship to drugs: *PIHKAL* and *TIHKAL.*

on Mexican methedrine labs, see:
- "The China Connection: Globalization and the Narcotics Trade" by Eduardo Porter, a NY
Times editorial, August 2nd, 2007

on Mexican drug-related violence and corruption, there have been countless articles. See,
for example:
- "Drug War Causes Wild West Blood Bath" by James C. McKinley, Jr. in the NY Times,
April 16th, 2008
- "Acting Chief of Police of Mexico's Federal Police Slain as Struggle With Cartels
Continues" by James C. McKinley in the NY Times, June 1st, 2008

on the impacts of the Drug War on the environment in Latin America and on U.S. society,
see:
-the Epilogue-"The Madness of the War on Drugs" by Michael Stewartt and Ethan
Nadlemann in *Visionary Plant Consciousness*, edited by J.P. Harpignies (Park Street Press,
2007)

-*Wages of Crime: Black Markets, Illegal Finance, and the Underworld Economy*, by R.T. Naylor
(Cornell University Press; Revised edition, 2005)

-United Nations' International Narcotics Control Board (INCB): www.incb.org

-The National Community Pharmacists Association (NCPA):
www.ncpanet.org

-The National Center on Addiction and Substance Abuse (CASA) at Columbia University's
report, *Under the Counter: The Diversion and Abuse of Controlled Prescription Drugs in the U.S,*
July 2005 www.casacolumbia.org/
Note: CASA is often an unreliable source of drug data as they have an extreme pro "war on
drugs" bent, but they may be a bit more objective on this topic of prescription drug abuse
than on the use of drugs associated with the "counterculture."

on the international black market in prescription drugs, see:
-"Prescription abuse outstrips illegal drug use, UN warns" by
Alan Travis, in The Guardian, March 1, 2007

-The Drug Policy Alliance, headed by Ethan Nadelmann, is the country's best activist group on changing our insane drug policies: www.drugpolicy.org

on the U.S. Supreme Court case on Ayahuasca, see:
-Chapter 14, "The Extraordinary case of the United States Versus the Uniao do Vegetal Church" by Jeffrey Bronfman, in *Visionary Plant Consciousness*, edited by J.P. Harpignies (Park Street Press, 2007)

on U.S. prison stats and drugs, see:
-Sabol, William J., PhD, Couture, Heather, and Harrison, Paige M., "Bureau of Justice Statistics, Prisoners in 2006" (Washington, DC: US Department of Justice, December 2007)
-Harrison, Paige M. & Allen J. Beck, PhD, "U.S. Department of Justice, Bureau of Justice Statistics, Prisoners in 2005" (Washington, DC: US Department of Justice, November 2006)
-Scalia, John, "US Department of Justice, Bureau of Justice Statistics, Federal Drug Offenders, 1999 with Trends 1984-99" (Washington, DC: US Dept. of Justice, August 2001)

on average sentences for various crimes, see:
-"US Department of Justice, Bureau of Justice Statistics, Federal Criminal Case Processing, 2000, With Trends 1982-2000" (Washington, DC: US Department of Justice, November 2001), p. 12, Table 6

on drug incarceration rates and racism in New York City, see:
-"Weeding Out Blacks and Latinos: new study outlines racial disparity in NYC's staggering number of pot busts" by Sean Gardiner, in the Village Voice April 30-May 6, 2008
-"Blunt Justice: The NYPD's Hidden Crusade Against Marijuana Furthers a Racist Agenda" by Nat Hentoff, also in the Village Voice, May 7-13, 2008

on national incarceration rates, race and drug arrests, see:
-"Inmate Count In U.S. Dwarfs Other Nations" by Adam Liptak, in the NY Times, April 23rd, 2008;
-"Reports Find Persistent Racial Bias in Drug Arrests" by Erik Eckholm in the NY Times, May 6th, 2008
-NY Times editorial "Racial Inequity and Drug Arrests" (May 10th, 2008)

-The Craig Haney and Philip Zimbardo quote is from "The Past and Future of U.S. Prison Policy: Twenty-five Years After the Stanford Prison Experiment," in the American Psychologist, Vol. 53, No. 7, July 1998, p. 721.
-The General Barry McCaffrey quote is from his keynote address at the National Conference on Drug Abuse Prevention Research, National Institute on Drug Abuse, September 19, 1996, Washington, DC

-The study on popular music content regarding drug and alcohol use by a team from the University of Pittsburgh School of Medicine led by Brian Primack is in the Archives of Pediatrics and Adolescent Medicine, Volume 162, No. 2, pp. 169-175, February 2008

-H. Rap Brown's famous quote from the 1960s that I paraphrase was actually: "Violence is as American as cherry pie" but for some reason it got changed to apple pie in the public imagination, perhaps because apple pie seems more archetypally American.

SEXUAL BEHAVIOR

"I can resist everything except temptation."—Oscar Wilde

I realize that intelligent, worldly people reading this might very well ask why I would bother discussing sex in an essay that is purporting to question societal norms. If there is one domain in which our society has had its assumptions radically transformed in just a few decades, sexuality has to take the cake. Even for a period of ever more dizzyingly rapid technological, economic, geopolitical, and socio-cultural upheavals, the changes to our sexual norms have been extraordinary, and the dust has far from settled. One could even make a credible argument that there are, in fact, no society-wide sexual norms these days.

We certainly are still in the midst of complex, fluid shifts about sexual expression, and it's obviously among the most passionately contested realms of contemporary life, one in which attitudes are likely to be dramatically different depending on one's age, region, neighborhood, social class, and ethnicity. This has of course always been true to some extent. Sophisticated elites have always had different behaviors than peasant farmers, but those differences are certainly more starkly pronounced today than at any point in recent history. We can now flip a channel and go from hard-core porn to an evangelical preacher in nanoseconds, and there is no imaginable (or unimaginable) human behavior that can't be found online. This is a country that contains both a huge "Bible Belt" and an ever-growing Las Vegas, and not a few born again Christians who go to Las Vegas on vacation! That's not that surprising a paradox, perhaps, since the southern "Bible Belt" regions of the U.S. have the highest divorce rates (much higher than the more liberal and secular Northeast) and the earliest average age of sexual initiation in the country.

And not only are sexual norms in flux, but figuring out what's actually going on is far from easy. In fact, finding reliable data about many aspects of sexual behavior in our society, it turns out, is pretty close to impossible. The emotionally charged nature of the topic, the covertness of many of the behaviors, the unreliability of responses to surveys, extreme disagreements among various "experts," and the sometimes complete dearth of figures on many sexual subcultures make it a maddening area to wander into. I was a bit surprised discovering this since I had (very naïvely, it turns out) assumed that after Kinsey's groundbreaking work sixty years ago (which, whatever its methodological flaws and the extraordinary controversy it generated, put this field of inquiry solidly on the map) surely reams of solid data about every nook and cranny of sexual life would now be available.

To some extent it's true that there is a lot of data. There are indeed quite a few aspects of sexuality that have been extensively researched. Since Kinsey, Masters and Johnson's work on the physiology of arousal in the 60s, John William Money's work on gender roles and identity, then the Janus Report on sexual behavior in the 90s have been just some of the noteworthy markers in this field, and many other researchers, including at places such as the Society for the Scientific Study of Sexuality and Kinsey's heirs at the still active Kinsey Institute, continue to make contributions (and on occasion unleash controversies). With the emergence of AIDS, research on sexually transmitted disease obviously became a priority, even during conservative administrations, and one can find, for example, hundreds of studies on condom use (why they break, cultural reasons men fail to use them…). You can also certainly find out just about anything you've ever wanted to know about "erectile dysfunction" since drug company funding is ample for such work for obvious reasons given the sales figures for Viagra and Cialis and their ilk.

We certainly live in different times than Kinsey. The LGBT (Lesbian/Gay/Bisexual/Transgender) movement is an increasingly accepted socio-political force. There are many, many specialized books published each year on a wide range of medical, psychological, cultural, social and political aspects of sexuality. In fact, with the emergence of new groups of academics reflecting the shifts in the larger culture, whole new fields have emerged, ranging from the booming discipline of "Queer Studies" to even a few instances of serious work by present or former workers in the adult entertainment world who have become academics. One good example of the latter is the book *G-Strings and Sympathy: Strip Club Regulars and Male Desire* by

Katherine Frank, a feminist anthropologist and former stripper who used her job to interview a wide array of male patrons of strip clubs over a period of a few years and produced some thoughtful and insightful original research. There have been a few serious, academic conferences on S+M, though one that included that topic at the State University of New York at New Paltz caused a major furor in New York State's political establishment a few years ago. In general one might get the impression that, despite occasional brouha-has, when it comes to sex, no stone has been left unturned, especially since, beyond academia, talk shows, films, mainstream TV programs and women's magazines all routinely delve into many topics and portray behaviors that would have seemed far too risqué in previous eras. Why the porn star Jenna Jameson even had a billboard at Times Square for a while not long ago.

It turns out, however, that that this superficial appearance of openness and transparency is once again somewhat illusory. In fact, in some ways the study of sexual behavior never fully recovered from the backlash to Kinsey's work. America, we all know, has extremely conservative, archaic, puritanical strands in its DNA that remain vibrantly powerful. One major factor leading to the deep-seated stagnation of the U.S.' political life in recent decades is that the socially conservative right is so obsessed by its visceral revulsion to those Dionysian cultural forces that emerged throughout the late 19th and 20th Centuries and exploded in the 1960s that it is stuck in a mode of per-manent, rabid rage.

Funding for big, well-designed surveys that would offer up more realis-tic portraits of American sexual behavior is, by and large, simply not avail-able. A lot of small studies in limited areas are tolerated, but large-scale stud-ies into touchy topics in this domain are a virtual taboo because conserva-tives, remembering the powerful impact Kinsey's work had, view such research as a way to legitimize behaviors they abhor. As with the decriminal-ization of "soft" drugs, the right will fight tooth and nail to prevent it, while what passes for the "left" in mainstream U.S. politics is unwilling to expend even a modicum of political capital to push for it because it involves politi-cal risk. Sexuality is still such fiercely contested terrain in our culture that many researchers have internalized fears of exploring the thorniest topics and now tend to censor themselves, not only because they realistically fear losing their funding but also because they fear becoming the brunt of fierce attacks if they dare court controversy.

It turns out their fears are well founded. The right has certainly been very frustrated by its overall failure in the larger culture wars, above all its inability to staunch the evolution of far more tolerant sexual attitudes, especially in younger generations, but it has also become better organized and more sophisticated and can still make life miserable for those it goes after, especially since it has benefited from connections to powerful allies in the Bush administration and the Republican party in the last few years. Leading socially conservative organizations such as Focus on the Family and the Family Research Council and other groups now actively monitor academia and research and start campaigns to discredit professors and work they object to. These efforts mirror national initiatives spearheaded by such figures as the notorious David Horowitz and Daniel Pipes that monitor and defame professors viewed as insufficiently pro-Israel and/or too left leaning. In 2003, the Traditional Values Coalition, representing over 40,000 churches, compiled a list of some 150 researchers doing work it objected to, a lot of it on sexuality, and brought it to the attention of sympathetic conservative politicians. As a result Congress threatened to shut down several sex studies by well-respected researchers in 2003, and government health officials refused to finance a proposed initiative by several major universities to train students in studying sexuality.

And the "abstinence only" sex-ed obsessions of the Bush administration were about as successful as Nancy Reagan's "Just Say No" campaign in the drug arena. Those groups of Christian teens who take pledges to delay sex until marriage are covered in the media as an exotic subculture, because teenage sexual activity is largely viewed as a given at this point. Teen pregnancy rates are still much higher than in Europe, though they have, mercifully, come down in recent years, but this has as much or more to do with increased condom and birth control pill usage and the popularity of oral (as opposed to penetrative) sex among teens than with modest reductions in teen sexual activity. The rates of STDs, especially Human Papilloma Virus (HPV) and Chlamydia, among teens (over 25%), indicate that this is a very sexually active group (as it has been, obviously, for the entire trajectory of our species-it's when males produce the most sperm and females are the most fertile).

As a result of the paucity of good research, there are many key areas of sexual behavior we know very little about. We know, for example, that the Internet is radically and rapidly changing courtship rituals and dating and the quest for sexual stimulation, but we really don't have reliable data on the details of these profound social transformations. On a much deeper level, we don't even really know much about how people form sexual identities, and the most controversial areas, such as studies of pedophilia, are so contentious that most researchers avoid them like the plague. For social conservatives only the pure demonizing of pedophiles should be allowed, because seeking to understand the phenomenon might perhaps, they fear, elicit some compassion for deviants. This certainly seems strange to those of us who think that it helps to actually understand a problem as deeply as possible to address it as effectively as possible.

This lack of understanding is certainly one of the factors that led to a wave of extraordinarily bizarre episodes during the Reagan and Bush I era, i.e. throughout the 1980s and into the early 1990s. Around the country, in a number of high profile cases, teachers and groups of parents of very young children in daycare and pre-schools were accused, convicted and imprisoned for large-scale, organized child molestation based solely on the testimony of impressionable children coaxed by their interviewers, often "specialists" with outlandish psychological theories, with no shreds of corroborating evidence. The defendants were often accused of being Satanists who had performed bizarre rituals in conjunction with these alleged incidents of child abuse. A whole industry of "experts" on such abuse and on the mysterious phenomenon of "repressed memory" emerged. The accused had almost no defenders and were railroaded in a hysterical atmosphere.

It started in 1982 with a Kern County, California child abuse case, followed by the most famous of them, the McMartin Preschool trial in Los Angeles, which erupted the following year. A whole wave of cases across North America (and some in England, Australia and New Zealand) subsequently popped up. To name only a few from later in the 80s into the 90s: the Wee Care Nursery School in New Jersey; the Glendale Montessori case in Stuart, Florida; the Little Rascals Day Care Center scandal in Edenton, North Carolina; the Ingram case in Olympia, Washington; one in Martensville, Saskatchewan; the Praca daycare center in the Bronx; and, finally, one of the most bizarre of all and the last hurrah of the genre in this wave, the Wenatchee sex rings case in Washington State, starting in 1994. Many people's lives were destroyed; some were jailed for years. By the mid to late 1990s, some form of sanity began to prevail, and nearly all these cases were overturned, though a few people served incredibly long prison terms. Perhaps the last to be released, in 2004, was John Stoll-he had served 20 years for 17 counts of child molesting before nearly all his accusers came forward and said the assaults he and three others were accused of had never happened, and that they had been manipulated by investigators when they were 6 to 8 years old. None of the children had been medically examined at the time and no physical evidence was presented at the trial. The whole 80s and 90s pedophilia craze may have been the closest thing to the panic surrounding the Salem witch trials in modern times.

In retrospect it's astonishing these accusations were taken seriously. In the Kern county episode, charges were first made by a step-grandmother with a history of mental illness. She accused her grandchildren's parents of using the kids in porn and prostitution, and the coerced children then also fingered the character witnesses for the defense, and the parents and their witnesses all got 240 year sentences in '84 and only had their convictions overturned in 1996. The McMartin case, the longest and most expensive trial in U.S. history, involved incredibly wild accusations of hidden tunnels, animal sacrifice, orgies and satanic rituals, all ultimately revealed to be patently absurd years later. In another such episode, the Fells Acres Day Care Center case, children told of being abused by a robot and a clown in a hidden room and of being penetrated with long knives (which miraculously left no injuries). Their testimonies were so consistent, it was clear they had been coached.

Another grotesque miscarriage of justice was the conviction of Kelly Michaels, a New Jersey nursery school teacher, for supposedly assaulting 33 children. She was sentenced to 47 years on totally absurd charges, based on the testimony of an "expert" on such conditions as "child sexual abuse accommodation syndrome." She served five years before her case was overturned. There were many other cases with equally unbelievable stories, which implicated whole groups of adults in epic child abuse, all resulting in convictions, and just about all thrown out later on. The wildest of all was the Wenatchee, Washington saga. In '94/95 cops and social workers embarked upon what they called the most extensive child sex-abuse investigation in U.S. history. Eventually forty-three (!) adults, including parents, a clergyman and Sunday school teachers in this out of the way town in the Eastern Cascades, were arrested on 29,726 charges involving 60 children. No physical evidence supported the charges. The only real "witness" was a thirteen-year-old girl, who just happened to be the foster daughter of the cop who was the lead investigator of the case.

Here we have an archetypal mass hysteria, a form of collective madness (sometimes called "moral panics"), but, while there have been some books and good TV exposés about these episodes, very little attention is focused on them today, and I really don't think we have collectively grasped the full implications of this wave of mass insanity that swept the English-speaking world for nearly fifteen years. Granted, we know more now about the fantastic imagination and malleability of children's stories when faced with questioners with an agenda, and about fabricated memories, but still, the terrifying gullibility of juries and the media and the ready willingness of the public to accept totally unfounded, preposterous accusations reveal the real risks of deep ignorance about human sexual behavior. Yes, there are pedophiles, but they don't take over whole towns or schools and build elaborate secret tunnels, à la *Invasion of the Body Snatchers*.

To be absolutely clear, I'm not at all saying there is no such thing as pedophilia, or that it's not a serious problem. It's next to impossible to be sure of the true prevalence of sexual abuse of children because few pedophiles seek treatment of their own accord, and we just don't know how many individuals have pedophilic fantasies but never act on them or aren't apprehended when they do. Probably less than 5% of such abuse cases are even reported, according to several estimates, but a couple of surveys of adolescents and people in their 20s in Canada and the U.S. found that around 30% of the females and 15% of the males had suffered "unwanted sexual contact" before the age of 17. By far most of those incidents among the girls were from other adolescents though, so most of these cases were not true pedophilia. Also, active pedophiles tend to be compulsive and to be serial abusers, so a very small group of them is most likely responsible for a big share of child sex abuse incidents. Still, the point is that quite a few young people are victims of abuse in general and a not insignificant number to sexual abuse of some form and that a lot of it goes unreported. Anecdotally, several people I knew quite well in my youth had been victims of sexual abuse when they were kids in my neighborhood, sometimes a few doors down from my family, I found out much later in life, so it's a topic I take very seriously.

A society's primary responsibility is the protection and nurturing of its young, so a society has an obligation to seek to restrain all forms of child abuse. But pedophiles, like nearly all other sexual beings, do not choose their inclinations. We have no choice but to incarcerate those who can't control their urges, but they are still human beings, and the more we understand them, the better chance we have to prevent or at least radically reduce pedophilia and to contain the damage it causes without ruining innocent people's lives.

It is important to attempt to think our way clearly through these difficult issues by avoiding oversimplification and hysteria and the lumping together of all sexual acts involving minors into the same category. In the last few years a number of cases involving female high school teachers caught having sex with their underage male students have garnered a great deal of attention. One could sense the glee of conservative commentators whose basic attitude was: "OK. You women wanted equality and an end to gender bias, so now you should suffer exactly the same legal repercussions as a male teacher seducing a young woman would receive." And feminists were hard-pressed to argue otherwise, so almost none of them show any sympathy for these women. I don't dispute that sex between teachers and students is almost invariably a very bad idea that requires disciplinary action and in many instances perhaps some legal sanctions as well, and that a mass society generally has no choice but to enforce laws across the board. But I would also argue that each case is unique, and that there is a very good chance that far less psychic harm is done to young men in many of these cases than would be the case if the gender equation were reversed. An ideal legal system should be able to attempt to judge each case based on the specific factors that define it, and judges often are, in fact, called upon to make these types of subjective calls in juvenile and child custody cases.

I think one can be an intelligent feminist who believes passionately that women are every bit as capable and intelligent as men, that they should be paid as well as men in comparable jobs, and so on, and still understand that men and women are also different in many ways and that a fifteen to sixteen year old boy is often far more likely to be psychologically "ready" for sexual initiation than a girl of the same age, and far more likely to seek it out. This is a sort of double standard, I admit, but one based on psychosocial reality. I don't dispute these teachers erred and should in most cases suffer some consequences, but to automatically lump them together with child molesters seems to me grossly unfair. There are cultures in which young men's sexual initiation by older, experienced women is widely accepted, and, in an ideal world, if done delicately, that strikes me as a cultural institution with potential merit, given how sexually clumsy and ignorant about women most young men are in our own culture.

But let me return to the task at hand, since I can't possibly cover even an iota of the issues involved in sexual behaviors. To recapitulate a few of the points I've been trying to make so far: the norms that may currently exist are certainly a fluid and rapidly shifting moving target; our society is far more tolerant in this domain than it used to be, but sex is still a highly contested battlefield in the culture wars; and our national attitudes toward sexuality are paradoxical and fractured in that we now allow the near ubiquity of far more provocative sexual material than in previous generations, but we are still very squeamish at our core and discourage the serious study of many key areas of inquiry in the field.

As I indicated at the onset, my focus in this book is mostly to explore the contrasts between the current underlying assumptions of educated elites and actual social reality in a few specific areas, so I am above all looking for discrepancies between widely accepted ideas and the real behavior of people on the ground. In the domain of sex, there are certain behaviors that would have been worth delving into a few years ago in a text such as this: the actual numbers of homosexuals in the population or the declining prevalence of married couples, say, but these barely elicit a reaction or much controversy these days among sophisticates.

Attempts to determine how many people in the population are homosexual or have had homosexual experiences are interesting, however, because they once again offer a case study that illustrates the great difficulty of getting exact figures that specialists agree upon in these domains. Kinsey, the first to really try to rigorously study the question, is widely remembered as having found that 10% of the population was gay, though that's an oversimplification. His view was actually more nuanced: he felt sexuality was more fluid, so he used a 0 to 6 ranking method that went from "0" indicating completely heterosexual tendencies to "6"-completely homosexual ones. Among his findings was that some 46% of male subjects had "reacted" sexually to both sexes at some point, 37% had at least one homosexual experience; 11.6% of white males 20 to 35 were ranked as 3s (fairly evenly bisexual) and 10% were "more or less exclusively homosexual" for at least a few years at some point in their lives. On the female side, roughly 5 or 6% were ranked as 3s, while 2 to 6% aged 20 to 35 were pretty much exclusively homosexual.

Now, besides a lot of moral panic and backlash, Kinsey was also criticized by some statisticians for his methodology, especially his sample selection, which was said to be unrepresentative of the whole population. For exam-

ple a quarter were or had been inmates and 5% or so had been male prostitutes, and those willing to answer such intimate questions in that repressive
era were seen as an atypical self-selected group. Kinsey's successor at the
institute he had founded, Paul Gebhard, worked hard for many years to correct these flaws and recalibrate the data, removing prisoners' responses for
example, and this led to the publication of *The Kinsey Data: Marginal
Tabulations of the 1938-1963 Interviews Conducted by the Institute for Sex
Research*, which, somewhat surprisingly, found that Kinsey's major estimates
held up pretty well, with only marginal changes.

But a more recent meta-report, *American Sexual Behavior: Trends, Socio-
Demographic Differences, and Risk Behavior* by Tom W. Smith of the National
Opinion Research Center at the University of Chicago (updated in 2003),
reviewed a series of recent national and international studies and concluded
that only about 2 to 3% of sexually active men and 1 to 2% of sexually active
women were currently engaging in same gender sex. He stated that 3.4% of
sexually active males had had a male sexual partner in the previous 12
months, 4.1% during the previous five years, and 4.9% since the age of 18.
That 4.9% is certainly light years from the 37% Kinsey said had had at least
one lifetime same sex encounter. Smith did find that gay men tend to con-
gregate in the largest cities, and that in those regions the rate can indeed be
in the 10% range (or is it that people in big cities are less frightened to be
honest??).

What's clear is that it's often really hard to even define something as fluid
as sexual identity for quite a few people, let alone categorize them and count
them accurately when honest answers are hard to be sure of since the fear of
being stigmatized (or worse) is still so understandable. In any case, whatever
the accurate numbers are (and after looking at these and other studies on the
question, I certainly have no better idea than when I started) most people in
the sophisticated elites finally now think of homosexuality as a perfectly routine phenomenon, one whose status has ranged, historically, from fully
accepted in certain contexts (ancient Athens or Sparta) to totally taboo, but
that has always involved a minority in every human society and that is also
far from uncommon in the animal realm, so clearly "natural" in every sense
of the word. The dominant view (again, among sophisticates) is that it most
likely has a genetic component, so that it is not a choice but a hard-wired
tendency that some are born with that must be associated with some bene-
ficial adaptive traits, or it would have died out long ago. So, since I am try-

ing to look at behavior that is not readily socially accepted and yet prevalent, homosexuality per se is of no interest to me in the context of this discussion, in that it's, for the most part, no longer viewed as unusual. It's now an accepted palette in the range of erotic identities.

The mutation of the average household and family unit is another example of a situation that once shocked but is now widely accepted. Not long ago, the 50s sitcom happy suburban nuclear family, with both parents married just once and with 2.3 kids (who are the actual genetic offspring of both parents), was still the de-facto ideal, long after it had stopped being a majority of households. The high divorce rate and the "breakdown" of the "traditional" family were widely bemoaned. That moaning still goes on, of course, especially among cultural conservatives, but it's far more muted. Now, when census data revealed that, in 2005, for the first time ever, more than half of U.S. women (51%) were living without a spouse in the house and that married couples now constituted a minority of households, it barely raised an eyebrow.

By and large, while stable families are viewed as a good thing across the ideological spectrum, and the prevalence of single mothers in poverty in certain communities is widely seen as a serious social problem, the idea of what a family is has become far more expansive. Professor Stephanie Coontz, probably the nation's leading expert on marriage and the author of *Marriage: A History*, says that marriage has changed more in the last thirty years than in the previous three thousand. With a divorce rate that hovers at somewhere between 50 and 55% and a society that now not only finally provides women with employment opportunities but actually makes it economically impossible for most of them not to work (though it doesn't pay a lot of them nearly enough when they do, nor offer them affordable daycare), modern capitalism has seen to it that the social conditions for 50s style nuclear families simply no longer exist, and by now nearly everyone understands that, whether they like it or not. While the culture is cyclical and there are occasional outbreaks of nostalgia for a bygone era of clear sex roles and white picket fences (or at the most extreme some growing pockets of polygamist enclaves in the Southwest), we're not going back (to an era that actually never really existed as portrayed anyway).

One bizarre form of such nostalgia that highlights by its very hyper-manic excesses just how threatened the old-style nuclear family ideal really has become is a new form of over-the-top wedding fetishism. For a certain sizeable subset of women weddings have become more than understandably emotionally charged and deeply consequential bonding rituals. A whole industry has emerged geared to insanely expensive, obsessively organized events that seem more like potlatches for control freaks than marriage ceremonies. This growth industry, which employs the expected platoons of matchmakers, planners, bakers, caterers, couturiers and so on, has countless glossy magazines and several "reality" TV shows (Bridezillas, etc.) dedicated to it, including at least one that features exercise trainers helping brides-to-be desperately trying to "get in shape" for the big event.

American romantic comedies have almost always ended at the wedding, as the two soul mates destined to be together finally overcome all the mishaps and misunderstandings and obstacles and villains to marry and head off to domestic utopia. Our culture's obsession with weddings is clearly nothing new, but the current version is so grotesquely overdone that it is hard to believe that it isn't intentionally self-satirizing. The wedding has become a sort of Teilhardian Omega Point, or to borrow from the counter-cultural philosopher Terence McKenna, a "transcendental object at the end of time" (or, to be snide, in retrospect, for quite a few, a black hole). It's also not surprising that the actual long-term process of marriage with all its complexities and compromises receives less pop culture attention, and when it is focused upon it is usually to discuss ways of saving or enlivening what is widely recognized as a problematic endeavor that requires a lot of remediation and reanimation.

It's interesting that as wedding fetishism sweeps the U.S. very different trends are occurring in other places. In France, for example, a relatively new form of civil union, which provides some of the legal benefits of marriage for cohabitating couples but is less binding than marriage, and which was originally designed for gay couples, became so popular among heterosexuals that, for a while, it outnumbered marriages, which are in rapid decline. Europe's formal institutions have become far more open to change and willing to experiment in the wake of social transformations than ours have in recent years. Here in the U.S., we seem to stumble forward as we grasp at nostalgic straws.

In a manner similar to "Western" novels and later films, which mythologized the West once the "frontier" was in fact "closed," some current subcultural trends (retro fashions, archaic dating guidelines and sex roles) mimic aspects of earlier eras when matters pertaining to gender seemed more clear-cut, but this aping is either so exaggerated or inescapably infected by the ubiquity of irony that it is not at all convincing, because the objective conditions surrounding even those who adopt these nostalgic yearnings have changed. The "old-school" woman who wants a husband who will be the provider most probably still wants all the perks of hip modernity and is very likely to have to work anyway unless she is in a very small privileged minority. Even most of the right wing has adjusted to this reality: some of the right's most strident advocates are dynamic career women, some of whom even on occasion describe themselves as feminists. Even the moose-shooting, fundamentalist Christian, arch-reactionary woman Republican Vice Presidential candidate in the 2008 U.S. election called herself a feminist at one point in the campaign.

One category of marriage-related, socially frowned upon behavior that periodically receives a lot of attention in our culture when famous people are caught straying is infidelity. It's yet another example of a phenomenon for which it seems impossible to get uncontroversial statistics, and in which camps with different ideological biases put forward radically different numbers. Interestingly, a few feminist authors of the 70s and 80s and some contemporary culturally conservative Christians tend to cite very high figures for infidelity. This seems to suit their respective agendas: the feminist writers were eager to undermine the patriarchal aspects of marriage and the Christians want to underline the moral decay of modern life.

I know I'm above all focused on the U.S. but infidelity is one aspect of sexual behavior that apparently varies a lot in how it is addressed in different cultures. In a recent book, *Lust in Translation: The Rules of Infidelity from Tokyo to Tennessee*, Pamela Druckerman says that cheating is of course frowned upon and carried on secretively everywhere, but that the Japanese abhor indiscretion more than the actual infidelity and avoid confrontation, the Russians love a big fight and the customary penalty is for men to buy their wives off with serious gifts (furs, diamonds, Black Sea vacations), the French don't tend to feel as much guilt as Anglo-Saxons, and Latin Americans are heavily into the double standard as South-American men have some of the highest rates (as far as we can tell) of affairs but until recently could get away with killing their wives if they caught them cheating in a number of countries. North Americans seem more obsessed with honesty than just about anyone else (in theory at least). What studies there are seem to indicate a wide variation in prevalence as well, from highest in parts of sub-Saharan Africa to lowest in Australia. But, judging by the unreliability of U.S. statistics on the matter, I'd be careful not to jump to any conclusions. The discrepancies in infidelity estimates are even more extreme than in the case of homosexuality. They're, to be blunt, all over the place. This is, for obvious reasons, a domain in which it's even harder to design survey methods that are likely to elicit a high degree of truthfulness in respondents, or to be able to corroborate findings. In 2007 teams of researchers from Texas A&M and the University of Colorado interviewed 4,884 married women in live interviews and via anonymous online questionnaires. Only 1% of the women in the face-to-face interviews admitted to adultery in the past year but 6% did in the computer surveys.

The Associated Press released the following stats during the Clinton/Lewinsky affair: 22% of U.S. men and 14% of women admitted to at least one act of adultery at some point; 5% and 3% respectively admitted infidelity in the past year; 17% of divorces were officially blamed on it. According to a Time-CNN poll at the time 90% thought it was morally wrong, but 61% did not think it should be a crime. But other writers on the topic offer much higher estimates of its prevalence. Peggy Vaughan, the author of 1989's *The Monogamy Myth*, says: "Conservative estimates are that 60 percent of men and 40 percent of women will have an extramarital affair." Annette Lawson, author of *Adultery* (also 1989) cites between a quarter to half of married women and from 50 to 65% for men (by age forty). Maggie Scarf, author of *Intimate Partners*, (re-issued in 1996) estimates 50 to 65% of husbands and 45 to 55% of wives, again by age forty. Shere Hite, author of the famous *Hite Report*, probably has the record for the highest estimate, asserting that up to 70% of women who were married more than 5 years had strayed at some point

Here are some more supposed factoids gleaned from a range of different sources: affairs affect one of every 2.7 couples, 10% of extramarital affairs last one day, 10% under a month, 50% less than a year, 40% two years or more, very few more than four, one "expert" affirms. Only 31% of marriages survive a discovered indiscretion, according to one writer, but another cites a figure of 64%! People very rarely marry the person with whom they were unfaithful once they are divorced, under 3%, says another. 74% of men and 68% of women say they would cheat if they were guaranteed that they would not be discovered, according to one website, while another says only 10% would. Now I have no idea how most of these "facts" were compiled or if any of them are even remotely accurate, but they are very confidently bandied about in articles and online, as are slews of other studies of various types that offer a wide range of yet more radically different statistics. Clearly, no one has the slightest idea.

The meta-study I mentioned earlier, *American Sexual Behavior: Trends, Socio-Demographic Differences, and Risk Behavior,* is far more conservative in its estimates. It admits that there are not a whole lot of really solid studies to go by, but it bemoans "pseudo-scientific" claims and the "incredible misinformation from popular magazines, sex gurus, and others…" and cites more recent studies that describe a range of 3 to 4% of the married who have had a sexual partner besides their spouse in a given year and some 15 to 18% for lifelong infidelity. It further concludes that rates have probably gone up in recent decades, are more prevalent among younger couples and that men cheat about twice as much as wives.

Among the more credible studies are those of the National Science Foundation's General Social Survey (headquartered at the University of Chicago), which has been tracking data on Americans' opinions and behaviors since 1972. Its estimate till the 90s had been that each year around 12% of men and 7% of women "cheated." But the most recent of its studies find rather dramatic increases in adultery among both the old and the young in recent years, with women's rates now getting closer to men's.

Once again, who knows? The conservative figures sound pretty low to me, especially given how very rare complete sexual fidelity in the animal and primate kingdoms seems to be. The biggest estimates sound exaggerated. I would guess the truth lies somewhere between the lower and higher estimates, but I really have to admit I have no idea, and I'm pretty sure, as I mentioned, that no one else really does either. Even an expert on the neurology of love, Helen Fisher, an anthropologist at Rutgers, has been quoted, while discussing promiscuity and monogamy, as saying "We don't know anything."

One thing I do strongly suspect, however, is that if you threw in a new wrinkle: "virtual infidelity" online, the rate would skyrocket. I base this suspicion mostly on the behavior of people I know and on a lot of other anecdotal evidence because (I know this is starting to sound like a broken record) there is even less reliable data (if that's possible) when dealing with Net-based sexual phenomena than with longer studied areas of inquiry such as homosexuality and infidelity. The Internet has burst upon us and is impacting nearly every aspect of social life, but very little serious, well-designed, large-scale work has yet been done on its effects on psychosexual life. A culling of tidbits from a range of websites on the topic of online affairs included such nuggets as: only 46% of men believe that online affairs are adultery; one third of divorce litigation is caused by online affairs; 8 to 10% percent of Internet users become hooked on cyber-sex; 38% of people have engaged in explicit sexual online communications; 31% of people have had an online communication that has led to actual sex; and so on. All these factoids have to be taken with pounds of salt, but there is little doubt that cyber-based eroticism is an enormous phenomenon, and that it has at the very least radically boosted access to emotional infidelity. I am really curious if cyber-sex is in some cases replacing physical sexual contacts or if, conversely, it's making it easier for people to contact each other so they can then "hook-up" in the actual "meat world." Clearly both are happening but I wonder if the first is more prevalent and the start of a "de-physicalization" of sex is underway. The Net has certainly launched pornography, erotic imagery of all types and sexual subcultures into whole new stratospheres of accessibility.

The increasingly easy access to porn, first with video, then dramatically boosted by cable TV, and finally mushrooming into cyberspace has made the genre a far more accepted feature of modern life, one routinely joked about by late night talk show hosts in a manner that, like drug use, implicitly recognizes that the comedians are intimately familiar with the topic and that assumes most of the audience is too. A few of the principal porn stars (Ron Jeremy, the aforementioned Jenna Jameson) have now developed even wider name recognition among the general public and mainstream media than Linda Lovelace once did.

Some aspects of the porn business are difficult to track because nearly all of the companies are privately held and don't release their sales figures. Estimates of the income of the entire (legal) U.S. sex entertainment industry in 2006 were in the range of 12 to 13 billion dollars. This includes video rentals and sales (rapidly decreasing as everything moves online), web site income, TV pay-per-view, strip clubs, magazines, etc. This is more than the combined revenues of all the professional football, baseball, and basketball franchises. This is no longer the porn of dingy shops and dank peep shows. It's a major industry that now includes, besides the slew of San Fernando Valley independent entrepreneurs, some major household name corporate players (GM, AT&T, Marriott, Comcast) that love the high profit margins that characterize the business. One of the most lucrative niches is still pay-per-view porn on cable TV in hotel/motel rooms.

Comcast, the biggest cable TV company in the country, which almost took over Disney in 2004 (the deal ultimately fell through), is probably still the biggest single distributor of porn, though cable companies don't as a rule break down their earnings from porn in their financial reports, so educated guesses have to be made. One wag pointed out, as the merger was looking likely in '04, that, apparently "This is a company...that is perfectly at ease bringing you both "Boob Mania 6" and "Toy Story 2." But cable TV and video sales are in decline, as more and more human activities move into cyberspace, where they're paradoxically both more hidden and luridly public on a mass scale.

Pornography and "adult entertainment" were, in fact, fundamental factors in facilitating the Internet revolution. They provided the only stable revenue stream for online entrepreneurs as the Internet was first trying to get established. To this day, porn most likely still constitutes the biggest single use of the Internet, at least for men. According to comScore Media Metrix, 71.2% of males 18-34 visited a porn site in the month of October 2003. Other studies list such statistics as: a quarter of all search engine requests are porn-related; 12% of all websites are pornographic; 90% of 8 to 16 year olds have viewed porn online; the average age of first Internet exposure to pornography is 11; 12 to 17 year olds are the group with the most frequent visits to porn sites; 20% of men and 13% of women admit accessing porn while at their jobs. Again, I really doubt most of these claims are completely credible or verifiable, but I feel quite confident saying that if you're a parent of a young teenage boy or the wife or girlfriend of a man, and you think he hasn't accessed porn online recently, the odds are excellent that you're wrong.

The most perennial of the socially frowned upon sexual activities is of course prostitution. It's legal or de facto decriminalized in specific jurisdictions in some European countries but still illegal in most of the world including the U.S. except for a handful of rural Nevada counties. It's been a permanent feature in all large-scale organized human societies, and, primatologists tell us, a version of comparable behavior exists among many primates, including chimpanzees and macaques. A recent paper on Indonesian macaques in the journal Animal Behavior was called "Payment for Sex in a Macaque Mating Market." It tracked how male macaques traded grooming for sex. Chimps are known to use meat as a currency for sex, but I'm guessing bonobos are so promiscuous and pansexual it probably wouldn't make sense in their social groups.

I realize that there are gay prostitutes (maybe 20% of people arrested for prostitution are male) and gigolos, and, horribly, more and more child prostitutes, but the bulk of the business is heterosexual, adult prostitution, so that's what I'm focusing on here. Prostitution has of course long been studied, but here too solid data is scarce. The National Task Force on Prostitution suggested in the 1980s that over one million people in the U.S. had worked as prostitutes (perhaps a tad under 1% of adult American women), but the only solid data is from law enforcement statistics, and they nearly all pertain to street prostitution, which is today a small share of the trade (at most 20% according to the few credible estimates).

The most recent gathering of the American Economic Association featured a controversial presentation by Steven Levitt, economics professor at the University of Chicago (and co-author of the bestselling *Freakonomics*) on the preliminary results of a study he conducted with Sudhir Venkatesh, a brilliant young Columbia sociologist, called "An Empirical Analysis of Street-Level Prostitution." The study deals with hard-nosed analyses of the trade in a few Chicago neighborhoods: supply and demand factors, marketing, pimps' wage strategies to retain their most lucrative earners, and some number crunching on risks (violence, arrest, sexually-transmitted diseases). One interesting factoid was that prostitutes were far more likely to have sex with a cop than to be arrested by one. Other papers at the conference included one on the difference between street prostitutes and ones working in brothels in Ecuador in terms of wages, condom use and rates of STD infections, and another subtitled "An Econometric Analysis of Strip Club Patrons." Venkatesh has also done studies of top-tier "call girls." So, micro-studies go on, but real macro studies are non-existent, so, in fact, no one knows the actual size of the prostitution business.

One conclusion to emerge from these and most serious studies on prostitution is that illegality increases public health risks because suppression has never worked and it's better for both the women and the public to at least attempt to monitor and regulate the trade, though no one pretends that would stop all the hardships and abuses that accompany prostitution, especially at the street level. The level of violence suffered by street prostitutes, who are often in dire economic straights and not infrequently strung out, has always been very high. Also these days, some big, even more nefarious new players have entered the prostitution field: highly lucrative, ruthless international criminal operations that dupe, kidnap and smuggle young women from poor regions, especially parts of Eastern Europe, Central America, and Asia, and force them into prostitution and near slavery. These human traffickers operate at a far higher level of global organization and savagery than the grimy, "free market" street commerce the new breed of hip, *Freakonomics*-style economists like to do iconoclastic studies about.

Today street level prostitution is a relic reserved for the poorest segments of the population. The telephone had already moved a lot of the business indoors ("call girls"), but now, especially for middle class and well-to-do clients, the Internet here too, as with finance, espionage, activism, merchandising, advertising, letter writing, porn and dating, is changing everything. And as prostitution has moved away from the visibility of the street, it's even harder to track or measure and the social pressure to crack down on it lessens, despite the news generated when the occasional high-profile politician is snagged when he is found on the client list of a busted high-end "escort" ring. In general, to date, very low percentages of such operations are busted, except during periodic crackdowns. They tend to attract law enforcement's attention only when the scope of their operations becomes too ambitious and serious sums are too obviously escaping taxation, or when someone being investigated for other reasons leads police to an operation (as in the recent case of former NY Governor Spitzer). The women in the rarefied world of the high-end trade and even some in its middle tiers may not be completely immune to occasional risk and violence, and some of them probably have been led to this career choice by difficult childhoods and dire circumstances, but those in the higher echelons of the trade are also, in a sense, successful entrepreneurs. They have every reason to be discreet, as do the clients, so it's a world that usually escapes public scrutiny, the inevitable occasional scandal and crackdown aside.

Similarly to the significant economic opportunities offered by drug dealing in poor neighborhoods for the toughest and most resourceful street entrepreneurs, or to high seas piracy long ago (and still in Somalia and South Asia), or to bootlegging for the generation of the 1920s, sex-related work, from stripping to prostitution, is by far the most lucrative work option available for many women outside the most educated and connected elites. In a fairly ruthless capitalist economy with very imperfect safety nets and ever less social upward mobility, the immediate potential financial rewards are just too great. If one gets in a jam and desperately needs substantial sums of money for oneself or one's family, there just aren't many options for poorer, and sometimes even middle class women.

As is the case with most prohibitions, illegality increases the cost of the contraband, and so the higher wages increase the temptation-a classic vicious cycle. And the demand has been steady since the dawn of history. I'm not a biological determinist, and I'm sure culture is a crucial factor in any social phenomenon, but one has to respect facts on the ground and to be realistic. Most men are likely to behave as most men always have. Some men who are in relationships already just crave erotic variety, novelty, and the strong lure of sex without commitment, but quite a few men may have no other viable options for sex-migrant workers; soldiers away from home; those too socially inept or physically unattractive or financially unsuccessful or troubled to establish successful pair bonds. In any case, whatever the reasons, there has never been a society without prostitution, no matter how harsh the penalties or how strong the social stigma. As I write this the police chief of Tehran, Iran, who had been leading an aggressive crackdown on "immodestly dressed" women in that far from sexually tolerant society, was arrested during a raid on a brothel, where he was found cavorting with six naked prostitutes.

But I digress. The main question that interests me in the context of the present text is how many men have frequented or regularly frequent prostitutes. As with many of the behaviors I've been looking at, it's illegal. It's also almost universally condemned socially (as opposed to, say, marijuana use, which is illegal but viewed as routine and morally neutral in quite a few milieus), so no one involved is likely to be too eager to discuss it honestly. Very little research on patrons of prostitutes has been done. In one British study, 50% of clients were found to be married or cohabiting. Kinsey found that 70% of adult men had engaged in prostitution at least once.

One interesting study done in 2000 under the auspices of The National Academy of Sciences ("Prostitution and the sex discrepancy in reported number of sexual partners") sought to account for the puzzling fact that, around the world in all surveys, men invariably claim to have had vastly more sexual partners than women do. The report cites a glaringly obvious mathematical problem: "This finding is puzzling, because in a closed population of heterosexuals, men and women actually have the same number of sexual partners in the aggregate." Men must be radically over-reporting and/or women must be under-reporting the number of their partners, or another factor has to be in play. The study concludes that while that over and under reporting does factor in, prostitution is the main missing piece of the puzzle, and men aren't admitting that aspect of their sex lives.

The aforementioned *American Sexual Behavior: Trends, Socio-Demographic Differences, and Risk Behavior* report admits: "Information about women who work as prostitutes is scant, and knowledge of their clients is sketchier still." It lists and discusses just about all the main recent studies on the topic and finds large discrepancies and inconsistencies in the data. It's pretty obvious that it's impossible to get honest answers from people about this behavior in surveys, and that it's just too covert an activity to measure accurately. The few well-designed studies are of street level prostitution, which, as I mentioned, is a small tip of the iceberg at this point and not at all representative of the larger phenomenon.

Surveys of men have been laughably unhelpful. One survey reported that 0.6% of men had hired a prostitute in the past year, 5.9% within the past five, and 16.3% at some point, but these figures are completely inconsistent and make no sense. The five-year figures are more than double what would be expected based on the annual figures. In another survey of a group of 15 to 29 year old men in 1995 0.7% admitted they had seen a prostitute when filling out a written form, but 2.5% of them admitted such behavior when using a computer-assisted audio questionnaire. It's pretty obvious one can't trust any of this data. Those figures are absurdly low. The exact numbers aren't knowable, but there is no doubt that prostitution is a huge business, and so it's obvious a lot of men have at some point purchased a prostitute's services, and a not insignificant number must do so quite often. Even if Kinsey's 70% is unlikely, it's probably a much higher percentage than polite society would be comfortable admitting. David Elms, an online entrepreneur, created a website, The Erotic Review, which has advertisements for escort services and prostitutes and encourages clients to rank them in several categories of performance on a 1 to 10 scale. It's the biggest site of its type, but it's still only one site, and it is estimated to get between 500,000 to 1 million visits each month. So, if you're a woman and you have a boyfriend or a husband and you think he's never visited a prostitute, you may be right, but there's also a pretty good chance you're wrong, and very little chance he'll tell you the truth about it if he has.

Finally, since my subject is normality, I can't avoid looking at what our society's mental health establishment labels as sexually deviant tendencies. Here too I am interested in how many people there really might be among us whose sexual identity or behavior would be considered anomalous by contemporary standards. Like so many other aspects of sexual life, these norms have changed and continue to change in rather startling ways. Strip clubs may be perceived as a bit seedy, but they've entered the mainstream in that it's expected for bachelor parties to take place there and that nearly every male would have visited one at some point, and groups of women go to see male strippers (though that's usually a far more innocent, festive, jovial affair than the tense, charged atmosphere when men are the patrons). Pole dancing is taught as a workout option in health clubs; lap dancing can't be far behind. A few strip club chains are publicly traded companies.

Soft-core S+M imagery, to cite another example, has now long been routine in a great deal of fashion, advertising and entertainment. Tight leather offends only animal rights activists. Props such as blindfolds and handcuffs and vibrators are widely viewed as fairly lightweight sex toys and barely raise eyebrows (dildos are probably not quite there yet). Madonna's embrace of erotic spanking a few years back seemed far more innocuous than scandalous. Janet Jackson's recent albums deal forthrightly with masochistic sexual themes and pass almost unnoticed (the poor girl got far more grief for inadvertently exposing a breast during the Super Bowl). Cross-dressing may be made fun of in many films or comedy routines, but it's largely affectionate: the zany, lovable transvestite has become a common iconic character in mainstream cinema. So, other than obviously, understandably total, permanent (let's hope) taboos such as all forms of non-consensual sexual violence, incest, pedophilia, child porn, self-harm, cannibalism (à la Jeffrey Dahmer), and so on, is anything off-limits and/or viewed as abnormal? Well, yes, there still is a whole lot, as it turns out, and reactions to the predilections in question on the part of outsiders to the phenomena range from mere amused puzzlement to complete ignorance or incomprehension to downright revulsion.

Forgive the broken record, but it turns out that the actual number of aficionados of various offbeat sexual tendencies or subcultures is even more impossible to tabulate than infidelity or prostitution, because very few people seek treatment to "cure" their tendencies, either because they realize it's very unlikely that can be accomplished, or, most often, because they're happy enough with their sexual lives as they are. The most common term to describe these practices or inclinations is a controversial one: paraphilias. It's controversial because the word has a negative connotation, and sexual minorities have good reason to be suspicious of a psychiatric establishment that until not long ago classified homosexuality as an illness. That said some people must be unhappy having urges that place them in a poorly understood minority, especially if their tendency is a really rare or widely reviled one.

Clinical psychiatric literature usually lists eight principal categories of paraphilias. The famous (or infamous) DSM (*Diagnostic and Statistical Manual of Mental Disorders*) I mentioned in the chapter on mental health says that for the activity in question to be technically viewed as an actual disorder it must be the only means of sexual gratification for six months and result in "clinically significant distress or impairment in social, occupational, or other important areas of functioning." There are probably far, far more people who have exotic sexual inclinations but are not narrowly sexually restricted or "impaired" enough to qualify for these DSM criteria for an official disorder. In other words they might really be into a fetish or two but not exclusively enough for it to govern their entire erotic lives or make their overall lives any more dysfunctional than anyone else's.

Also, the view of minority sexual tendencies evolves. For example, the few serious studies on S+M (or BDSM as it's now usually called) in recent decades have concluded the overwhelming majority of active members of these subcultures are just about as happy and well adjusted as everyone else, so the DSM has softened its entry on the topic. In Northern Europe sadomasochism is largely seen as a routine sexual predilection and not a disorder, and it was in fact formally removed from the official listing of disorders in Denmark in 1995, and there's a chance this could happen here, as it finally did with homosexuality. Still, it's one thing for specialists to no longer consider something a formal psychological disorder, but to most people it still seems edgily kinky. Also, European sexual attitudes are generally far more tolerant than ours, and that may not change in the near future. When Max Mosley, the British head of the Paris-based International Automobile Federation (Formula I auto racing's highest body), was surreptitiously filmed in a wild sadomasochistic session with a slew of dominatrices, the federation agreed with him that it was his own private business and voted overwhelmingly to keep him at its helm, and this despite Mosley's cursed family heritage (his father was the leader of Britain's fascists in the 1930s). It's hard to imagine NASCAR having the same response in a similar situation.

Besides pedophilia, the DSM lists: exhibitionism, fetishism (erotic excitement from specific inanimate objects or "non-sexual parts of the body"), frotteurism (urges to rub up against non-consenting others), masochism, sadism, transvestitism, and voyeurism. Some of these, such as fetishism, are whole universes with slews of substantive subcultures within them, each with many, many sub-categories. Others must surely be the province of much smaller groups of people. But these main paraphilias listed in the DSM are part of a much larger universe of unconventional sexual inclinations.

I went to the Wikipedia entry for "paraphilias," and I found the following big list in alphabetical order:

Abasiophilia: attraction to people who are lame or crippled and/or who use leg braces or other orthopedic appliances
Acousticophilia: sexual arousal from certain sounds
Agalmatophilia: sexual attraction to statues or mannequins or immobility
Algolagnia: sexual pleasure from pain
Amaurophilia: sexual arousal by a partner whom one is unable to see due to artificial means, such as being blindfolded or having sex in total darkness
Acrotomophilia and apotemnophilia: sexual attraction to amputation or amputees
Andromimetophilia (also gynemimetophilia): sexual attraction towards women dressed as men or who have had a sex change operation
Aquaphilia: arousal from water, including bathtubs and swimming pools
Aretifism: sexual attraction to people who are without footwear
Autogynephilia: love of oneself as a woman
Autoassassinophilia: sexual arousal from fantasizing about or staging one's own murder
Biastophilia: sexual arousal from assault and rape
Coprophilia: sexual attraction to (or pleasure from) feces (related to: Fecophilia-arousal from defecation or watching a partner defecate)
Covert incestiphilia: arousal from non-contact sexual behavior with a child
Dacryphilia: sexual pleasure in eliciting tears from others or oneself
Dendrophilia: sexual attraction to trees and other large plants
Emetophilia (also vomerophilia): sexual attraction to vomiting
Ephebophilia (also hebephilia): sexual attraction towards adolescents

Erotic asphyxia: sexual attraction from asphyxia (a.k.a. "breath control play," "strangulation," and autoerotic asphyxiation)

Erotic lactation (also galactophilia or lactophilia): sexual attraction to human milk or lactating women

Exhibitionism (also autagonistophilia or peodeiktophilia): sexual arousal by engaging in sexual behavior in view of third parties (also includes the recurrent urge or behavior to expose one's genitals to an unsuspecting person)

Food play: sexual arousal from food

Formicophilia: sexual attraction to smaller animals, insects, etc. crawling on parts of the body

Forniphilia: sexual objectification in which a person's body is incorporated into a piece of furniture

Frotteurism: sexual arousal from the recurrent urge or behavior of touching or rubbing against a non-consenting person

Gerontophilia: sexual attraction towards the elderly

Homeovestism: sexual arousal by wearing the clothing of one's own gender

Human animal roleplay: sexual arousal by having oneself or a partner taking on the role of real or imaginary animal

Hybristophilia: sexual arousal to people who have committed crimes, in particular cruel or outrageous crimes

Incestophilia: sexual attraction to a member of one's own family

Katoptronophilia: sexual arousal from having sex in front of mirrors

Kleptophilia: sexual arousal from stealing things

Klismaphilia: sexual pleasure from enemas

Lust murder (also homicidophilia or erotophonophilia): sexual arousal from committing (or trying to commit) murder-related to sadism, necrophilia, vorarephilia and blood fetish

Macrophilia: sexual attraction to giants or giant body parts (such as breasts and genitalia)

Masochism: the recurrent urge or behavior of wanting to be humiliated, beaten, bound, or otherwise made to suffer

Microphilia: sexual attraction to miniature people or miniature body parts

Mysophilia: sexual attraction to soiled, dirty, foul or decaying materials

Narratophilia: sexual arousal in the use of dirty or obscene words to a partner

Necrophilia: sexual attraction to corpses (includes necrosadism-sexual gratification derived by mutilating and dismembering corpses)

Odaxelagnia: sexual arousal associated with biting or being bitten

Olfactophilia: sexual stimulus with smells or odors

Paraphilic infantilism: sexual pleasure from dressing, acting, or being treated as a baby

Parthenophilia: sexual attraction to virgins

Pedophilia: sexual attraction to prepubescent children

Pictophilia: sexual attraction to pictorial pornography or erotic art

Plushophilia: sexual attraction to stuffed animals and/or people dressed in animal costumes

Pyrophilia: sexual arousal through watching, setting, hearing, talking or fantasizing about fire

Sadism: deriving pleasure, or in some cases sexual arousal from giving pain

Salirophila: sexual arousal by soiling

Schediaphilia: sexual attraction to cartoon characters

Sitophilia: sexual arousal by involving food in sex

Somnophilia: sexual arousal from sleeping or unconscious people-related to necrophilia

Sthenolagnia: sexual arousal from the demonstration of strength or muscles

Telephone scatologia: being sexually aroused by making obscene phone calls to strangers

Teratophilia: sexual attraction to deformed people

Transvestic fetishism: sexual arousal from the wearing of clothes typically associated with the opposite gender to the wearer

Trichophilia: sexual arousal from hair

Troilism: sharing a sexual partner with another person

Urolagnia: sexual attraction to urine, including urinating in public, on others, or on by others-includes Urophagia-sexual attraction to drinking urine or watching others drink urine

Vorarephilia (also gynophagia): sexual attraction at the thought of being eaten by or eating another person or creature-includes endosomataphillia-a sexual fetish of being within someone (a sub-genre is partial unbirthing-a sexual attraction to inserting an adult head into a vagina).

Voyeurism: sexual arousal through secretly watching others having sex (also includes scoptophilia-the recurrent urge or behavior to observe an unsuspecting person who is naked, disrobing or engaging in sexual activities)

Xenophily: sexual attraction to foreigners or aliens

Zelophilia: sexual arousal from jealousy

Zoophilia: sexual attraction to animals
Zoosadism: sexual gratification derived from causing pain and suffering to animals (includes Necrozoophilia and necrobestiality-killing animals)

Some Fetishes:
Anesthesia fetishism
Blood fetishism (also haematophilia)
Breast fetishism
Breast expansion fetishism
Crush fetish
Diaper fetishism
Doll fetish
Fat fetishism (lipophilia)
Foot fetishism (podophilia)
Garment fetishism
Hand fetishism
Hypno-fetishism
Impregnation fetish
Medical fetishism
Navel fetishism
Nose fetishism (nasophilia)
Panty fetishism
Pregnancy fetishism
Robot fetishism
Shoe fetishism
Silk/Satin fetishism
Smoking fetishism (capnolagnia)
Spandex fetishism
Tickling fetishism (acarophilia)
Total enclosure fetishism
Transformation fetish
Wet and messy fetishism: sexual arousal by having substances deliberately and generously applied to the naked skin

Some specifically Japanese terms:
Nyotaimori: sexual arousal by eating sashimi or sushi from the body of a (usually naked) woman
Omorashi: sexual arousal to one's or a partner's feeling of having a

full bladder
Tamakeri: sexual arousal from having a male kicked in the groin by a woman
Wakamezake: sexual arousal by drinking alcohol from a woman's body

And, apparently, there are variants unique to one individual or at least very rare, even rarer than the most obscure ones listed above: a man who was erotically fixated on automobile exhaust pipes; sneezing fetishists, etc. Obviously some of these paraphilias are clearly illegal: exhibitionism, non-consenting voyeurism, frotteurism, hebophilia, lust murder, necrophilia, pedophilia, raptophilia, telephonicophilia (obscene phone call fetish), zoosadism, zoophilia, etc.

I had at least heard of quite a few of the inclinations on this whole long list (though I was most often unfamiliar with their technical names). A few were new to me, and there are some fairly common ones I know of that I didn't see specifically referred to (masochistic piercing or candle wax dripping, say, or rubber or leather fetishes, or filming oneself having sex, or men into watching lesbian sex, and so on), so even a list this long is not exhaustive, or some of its categories are broad enough to contain dozens of subcategories not listed above within them. Some of these kinks sound so exotic that it's hard to imagine more than tiny handfuls of people being into them. Others are widespread behaviors that enter into many people's sex lives (biting, tickling, talking "dirty," enhancing sex with foods (remember the Japanese film, *Tampopo*?), smells and/or sounds and sensations). Some got me wondering–I'm an eco activist tree-hugger, literally and figuratively–am I (on top of all my other problems) a borderline dendrophiliac? Some seem to describe whole cultures or subcultures more than individuals: attraction to virgins is a fairly deep-rooted "family" value in more than a few cultures, including our own; kleptophilia sounds like a description of our economic and political system; homeovestism sounds like the definition of the fashion industry; and garment and shoe fetishism have consumerist variants that are probably more harmful (at least environmentally) than their more directly erotic expressions.

It is fascinating how our fundamental, hormonally induced physiological urges can wind up taking so many variegated pathways. The range of these behaviors extends from the extremely atavistic, with clear roots in core aspects of primate/mammalian biology (food, shit, piss, violence, grooming), to the obsessively refined (silk and shoe fetishes), to the technologically mediated (obscene phone calls or e-mails or online porn). The erotic imagination seems to be both prone to extremely narrow, obsessive fixation and to remarkable fluidity; and capable of taking us back to the primal and archaic or forward to futuristic fantasies of sex with androids/robots (à la *Battlestar Galactica* or *Blade Runner*). I wonder if the more complex and technological a culture becomes, the more unusual variations in sexual expression will occur. Are all these inclinations based on a few archaic urges that simply seem novel because they borrow new vehicles, or do entirely new kinks emerge with cultural and technological changes? The most purely animal behaviors may seem the most gross to those who don't share a taste for them, but they make sense because, while sex can certainly be a refined art, in its essence it demands a regression to the most primitive impulses and to infantile cravings (no surprise so many lovers engage in "baby talk" or just grunting). For that reason I find the more technologically oriented kinks more baffling than the primal ones.

I have encountered in my life quite a few people suffering from paranoid, delusional episodes, and these very different individuals in unrelated settings frequently reported the same, nearly identical plotline-that the FBI or CIA or NSA was sending them messages through their dental fillings. I always wondered if this was a completely new syndrome. Certainly such a narrative would not have been possible in a pre-modern era not so long ago before high-tech dentistry, radio broadcasts and giant intelligence gathering organizations with advanced electronic communications capacities. And why is this strange, unlikely storyline juxtaposing such odd, almost Dadaistically unrelated elements (umbrella + bowler-hat + urinal…fillings + radio messages + CIA) so widespread and so uniform among modern paranoids? Did cultural complexification simply add a wrinkle to a condition that would have taken other forms before (Satan talking to paranoid medieval serfs through their pitchforks?), or does it create altogether new ones? Certainly the human species' capacity to create extraordinary variations in art, music, architecture and languages is mirrored in the mind-boggling diversity of its sexual predilections and mental states. In a way our capacity for elaborate kinkiness is another indicator of our humanity: we're not only the most culturally creative and complex and high-tech of the apes, we're also definitely the most convoluted and twisted (and dangerous). We're not just the hairless or culturally complicated ape, we're the kinky ape.

Sexual inclinations that are not ours at best leave us indifferent; at worst they can horrify us. This is not all that different than religion or politics. If one is not a Christian the idea of a virgin birth (among humans anyway-parthenogenesis does happen on rare occasions among Komodo dragons and sharks, apparently) seems totally baffling. The imminence of Armageddon and the "Rapture" in the interpretation of the *Book of Revelation* by some fundamentalist American Protestants sounds like the wildest (and most perverse) sci-fi to someone who doesn't share that worldview, but if it's perverse, it's a very widespread religious kink in the U.S. Tibetans' reincarnation based succession to the major Lamas seems exceedingly odd to those of us who are not Himalayan Buddhists. To a disciple of Milton Friedman, socialism is a form of perversion (and vice versa). To Lenin, anarchism and Trotskyism were infantile disorders, etc.

Though land, religious and political passions have caused infinitely more bloodletting than our sexual variations, our reactions to forms of sexual expression we are uncomfortable with are more visceral and disturbing to us. We may kill each other far more over resources, politics and religion but we have a harder time talking about sex, or even wanting to talk about it when it touches on our personal or collective taboos. There is no doubt that sexual kinks can take almost incomprehensibly bizarre twists and turns. A form of pocket-sized pornographic books called "Stalags" that were wildly popular in Israel in the early 60s featured sexy, sadistic, female Nazi SS officers torturing prisoners and then at the end being brutalized, raped and killed in revenge. Nazi themed porn was very widespread throughout Europe in the postwar years as well. The film *The Night Porter* is a high-art reflection of this dynamic. Eros can seize us and transport our imaginations to the land of the pure Id and about as far from the politically (or morally) correct as we can imagine. Cultural conservatives feel that that is why these urges need to be resisted and suppressed or at least strictly canalized. Modern sophisticates say that's a hopeless battle and that letting at least all the non-harmful, consensual adult behaviors find expression is psychosocially far healthier.

These polar opposite attitudes have been at war for at least hundreds of years in their modern forms and are sure to continue unabated for hundreds more, but what I'm interested in here, as part of this effort to explore how many of us would qualify as "normal" by current standards is to find out how many of us are into one or more of these "paraphilias" or fetishes. And for the moment there just isn't any way to know. There haven't been any large or even medium-scale studies, to my knowledge, that have even tried to figure out a way to tabulate or even estimate how many people share these various inclinations. Ironically, I suspect the most comprehensive information anyone has compiled on a paraphilia may be the data on pedophilia and on websites that cater to pedophiles, because these are so actively tracked and studied by law enforcement, but the job of the police is above all apprehension, rather than comprehension.

One potentially rich source of information would be the porn industry. If one could get sales figures on specialized materials geared to specific sexual subcultures, this would offer some clues to their relative popularity. Unfortunately this is not possible because, as I mentioned, porn companies are usually privately held and don't release sales figures, and the biggest of these companies cater to the broadest possible market, so they don't focus that much on the most arcane stuff. The less well-known kinks are usually catered to by enthusiasts, who build swaths of smaller, independent, often free websites to share their passion with fellow travelers, rather than by bigger commercial porn enterprises.

Some trends can be tracked a bit: there is far more porn featuring older women protagonists, from their 30s up, even in a few cases into their 70s (a reflection of the baby boomer demographic and new trends in fitness, diet and aesthetic surgery?). While porn is still a largely male preserve and is almost sure to remain that way, more women do purchase porn than in the past. A subset of the porn business that caters to women and couples and gay women, often run by women, has emerged, and offers somewhat more refined fare. And porn to cell-phones is now the fastest growth segment of the industry outside the U.S, but not yet here. Such info bits tell us a little bit about the evolution of some aspects of our sexual culture, but hardly anything about the prevalence of various kinks.

In the pre-Internet era, going to video stores and to peep-shows and adult bookstores and counting and classifying the material by erotic tendency, and, if one could, getting some sales or rental figures from the stores to see what sold the most would have been an obvious research technique, though probably hard to pull off without seriously irritating the patrons and staff. But today to hunt for clues one has to go to the Web. One possible tack would be to pick one of these subcultures and to search the Web for sites that cater to its aficionados and to try to get a sense of how many sites there are, how many visits they get, and how well funded they seem. This wouldn't give you hard figures, but it might begin to give a researcher some sense of the scope of interest. To even try to do this rigorously would be an enormous amount of work.

One might for example, decide to study the S+M subculture in a city and seek out all the online and print ads for clubs and "dungeons" and independent dominatrices in that area and try to get some sense of the prices they charge and the volume of customers they would need to pay whatever the rents and utility bills and legal fees and bribes and other expenses are likely to be in that town, and then one could try to deduce the amount of patrons, how many are occasional, how many are frequent. This would only be the beginning, because these patrons are the active participants in the visible subculture who can afford to engage in it. For each one of them, how many no less obsessed but less active or poorer S+M-interested people are there who restrict their activities to cyberspace voyeurism? And even after all this, one would have to seek to determine how representative that city was by national or international standards. There are most likely going to be infinitely higher densities of such establishments per capita in San Francisco than in Omaha. It would be an interesting line of research, but who would fund it? And replicating such research for dozens of paraphilias would become prohibitively expensive. And random public surveys about such taboo topics, we have seen, rarely yield good results. There have been more targeted studies that placed ads in S+M magazines to interview aficionados of this form of Eros, which yielded interesting insights about the attitudes, psychology and social standing and incomes and so on of these folks, but the sample sizes were small and did nothing to help us determine how many of them there may be society-wide.

A more modest effort to just do some Web searches to get some sense of a phenomenon's scope can be instructive, but it's hard to be certain of one's impressions. One problem is that in many instances, when one picks a particular sexual kink, say foot fetishism, one is likely find an enormous amount of sites, more than even the most avid such fetishist will probably have time to explore in a few months or years. It would be easy to jump to conclusions and to suddenly deduce that half the male population must be composed of foot fetishists. The problem is that we're a very big country in a very big, wired world, and that an active subculture of a few hundred thousand people (three hundred thousand people are less than one tenth of one percent of the U.S. population) can generate an enormous slew of websites and online activity. I experimented with searching for websites catering to a random handful of the fetishes in that list as part of my research for this text. A few seemed fairly small with not much in the way of a Web presence, but more had a lot of sites devoted to them. There was no doubt that there were many fairly large, thriving erotic subcultures on the Web, and some were immense universes, with far too many websites to even visit a small fraction of them in one lifetime, but while that is somewhat revelatory, it still doesn't really offer any solid sense of how prevalent even the most active and dynamic of these subcultures are in the total population.

I can't prove it, but I do suspect that if one could count all the people who at least had their sexual tastes strongly colored by one or another of these "kinky" tendencies, it would be far bigger a group than we usually acknowledge. It would, however, mostly be men. Yes, of course there are some women who have offbeat erotic inclinations, more than was previously thought in fact. Not that long ago, for example, conventional wisdom in mental health circles was that sexual sadism didn't really exist among women. This turned out to be quite false. They aren't legion but such women certainly exist. Still, what few surveys have been done in sadomasochistic circles find that men outnumber women by 10 to 1 or more even among masochists, a kink often associated in the public imagination with women (*9 and 1/2 Weeks*, *The Story of O*, *Belle de Jour*). This isn't conclusive in that there could be many reasons women would be less likely to actively participate in such milieus, but there does seem to be pretty strong cumulative anecdotal evidence that male sexuality is far more prone to kink and fetishism than women's. I hate to generalize, but women seem to have a far broader, more holistic, more diffuse erotic inner landscape that is less prone to fixation on one object or stimulus or a narrow range of triggers. That is one reason women usually take longer to stimulate and require that a wider context of positive emotional circumstances be operative in order for their libidos to surge forth. Males seem inherently fetishistic in the sense that their sexual urges are often set in childhood or adolescence, when they, in ways we don't yet understand, imprint on certain narrow stimuli that will thereafter be the prime triggers of their libidos.

And after all, "normal" sexual tendencies in men are in a sense just the attraction to stimuli that most men in a culture are aroused by, and though some of these are fairly universal, they can vary quite a lot from one culture to another and one epoch to another. American men seem quite exuberantly fixated on large breasts, so this specific fetish is considered normal here.

This does not seem to be the case in many other places. Japanese porn is far more crotch-centric than breast obsessed, for example. The ancient Romans considered big penises grotesque; today they're a central object of fascination (at least in our porn). Ideals of pulchritude vary substantially in different eras and in different cultures. So, men who are "normal" are those who have wound up imprinting and fixating on those particular erotic stimuli that are dominant in their culture at that historical moment. Men who are attracted to big breasts and dream of threesomes are the standard in the U.S., those who are fixated on feet or calves or noses or only like to have sex upside-down underwater are not, but somehow the mechanism of imprinting and fixation must have been somewhat similar. It just hit a different target, a bit like goslings who will imprint on whoever or whatever is around at a certain point after their birth if mother goose is absent.

Of course some fixations are the most logical candidates for imprinting, hard-wired by evolution to be the most likely triggers. The basic physiological attributes of females of childbearing age, especially those related to reproduction, must have been attractive to most men, one way or another, in all societies or we wouldn't currently have 6 billion humans plus, and counting. It is therefore actually quite surprising how prone to outlandish (sometimes surreal) variations male libidinal fixations in fact are. I wonder if the fact that continued reproduction at our previous rates of fertility is now a danger to our species rather than a necessity for its survival is somehow subliminally encouraging more variation, more deviation from reproductively oriented sexuality. That's pure, wild speculation on my part though, and it certainly can't explain the origin of kinks, because we know the Romans and Etruscans and Greeks seem to have had a whole lot of them already.

One interesting aspect of how we view kinks is that our societies have historically considered the kind of sexual behavior that could more or less lead to reproduction as the most normal because it's the most "natural." There is an element of truth to that, but there are many other behaviors we generally tend to frown upon precisely because they are far too "natural," e.g. nudity, eating with our hands, public urination, biting our rivals. As Freud and countless others have pointed out, a great deal of the edifice of civilization is built upon trying to repress or distance ourselves from our "natural" origins. In that sense, some kinks (not the most atavistic) are very civilized indeed, in that they too seem to be ever more convoluted attempted escapes from the confines of nature.

Also it's long been widely commented about that many social behaviors that are not commonly viewed as sexual are clearly at least partially forms of displaced libidinal energy, and they can seem every bit as fetishistic as paraphilias. Women's (and increasingly some men's) sartorial or decorative obsessions or suburban men's cravings for power tools they'll never use or male automotive or audio equipment or sports fan fixations are obvious, oft-cited examples. So are some forms of compulsive eating and gambling and self-cutting. The classic Freudian view of sublimation of course views just about everything as displaced Eros, and I don't want to lapse into an oversimplified view of psycho-social dynamics, but at the very least I'd argue that it's not so easy to segregate sexual "deviancy" from other bizarre forms of social fixations, rituals and commodity and symbol fetishes (shoes, brands, flags, uniforms, sports teams) that are no more productive or rational and that might perhaps be triggered by similar mechanisms. These consumeristic fetishes, however, while ultimately far more devastating to the future of the biosphere than mere sexual kinks, are so "normal" they are largely invisible. But, again, I digress…

I realize that in the area of sexual behavior I haven't been able to come up with figures even as reliable as those already shaky ones for mental health or drug use in the previous chapters. We just don't know the real numbers for infidelity, prostitution, and paraphilias and maybe we never will. What I think I can say, though, based on looking at these various categories cumulatively, is that if you are a woman who has a boyfriend or a husband or a brother or uncle or male cousin or father or a teenage or adult son, and you think that he has never been unfaithful to a partner, or employed the services of a prostitute or had some sort of relationship to pornography, or been into some sort of unusual sexual propensity, then the odds are overwhelming that you are wrong on at least one (and most likely more than one) of those counts. How chronic and intense or infrequent and sporadic the behavior in question may be is another matter.

People in couples tend to want to believe the best of each other, especially in the initial parts of their relationships. My observations tell me that most heterosexual women, even the savviest and world-wise among them who have a sophisticated general sense of the male psyche, convince themselves that their own male partners are different than other men, even when yet another major figure is caught leading a double life. In just this neck of the woods in very recent memory two governors were forced to resign, one

(New Jersey's Jim McGreevy) for a gay affair, one (the aforementioned Eliot
Spitzer for hiring a prostitute), and Spitzer's successor, David Patterson,
quickly admitted his past infidelities (and drug use) before it would be
exposed. In just the past few days, the last conservative Republican
Congressman in the city, who had, incidentally, been one of President
Clinton's most moralistic critics during the Lewinsky scandal, was found to
have maintained a mistress and a daughter in Washington while posing as an
exemplary family man back home in his district on Staten Island. It's hard to
escape the evidence that a whole lot of men, maybe most, have trouble con-
taining their libidinal urges. But logic and Eros are not natural allies; perhaps
self-deception is best for one's mental health-after all, a tiny handful of
women are bound to be right about the virtue of their men...

As to the prevalence of deviation from erotic "normalcy" among
women, it's harder to be as definitive. They are certainly every bit as motivated by Eros as men and just as capable of delusional and irrational behavior (and deception) in actual relationships as men, and some of them are very
kinky indeed, but for the most part they just don't collectively seem to be as
driven, as compulsive and possessed by the pursuit of very specific erotic
triggers. Norms and compulsions for women have a richer social context.
Wedding and clothing and shoe fetishes, romance novels, Hallmark cards, and
so on may perhaps be the equivalents of male porn and fetishes for quite a
few women (or maybe they're more akin to male sports fetishism). It's a ter-
rible cliché, but evolutionary psychologists' claim that most women are pre-
disposed to being attracted to prosperous, socially successful, big and strong
men seems to be fairly hard to refute. Evolutionary psychologists have been
known to overstate their points. Natalie Angier, among many others, has
offered a cogent critique of the most egregious of these exaggerations, point-
ing out that culture is every bit as potent a factor as nature, that women can
at times be as violent as men, and so on, but even she describes in detail how
rare monogamy is in nature. There's no getting around some basic epiphenomena of evolution. Big strong guys or wily, assertive guys who could convince other people to do what they said were better bets as protectors of
infants.

Today, though, the romance novel/soap-opera archetype of the ideal
male has taken on ludicrous dimensions. He is rich, strong, handsome, powerful but loyal and considerate and compassionate (and even "in touch with
his feelings"), and rugged but tasteful (with just a streak of wildness and cru-

elty left). He's about as likely a concoction as the male fantasy of the super-model he passes in the street who really wants to give him a no-strings-attached blow job without exchanging a word even though he's a schlubby nobody (a daydream amusingly portrayed in the film *The Real Blonde*). Yes, women can definitely be kinky and deviate from norms, but, by and large, less frequently and weirdly than men. Tall, attractive women attracted to poor, short, weak men must certainly exist, because almost any behavior we can dream up probably exists somewhere, but they are probably even scarcer than dendro or zoophiliacs, or certainly than female sexual sadists. They definitely have fewer websites.

Notes:

-Alfred Kinsey's two landmark studies are: A.C. Kinsey, W.B. Pomeroy, C.E. Martin, *Sexual Behavior in the Human Male* (Philadelphia, PA: W.B. Saunders, 1948); and A.C. Kinsey, W.B. Pomeroy, C.E. Martin, P.H. Gebhard, *Sexual Behavior in the Human Female* (Philadelphia, PA: W.B. Saunders, 1953).
-The Kinsey Institute is at: www.kinseyinstitute.org/
-see also the 2004 "biopic" film "Kinsey" directed by Bill Condon.

-Paul Gebhard's review of Kinsey's data is in: *The Kinsey Data: Marginal Tabulations of the 1938-1963 Interviews Conducted by the Institute for Sex Research* (with Alan B. Johnson, 1979)

-Masters and Johnson main work on the physiology of arousal is in: Masters, W.H.; Johnson, V.E. *Human Sexual Response* (Bantam Books, 1966).

-John William Money, a professor of pediatrics and medical psychology at Johns Hopkins University until his recent death was a famous psychologist and sexologist known for his research into sexual identity and the biology of gender. He became very controversial for his role in sex reassignment surgery (see: the David Reimer case).

-*The Janus Report on Sexual Behavior* by Janus, Samuel S.; Janus, Cynthia (John Wiley & Sons Canada, 1993)

-the Society for the Scientific Study of Sexuality: www.sexscience.org

-Electronic Journal of Human Sexuality: www.ejhs.org

-*G-Strings and Sympathy: Strip Club Regulars and Male Desire* by Katherine Frank (Duke University Press, 2002)
for background on the academic conference on women's sexuality at the State University

of New York at New Paltz that caused a furor in New York State's political establishment, see:
-"Furor Over a Sex Conference Stirs SUNY's Quiet New Paltz Campus" by Karen W. Arenson in the NY Times, November 8, 1997

on the difficulty of doing sex studies and the efforts to prevent the funding of such studies by the Christian right, see:
- "Long After Kinsey, Only the Brave Study Sex" by Benedict Carey in the NY Times, November 9th, 2004

on right-wing intimidation of professors, see:
- "The Petition: Israel, Palestine, and a tenure battle at Barnard" by Jane Kramer in the New Yorker, April 14th, 2008

on STD rates among teenage girls, see:
- "Sex Infections Found in Quarter of Teenage Girls" by Lawrence Altman in the NY Times, March 12th, 2008

on the pedophilia and Satanism panics in the 80s and 90s, see:
- *Satan's Silence: Ritual Abuse and the Making of a Modern American Witch Hunt* by Debbie Nathan and M. Snedeker (Basic Books, 1995)
on the Ingram case in Olympia, Washington:
-*Remembering Satan: A Case of Recovered Memory and the Shattering of an American Family* by Lawrence Wright (Alfred A. Knopf, 1994)
on the McMartin case, see:
-the Emmy Award-winning HBO TV film: *Indictment: The McMartin Trial*

on studies on pedophiles' psychology, see:
- "A Profile of Pedophilia: Definition, Characteristics of Offenders, Recidivism, Treatment Outcomes, and Forensic Issues" by Ryan Hall and Richard Hall (Mayo Clinic Proceedings, April 1, 2007)
- "The Making of a Molester" by Daniel Bergner in the NY Times Magazine, January 23rd, 2005.

-*American Sexual Behavior: Trends, Socio-Demographic Differences, and Risk Behavior* by Tom W. Smith of the National Opinion Research Center at the University of Chicago (updated in April 2003)-GSS Topical Report No. 25, done for the General Social Survey (GSS) project directed by James A. Davis, Tom W. Smith, and Peter V. Marsden and supported by the National Science Foundation.

on the changes in family structures and marriage, see:
-"51% of Women Are Now Living Without Spouse" by Sam Roberts in the NY Times, January 16th, 2007
- *The Meaning of Wife* by Anne Kingston (Farrar, Strauss and Giroux, 2005)
-*Marriage, a History* by Stephanie Coontz (Viking, 2005)
-"25th Anniversary Mark Elusive for Many Couples: Divorced, Separated or Widowed by Then" by Sam Roberts in the NY Times, September 20th, 2007

-in my discussion of over-the-top weddings, the "Teilhardian Omega Point" is a reference to the French Jesuit priest, paleontologist and philosopher Teilhard de Chardin's idea that evolution was marching toward a supreme point of complexity and consciousness; author and counter-cultural philosopher Terence McKenna's notion of the "transcendental object at the end of time" is a psychedelically inspired variation on that Teilhardian idea.

on infidelity, see:
-the aforementioned National Science Foundation's General Social Survey at the University of Chicago at: www.norc.uchicago.edu/projects/
-*Lust in Translation: The Rules of Infidelity from Tokyo to Tennessee* by Pamela Druckerman (The Penguin Press, 2007)
-*Private Lies: Infidelity and the Betrayal of Intimacy* by Frank Pittman (Norton, 1990)
-"In Most Species, Faithfulness Is a Fantasy" by Natalie Angier in the Science Times, March 18th, 2008
-"Public Infidelity, Private Debate: Not My Husband (Right?)" by Jan Hoffman in the NY Times, March 16th, 2008
-"Love, Sex and the Changing Landscape of Infidelity" by Tara Parker-Pope in the NY Times, October 28th, 2008
-*The Monogamy Myth* by Peggy Vaughan (Newmarket Press, 1989)
-*Adultery* by Annette Lawson (Basic Books, 1989)
-*Intimate Partners* by Maggie Scarf (Random House, 1987, re-issued by Ballentine in 1996)
-*The Hite Report: A Nationwide Study of Female Sexuality* by Shere Hite (Dell, 1987)
-"the new position on casual sex" by Vanessa Grigoriadis in New York magazine, January 13th, 2003

on sales figures for the porn industry, see:
-"Indications of a Slowdown In Sex Entertainment Trade" by David Cay Johnston in the NY Times (January 4th, 2007)

on Comcast and porn, see:
-"Comcast cashing in on porn" by David Lazarus in the San Francisco Chronicle, February 13, 2004

-comScore Media Metrix offers Internet audience measurement and ratings: www.comscore.com/metrix

on prostitution, see:
-"Selling Sex: Economists let some light in on the shady market for paid sex" in The Economist, January 19th, 2008
-"Prostitution and the sex discrepancy in reported number of sexual partners" by Brewer et al (PNAS, October 2000, National Academy of Sciences)
-"Prostitution: A Difficult Issue For Feminists" by Priscilla Alexander in Frederique Delacoste and Priscilla Alexander's *Sex Work: Writings by Women in the Sex Industry* (San Francisco: Cleis Press, 1987)
-"Navy Officer Describes Working as a Prostitute: Testimony at Trial of So-called D.C. Madam" by Ginger Thompson and Philip Shenon in the NY Times, April 12th, 2008

-"The Diverse Crew of 4 Who Operated the Escort Service That Undid Spitzer" by Russ Buettner and Ray Rivera in the NY Times, April 7th, 2008
-"The Double Lives of High-Priced Call Girls" by Cara Buckley and Andrew Jacobs in the NY Times, March 16th, 2008
-"Chief of Police of Tehran Was Arrested, Iran Confirms" by Nazila Fathi in the NY Times, April 16th, 2008
-"Sex Trade Monitors a Key Figure's Woes" by Matt Richtel in the NY Times, June 17th, 2008
-"Payment for Sex in a Macaque Mating Market" by Michael D. Gumert in Animal Behavior (December 2007)

on the technical definition of paraphilias by the psychiatric establishment, see:
-the *Diagnostic and Statistical Manual of Mental Disorders*, fourth edition (DSM-IV) (American Psychiatric Press, 2000)

on the Max Mosley affair, see:
-"Possible Nazi Theme of Grand Prix Boss's Orgy Draws Calls to Quit" by John F. Burns in the NY Times, April 7th, 2008
-"Mosley wins court case over orgy" at BBC News, UK, Jul 24, 2008: news.bbc.co.uk/1/hi/uk/7523034.stm

-*Tampopo* is a 1985 Japanese comedic film about food, sex, clichés from Westerns, and other topics, directed by Juzo Itami.

-*Blade Runner*, directed by Ridley Scott, is a 1982 film based on Philip K. Dick's sci-fi novel *Do Androids Dream of Electric Sheep?*

-The (extraordinary) current Sci-Fi channel series about to enter its final season in 2009, *Battlestar Galactica*, created by Ronald Moore, also deals with human-android sex among its many themes.

on the "stalag" phenomenon of Nazi-themed porn in Israel, see the film:
-*Stalags* by Ari Libsker (Israel, 2007)
-*The Night Porter* (in its original Italian title *Il Portiere di notte*) is a controversial 1974 film by Italian director Liliana Cavani starring Dirk Bogarde and Charlotte Rampling that deals with transgressive sadomasochistic sex and Nazi themes.

a few notorious films about female sexual masochism:
-*9 and 1/2 Weeks* (Adrian Lyne, 1986)
-1975's *The Story of O* based on the 1954 erotic novel by French author Anne Desclos under the pen name Pauline Réage
-Luis Bunuel's 1967 *Belle de Jour* with Catherine Deneuve

-an interesting confessional piece on intense masochism: "Confessions of an extreme submissive" by Donna Larsen in the NY Press, June 30/July 6, 2004

MONEY

"People cheat, they steal, they lie,
for wealth and what it will buy.
Don't they know that on the Judgment Day
all the gold and silver will melt away…"
—Hank Williams (House of Gold)

"Behind every great fortune lies a crime." —(paraphrased from) Balzac

"…as through this world I've wandered
I've seen lots of funny men;
Some will rob you with a six-gun,
And some with a fountain pen."
—Woody Guthrie (Pretty Boy Floyd)

(Note: I wrote the bulk of this chapter in August 2008, before the collapse of global financial markets. The subsequent events did nothing to change the main thrust of my arguments, but I did make a few additions and edits to reflect the new, post September 2008 situation in the final edit of this chapter.)

It has almost become a cliché that discussing some aspects of our relationship to money can be more taboo than talking about sex. This is probably an exaggeration. It is very rude to ask strangers at a dinner party how much they make, but it's unthinkable to ask them to describe in detail their last few sexual experiences. Still, our attitudes to money are probably as complex, confusing and problematic, and the conundrums surrounding wealth and poverty have wider socio-political implications than those involving sex-they expose core contradictions in the very foundations of our social order. Money, by its very existence and unequal distribution, highlights more than any other symbol the perhaps un-resolvable tension between our self-centeredness and greed and our altruism and egalitarianism. These dueling sets of impulses lie at the heart of most of our enduring political and ethical struggles. On the one hand most or our religions and secular ethical systems preach generosity, compassion, and sacrifice, even self-abnegation; on the other hand messages overt and subliminal extolling winning at any cost, wealth, conspicuous consumption, comfort, and celebrity bombard us incessantly. The battle has become increasingly one-sided since the Middle Ages, but no society can jettison all pretenses of compassion and morality, as these serve as useful ideological barriers to a complete Hobbesian, dog-eat-dog nightmare.

Money often makes us feel dirty. Some Freudians even trace adults' styles of financial behavior to how they dealt with their shit as infants, but, even without subscribing to such an anal-ysis, it is obvious that the intrusion of pecuniary considerations is viewed as unseemly in quite a few domains of life. The problem is that it's rarely clear-cut. When someone buys us a present, or a wedding ring, for example, it is very poor form to ask how much it cost, as it would be to inquire about the cost of a wedding or funeral, and yet, many of us, if we are honest, would have to admit we are more impressed by such gifts or rituals if we think they were expensive. We see such contradictions in countless domains. U.S. laws prohibit the sale of organs or body parts for transplantation, something viewed as immoral here, but this is not true everywhere, and American citizens have been known to travel abroad to buy organs (some of them "harvested" under extremely dubious circumstances-including from kidnap victims or executed prisoners or the desperately poor) and receive transplants. A few U.S. doctors and economists in fact advocate a well-regulated domestic market for such organs. The sale of blood has long been prohibited, but "donor eggs" and sperm are now commodities (as are some cell lines/DNA of human beings). And the sale of babies is a taboo in our culture, but payments of all sorts have routinely been made in adoptions of foreign infants. These days hiring someone to have sex with you for an hour is frowned upon, but renting a surrogate mother's womb for nine months is apparently OK.

What was once unthinkable can become normal as domains of life previously viewed as sacrosanct enter the marketplace. This battle over what should remain part of the commons and what is open to commodification is one of the defining ideological struggles of our era. On some fronts we have made progress. Though poverty and gender roles still force billions of people around the world into conditions akin to indentured servitude, at least outright, legally sanctioned slavery and serfdom have been universally abolished (though Marxists persuasively argue money made serfdom unnecessary because a new, and far more efficient form of control, "wage slavery," emerged).

Many of our great religions' founders had mystical experiences that underscored human unity, and the Enlightenment ideas that birthed the modern, secular democratic state emphasized equality vis à vis the law, meritocracy, and social solidarity, but money can be the greatest of all dividers. Once most of humanity left the hunting and gathering life behind for agriculture, some form of currency became inevitable, and without money and credit highly organized, mass-scale, urbanized societies would most likely be impossible. Money is an unparalleled mass motivator and the essential fluid that lubricates modernity, but it is also the most effective breeder of large-scale inequality and injustice ever devised, and we really don't like to be reminded of the near impossibility of reconciling our supposed foundational egalitarian values with the extraordinary dominance of money in our society. After all, the cunning investment maxim attributed to Baron Rothschild-"Buy when there's blood in the streets"-tells us all we need to know: the nature of capitalism is to profit from someone else's misery. This is exemplified perfectly by Wall Street "sin funds" that invest in tobacco, alcohol, and gambling stocks. These are viewed as perfectly respectable investment vehicles that tend to do well perennially. For the overwhelming majority of financial analysts (aside from the dynamic but still fringe socially-responsible investing subculture), the only criterion by which to judge them is their rate of return; the misery they often leave in their wake is not part of the calculus. The market is, at best, amoral.

The Legal System:

Two areas that illustrate these contradictions most vividly in our own society are healthcare and the legal system. It is obvious to one and all that the wealthier you are the better your chance of getting high quality medical care or expert legal defense, should you need them. In the case of our legal system, equality before the law is supposedly a sacrosanct principle, but we all know the poorest among us get an overworked public defender when they face a charge, while the rich hire a team of high-priced attorneys, and we all know what the likely outcome is in each case. In one emblematic

Texas case, higher courts refused to overturn the murder conviction of an indigent defendant whose attorney slept through most of his trial. A 2007 Stanford Law Review investigation found that in immigration asylum cases, 46% of those who managed to appear with a lawyer were granted asylum versus only 16% of those too poor to afford one. And the better the lawyers the better the result. Georgetown University's legal clinic has an 89% success rate in such cases, and Human Rights First, which gets major law firms to handle some such cases pro bono, has a 96% success rate. Everyone understands the verdict depends far more on how good a lawyer you have than on the merits of your case. New York State's Chief Judge, Judith Kaye, recently admitted the state's judicial system was "severely dysfunctional" and "structurally incapable" of guaranteeing its obligation to provide poor defendants with adequate legal defense, and New York is a paragon compared to many U.S. states. Another totally accepted aspect of our jurisprudence is that in civil cases for say, wrongful death or incapacitation, how much money plaintiffs (or their heirs) receive depends on what their projected lifelong earning potential would have been. We measure the value of their loss by their potential income, something often closely linked to class, gender, education and ethnicity. This may or may not be fair, but it's far from an egalitarian legal concept.

As we look beyond the individual into the larger economic sphere, we see that when major corporations face lawsuits from citizens' groups or wronged individuals or communities, they not only have the resources to prevail in most cases, but they have in fact won over judges and nearly the whole political class to their way of seeing the world long before trials even begin through shared ideologies, and political donations and junkets and lobbying and advertising and revolving doors to seal the deal. Between 1992 and 1998, 230 federal judges (that's more than 25% of the total) profited from a loophole in judicial ethical guidelines to accept free vacations at resorts, under the guise that these were "judicial education" programs. The corporations paying for these pro-business "seminars" are frequently in federal courts resisting environmental and worker safety laws. No surprise that they usually get what they want from their golfing buddy judges. Some high-ranking judges even flout limits on extra-legal activities by sitting on boards of virulently antiregulatory activist groups funded by oil and other corporations. The issue of judicial independence is occasionally highlighted when a judge goes so far even the media take notice, as in the notorious duck hunting trip Dick Cheney took (before his now more famous grouse hunting, lawyer-shooting debacle) with Supreme Court Justice Antonin Scalia while that court had to rule on a case involving the Vice President, or more recently when the Chief Justice of West Virginia's Supreme Court, Elliott Maynard, was photographed dining on the French Riviera with the CEO of a major coal company while that firm had litigation pending in front of the judge's court, but the problem is far broader and deeply systemic. The entire judicial system is profoundly tainted. The fact that judges at the local level have to run for office and raise money further pollutes the entire process.

Jurisprudence has already been pre-cooked to the specifications of the biggest and most powerful players. Since a notoriously convoluted 1886 ruling by the Supreme Court, corporations receive many of the legal rights afforded individuals with few of the responsibilities. And should judgments go against them, they can use their endless coffers to take years to use every legal maneuver to delay and endlessly appeal till their opponents are ruined, exhausted, or dead. Petty thieves with "three strikes" against them in some states are sent to prison for decades for stealing pizzas, while CEOs who stole billions get slaps on the wrists, or, if they, on rare occasions, have to do some time, it's in a "Club Fed" not a San Quentin or Attica where so many prisoners are raped. Everyone understands that equality before the law is a fantasy in our society, but while occasional milquetoast reforms are enacted, no one in a position of real authority seems very inclined to make too big a deal about it. Late night comedians make endless jokes about how celebrities get away with murder (especially in Los Angeles), and everyone laughs along. Apparently this double standard, which is evident to everyone, is just something we have learned to accept and joke about.

Medicine:

Healthcare presents an even more muddled ethical picture. Doctors are theoretically bound by the Hippocratic oath to treat all patients alike. When we hear the emergency room of a private hospital turned someone in real need away because he couldn't pay, we feel revulsion. And yet, medicine is above all a huge business. Doctors are intensely lobbied by pharmaceutical and medical equipment firms bearing lunches and gifts and "educational" junkets in tropical resorts to prescribe expensive (i.e. lucrative) new drugs and tests to their patients, whether they really need them or not. All serious studies of the matter have found that doctors are very prone to being influenced by these lobbying efforts. They do, by large majorities, prescribe the new drugs pitched to them by the drug reps who have wined and dined and gifted them, and doctors order far more frequent expensive tests when they have bought a fancy diagnostic device they need to make payments on or are partners in an MRI operation. The companies wouldn't be spending hundreds of millions of dollars on such marketing efforts if they weren't paying off handsomely.

Maybe most doctors still care about their patients' health, but, consciously or not, it's very far from their only consideration in the treatments they choose. And analyses of papers in medical journals definitively reveal that new drug studies that had been funded by drug companies were far more likely to review a new drug favorably than those funded independently, and given the realities of the modern medical economy, there are very few researchers who don't directly or indirectly somehow depend on the coffers of private companies at some point. A recent scandal has in fact revealed what astute observers long suspected-that many supposed studies of new drugs were written by the giant drug-maker Merck, which then had prestigious doctors sign them before they were published, and that other pharmaceutical companies are surely doing the same thing. And as I write this the U.S. Senate has been holding hearings to examine the financial dealings of the American Psychiatric Association because a study has revealed that psychiatrists who received at least $5000 dollars from makers of new antipsychotic drugs were three times more likely to prescribe those drugs to children (an unapproved use of these drugs) than doctors who had received less or no money. The entire process of drug company research and promotion is, at best, highly suspect.

Obviously equal access to healthcare does not exist in our society, and no one even pretends it does. Vast discrepancies exist in the quality of healthcare between regions, social classes, and ethnic groups. A recent study by researchers at Dartmouth found that African Americans with diabetes or vascular disease were five times more likely to have a leg amputated than whites, and women in Mississippi far less likely to have a mammogram than ones in Maine. And, unlike in the legal realm in which they at least have to pay lip service to equal rights for all, hard-line conservatives don't view access to healthcare as a right.

As everyone knows, we are facing a major crisis regarding the rapidly rising costs of medical care. Besides the ridiculous inefficiency of the giant insurance companies' bureaucracies, which siphon off well over 20% of healthcare dollars and whose profits depend on denying coverage to as many people as possible, a dirty little secret is that the lion's share of medical expenses are incurred by very expensive, labor intensive, high-tech medicine used for people in the very late stages of life, often the last few months. By nearly any measurement, the U.S. has the most expensive per capita public health system in the industrialized world, and also one of the worst and least efficient. We are 45th in the world in life expectancy and near the bottom in infant mortality among the "developed" nations.

We could in fact fashion a very good medical system that covered everyone affordably, and that was especially geared to childhood health and nutrition (the most important point of intervention to shape good lifetime health outcomes) and preventive medicine and to addressing nearly all conditions throughout life, including much dentistry and mental health. We would, however, have to, besides cutting out the parasitic insurance middlemen and limiting the power of the big pharma companies, force everyone to be part of the system and radically curtail the overuse of the most expensive diagnostic tools, such as MRIs and other imaging technologies. In 2004, over 100 billion dollars was spent in the U.S. on medical imaging procedures, which averages out to $350 for every single person in the country. The profit motive (many doctors invest in diagnostic labs) and fears of malpractice lead to the massive overuse of these and other highly expensive high-tech diagnostic tools.

More controversially, we would most likely also have to deny public coverage for a few of the most expensive, high-end surgical procedures, such as the most expensive transplants, for everyone. The rich would go and get those things privately of course and extend their lives a little bit on occasion. Others who needed them would die. This would be brutal and grossly unfair, and I'd be royally bummed out if I were one of the ones turned down, but our system is brutal and grossly unfair now, and is only getting worse and isn't about to become fair. If we could acknowledge the reality, as distasteful as it might be for the egalitarians among us (myself included), we could create a system that was vastly better for the overwhelming majority and for the greatest common good than what we have now. It would be a death sentence for a few, but it would radically enhance overall public health and probably increase overall life expectancy.

But what I am saying is completely taboo. We can't admit openly that:

money has created an unequal society, the power dynamics on the ground make changing that impossible for the foreseeable future, and we therefore have to find solutions in that context. We can't openly admit governments and large bureaucracies by their very natures portion out benefit and pain and life and death with every major decision, and that even by not choosing, we inevitably choose winners and losers and let some live longer and some die sooner. If I thought a socialist utopia and the abolition of money were possible in the near future, I would be all for it, but the chances for that are nil. So we are stuck. We have to pretend to hew to pristine principles, and so all plausible solutions are off the table. Money not only makes us feel dirty; it also causes us to lie to ourselves about reality. It's a classic "catch-22"- because life is sacrosanct we can't debate whether prolonging it a few months for a small minority is ruinously expensive and preventing a much better overall public health outcome for the vast majority. But, by not discussing it, we let millions go without minimally adequate healthcare and cause many to die prematurely anyway. By pretending we can one day solve it all without perverting our supposed principles, which we are perverting anyway, we let the system keep deteriorating and head to an inevitable major crisis.

Corruption:

As I mentioned in the introduction, we tend, most of the time, to react to each instance of corruption we hear about through the media as a discrete narrative, and we get caught up discussing the details of the most recent specific episode and the cast of characters involved. Even those hard-bitten types who claim to be cynical about the world and reflexively say that all politicians are dishonest and all the rich are crooked get sucked in, and even they don't really take the time to grasp just how pervasive and systemic corruption is at every level of our social order.

So far even the current massive financial global meltdown, the most serious since 1929, hasn't really changed that dynamic. Yes, people are now finally skeptical about the morality of Wall Street insiders and enraged at the crisis they have wrought, but there isn't much depth to the critique. Most business commentators are quick to absolve most of the business class of any moral failing. They place the blame on a small group of people and on a "system" that got a little bit too exuberant for its own good. In a sense it's an improvement that they're willing to think systemically, but they're using talk of the "system" to deflect responsibility, not to probe more deeply into the core issues at play. And they still dare whine incessantly about how we must be careful lest we throw out the baby with the bathwater and stifle the "creativity" of the financial markets. But I'm not mostly concerned in this text with run of the mill corruption such as the abuses of financiers and speculators, as gargantuan as the current ones are. I'm interested in getting to the root of our deeper conundrums involving money itself, to the inescapable corrosive corruption it brings to our lives.

The core problem isn't predominantly that individuals are inevitably fallible and greedy (though they often are), it's that most of our society's institutions are structured in such a way that corruption is inevitable. We often put lowly paid people in positions in which they are asked to control or regulate highly lucrative activities (customs agents, narcotics or vice squad officers, building inspectors). Furthermore, countervailing moral forces that would discourage corruption are very weak. In a pluralistic society with many different cultures and subcultures, there are a lot of disagreements about norms and morality, whatever the law might say, but the one thing nearly everyone shares is the desire for wealth and comfort and possessions. Since the main glue that holds modern society together, especially in the U.S., is this lure of material advancement and enhanced prosperity while there is far less agreement on ethical matters, how can we be surprised if many people are willing to bend inconvenient rules for a piece of the pie? They've seen that those who have the biggest pieces of that pie rarely got there by being impeccably moral, so they don't see why they should have to. And it's absurd to expect ambitious people who have few options beyond dead-end, low wage jobs, not to gravitate to the few avenues for substantial profits open to them, whatever the risks. They always have, and they always will.

To add to the problem, nearly all the decisions within the institutions, large and small, that regulate and shape our lives are made in immense, foggy ethical grey areas. Often ways of doing business that are technically legal are far more ethically revolting and socially harmful than actual criminal violations of statutes, but the media discourse that is the ever-present background soundtrack to our lives lulls even the most skeptical of us into a semi-somnolent, unconscious sense that our social order is, while flawed and prone to periodic abuses, basically rational and governed by moral rules. This assumption has it backwards. I would argue that in the context of our societal architecture and our moral landscape money by its very nature causes our economic and political systems to be fundamentally, profoundly, systemically corrupt, or at the very least hyper-prone to corruptibility, even if some rare, exceptional, honest and incorruptible individuals can be found within them from time to time.

In a now predictable and tiresome cycle, when dramatic, overt sins are exposed, we awaken briefly, make some reforms, and then drift back into our deluded coma, but in most of our large bureaucracies and systems, public or private, it is corruption that is the norm, reform the exception. We will certainly go through another major round of reforms now that the world's financial architecture has revealed its fragility (and insanity), but I am depressingly confident that exuberant, pervasive new forms of corruption will emerge after a while. The founding fathers of the U.S. understood the inevitable dangers of power and sought to build into the fledgling republic's political structure a system of checks and balances, but money is the most pervasive form of concentrated, corrosive, fluid power-it can undermine any structure.

A thorough case to prove this point would take massive tomes to document, and other people have done it already quite well, so I will content myself with offering a few revelatory anecdotes at different levels of power (local, national and international) to illustrate my argument. Some of the most obvious examples, such as: pervasive organized crime control of some unions and industries in big cities, the awarding of precious water rights to a tiny handful of rich farmers in California and Arizona or sugar barons in Florida, Congressional "earmarks" and massive corporate lobbying at all levels of government, the frequent appearance of precise phrasing that benefits a single rich contributor mysteriously inserted into a Congressional bill in the middle of the night or into a trade treaty, the outright giveaways of public resources in grazing allotments or mining rights to big interests at great loss to taxpayers, the mind-boggling tax breaks and subsidies given to developers and giant retailers and oil companies and sports team owners and rich farmers, the aforementioned wining and dining of judges by polluting corporations, multinationals bribing amenable foreign leaders and helping overthrow and assassinate less cooperative ones, the complete complicity of banks and tax havens in shielding the looted fortunes of dictators and drug lords, etc, etc, have been so widely discussed elsewhere that I won't bother retreading most of that familiar ground.

The main point I seek to drive home is that these are norms, not exceptions; they are the way business gets done. They are often, in fact, crucial structural underpinnings of the "official," aboveground economy. I acknowledge that someone reading the litany above could justifiably point out that some of those situations are not as grievous as they once were, are being discussed and new safeguards are being enacted. This is true in a few of those instances, but corruption, like performance-enhancing drug use, is always a few steps ahead of regulators. It is, if nothing else, impressively dynamic in its capacity to implant itself into every hidden nook of collective life, and like fungal mycelia or an ailanthus, flourish in the dark before eventually blooming into extravagantly creative and potent novel forms.

Routine tax breaks and the standard processes involved in creating laws and regulations and awarding most major government contracts, all usually perfectly legal or close enough, are far more grotesquely unfair and corrupt in their essence and damaging to the public good than actual, outright graft. I challenge anyone to read New York Times financial reporter (and lifelong Republican) David Cay Johnston's impeccably researched and devastatingly convincing *Perfectly Legal: The Covert Campaign to Rig Our Tax System to Benefit the Super-Rich-and Cheat Everybody Else* or his more recent, *Free Lunch: How the Wealthiest Americans Enrich Themselves at Government Expense and Stick You With The Bill*, and not arrive at the same conclusion.

We have to wean ourselves from this idea that we can "root out corruption" by mildly tweaking the system and learn to understand that our entire economy and system of governance are not only congenitally prone to corruptibility but corrupt in their very essence. The entire history of power, of governance, of bureaucracy, and especially of capitalism is inextricably linked to corruption (and violence). But we go from scandal to scandal: the massive railroad scams of the 1870s that shaped the patterns of land ownership in the Western U.S. for generations; countless other robber baron and large trusts' predations and the building of the nation's economy on the back of sweatshop labor (and the gunning down of striking workers by Pinkertons and protesting veterans by General MacArthurs's troops); the vicious violence of Rockefeller and Standard Oil to corner the oil market that structured the world's oil trade into the present; the CIA's tacit wink at the heroin smuggling of its Golden Triangle ex-Kuomintang warlord and Corsican and Sicilian Mafia allies (and later the coke dealing of the Nicaraguan Contras) which helped shape the modern, planetary illicit hard-drug economy; the 80s Savings and Loan debacle, Enron and company, and just now the mortgage meltdown and the proliferation of ever-more insanely compli-cated leveraged derivatives-all of which contributed to exacerbating our ever more skewed concentration of wealth, and then finally collapsed on us all.

These are again and again portrayed as aberrations or, among the more sophisticated, viewed as normal, necessary episodic outbreaks of fever in an otherwise healthy organism. This is absurd. Many of these earlier episodes were not epiphenomena of an otherwise healthy capitalism: they were foun-dational in creating our most basic national and global economic structures, as Russian oligarchs and Kremlin insiders or Iran's Revolutionary Guard and ruling mullahs are today shaping the economies and the distribution of wealth and power in their societies for generations to come. This is even truer of China. Philip Pan's *Out of Mao's Shadow* details how connected party officials and Chinese military and intelligence operators have shifted to becoming a brutally exploitive capitalist class. The Industrial Revolution from the enclosure of the commons on was birthed in blood and corrup-tion, and we were deluding ourselves when we thought we had escaped that pattern. Corruption does not get cast out like Satan; it's right there at the Creation. As far as economies go, it just may be "the Word."

Hobbesians would argue that this is due to "human nature;" Marxists point to the exploitation of labor; yet others point to the massive scale of our societies and institutions, so far removed from our small-pack primate ori-gins and our long history in smaller communities where power was trans-parent and social controls more obvious. It's true that the more complex the social order, the more covert corruption thrives, because it can handsomely pay the best minds to devise diabolically clever, impenetrable tax dodges, financial schemes and endless chains of dummy companies and incompre-hensible derivatives. The algorithm is a far more effective and lucrative weapon in theft than a firearm, and much harder to trace. Whatever the ulti-mate causes of corruption, though, and whether it's ultimately a soluble problem or not, let's at least face the truth and admit the problem is com-pletely systemic, and that minor tweaks will never succeed in reforming our system of governance and our habitual ways of doing business.

The New York Grime:

Let me offer a few anecdotes to illustrate what I'm ranting about. I'll start at the local level. As a lifelong New Yorker, I've seen countless municipal scandals come and go. I don't think New York City is much more corrupt than most American cities (and it's positively angelic compared to Lagos or Sao Paulo or Naples or Palermo or Moscow or Shanghai or Mexico City), but it's the biggest and older than most, with more entrenched power brokers and an active tradition of local investigative journalism that periodically exposes the ever-present rot under the surface of public life, so there is a rich record of greed and theft to look at. There have been many, many histories of the famous Tammany Hall period and of other particularly "colorful" epochs in the metropolis' trajectory, so there's no point rehashing all that history. I'll just offer a few snippets of relatively recent and contemporary municipal machinations.

First, one needs to understand that one reason those in the educated elites, including those who work in the news media, don't realize how pervasive corruption is in the trenches, the mean streets of daily life, is because they are generally not in positions in which they encounter it on a regular basis. They lead shielded lives. They aren't contractors trying to get building permits, or small shop owners trying to survive by supplementing their meager incomes by selling weed or taking bets, or small businesses trying to get city contracts, or undocumented immigrants desperately trying to get papers. The biggest, most lucrative frauds of course take place in the rarefied universes of large government contracts and corporate and big developers' suites, but those are far more rarely exposed, and when they are, they don't have the same juiciness, the visceral aura of grime and sweat and cheap cigar smoke that makes the earthier stories so appealing to the tabloid-reading public.

I was born and raised in Queens, a borough of New York City, in a mixed middle and working class area. When I was a bratty kid in the late 50s and early 60s, as I drank my egg-creams and milkshakes in my local luncheonette on Union Turnpike reading the comics with my friends after riding our bikes around or playing football, none of the teenage punks and adults hid the fact that they were playing numbers or placing sports bets with Mister Meyer, the very sweet, Holocaust survivor owner. And I heard the stories of local politicians and saw the get-out-the-vote operations (including cops) handing out money on election day, and no one acted as though all this were anything but absolutely routine. Some larger-than-life lowlifes dominated the political scene. One county boss, Matthew Troy, who was finally convicted of grand larceny, in later years after his exit from politics was invited to law schools to describe to students how business was done: a State Supreme

Court judgeship went for $75,000, a lower court job for $35,000. His successor as head of the Queens Democratic Party machine was Donald Manes, who committed suicide after finally being caught in one of the most notorious scandals in NY history, the systematic looting of the Parking Violations Bureau (there is a good fictional film about this era of Queens politics: *The Yards*). No one I knew who grew up in Queens was surprised by any of this, nor did they think Queens was any different than the other boroughs of the city. It was the way things were done, and it still is, though the scams tend to be a bit less obvious and a tad more sophisticated.

Those who are savvy and have to deal with life on the streets know that the Police, Building, Transportation and Water and Sewer departments, to name only a few, often require "special handling." And the history of private trash haulers and construction unions are so notorious and well documented I won't bother to dwell on them, except to mention that abuses in these realms are far from just history. As I write this, the man who controlled 80% of the trash hauling in southwestern Connecticut pleaded guilty to mob-linked racketeering and surrendered 25 of his businesses and $100 million dollars in forfeiture, and the Schiavone Construction Company, one of New York's biggest building firms, which has received at least two billion dollars in contracts in recent years on such high-profile mega projects as the Second Avenue subway tunnel and the Croton water filtration plant, was recently exposed as heavily linked to organized crime.

Just recently, a slew of building accidents resulted in the death of (so far) fifteen construction workers in a few months. In a familiar pattern, the head of the Buildings Department was forced to resign after a particularly spectacular accident when a giant crane fell into an apartment building on Manhattan's East Side, killing seven, and as, typically, patterns of rushed permits, lax or faked inspections, mob ties, payoffs to the city's chief crane inspector, and other shenanigans came to light. It turns out the construction boom required far more crane operators than were available, so a slew of incompetent ones were slipped the answers to the licensing tests and pressed into service. One union official admitted in his testimony that one operator "couldn't write his name," let alone pass a licensing test.

To cognoscenti this was totally par for the course. For some 200 years this department (that now has a $12 billion dollar budget) has seen one baroque scandal after another, and those are just the few that are exposed. Its problems are perennial and intractable. In 2002, just to stay recent, 19 of the department's 24 plumbing inspectors (including all the top supervisors in 4 of the 5 boroughs of the city) were charged with extortion and bribery. In 1996, 42 elevator inspectors were suspended and 18 ultimately convicted of extortion. Developers' billions are what makes the city go, and they are desperate to get their permits approved quickly, and inspectors, like cops and firemen, don't make a whole lot. It doesn't take a genius to figure out the result.

On the police front, cops and criminals form an ecosystem. They have to share information and to accommodate each other in myriad ways. For the police to gather intelligence they have to enforce laws selectively and offer carrots as well as sticks. The dividing lines can't help but get blurry, and the temptations faced by narcotics and vice squads are overwhelming. Many cops moonlight as security guards because their salaries are quite low. They are exhausted and bitter. When they catch drug dealers or pimps with wads of cash or piles of drugs, it is very easy to understand their rationale for wanting to supplement their incomes, so the cyclic scandals that rock police departments every few years are tediously predictable. Each time another commission is appointed to study the problem, a higher degree of scrutiny is put in place for a few months, and then life eventually returns to normal, till the next "scandal"-i.e. a brief look beneath the veil at the underlying code that runs "the Matrix."

One anecdote I love because it happened close to where I grew up is the story of John M. McNamara, a Long Island car dealer who was convicted a few years ago of one of the largest corporate frauds in U.S. history to that point-bilking General Motors of 422 million dollars, which he cleared in profit by borrowing over 6 billion dollars for non-existent vans. Mr. McNamara only got 5 years in jail and got to keep a couple of million and a very nice house because he supposedly helped federal prosecutors in their investigations of political corruption on Long Island, though they failed to convict anyone on the basis of his information. One has to admire what a mere car salesman with a bit of chutzpah can accomplish in the land of opportunity.

I could go on and on endlessly just focusing on New York City's countless arenas of petty corruption. A number of judges in my borough of Brooklyn have been charged recently with accepting bribes to favor husbands in divorce cases and a bunch of lawyers were caught in a very common, very lucrative scam-using the role of legal executor to loot elderly

clients' assets as their mental powers wane. Real estate scams and unscrupu-
lous contractors and vicious predatory lenders (including major corporations' household lending arms) routinely steal houses from the elderly poor,
most of them black and Hispanic, by trickery. Western Union makes obscene
profits on the remittances immigrant workers send home to support impoverished family members. Till just recently phone companies that had
monopolies on phones in prisons were allowed to charge insanely high rates
to inmates and their family members-often among the poorest of the poor.

While I was working on this chapter, it was revealed that the New York
City Council has had a sort of secret annual slush fund of close to 400 million dollars, which permitted council members to have complete discretion
in distributing funds to non-profit groups in their districts, and, unsurprisingly, quite a few were generously funding small organizations heavily staffed
by their relatives. A few days later four local Department of Education
employees were indicted for soliciting bribes from school bus companies to
give them favorable treatment in safety inspections, and the Attorney
General of the state announced he was investigating both a 30 million dollar home-healthcare scam centered in the city's Russian community that
seems to have links to prominent Hasidic political fundraisers, and, totally
separately, millions of dollars in illegal government pensions granted to hundreds of politically connected lawyers at all jurisdictional levels across the
state, a sort of festering, low-level mode of political patronage going back
decades. Then two officials of the city's child welfare agency were charged
with creating phantom adoptions to pocket funds aimed to aid disabled children. I could go on and on. There is nothing unusual in all this: by New
York standards, it's a fairly unexceptional monthly or even weekly news
roundup.

And let me reiterate, I'm only using New York anecdotes because I live
there and they are often colorful, but it is by no means the worst case. One
only needs to look at the long, continuing history of scandals in the Chicago
or Los Angeles or New Orleans or Philadelphia police forces, or at Texas
redistricting scams, or at decades of faked evidence in a number of crime labs
around the country, or at the fiscal woes of San Diego a few years back, or
more recently to the financial fiasco engulfing Birmingham, Alabama, where
a few fast-talking investment bankers (the main one a JP Morgan Chase
managing director) talked some corrupt (or perhaps only imbecilic) county
officials into some insanely complicated hedges and interest rate swaps (so

the bankers could reap high commissions on every transaction) to pay for sewer system repairs. The deals went spectacularly sour, and the county and city now face a massive bankruptcy, owing close to 5.4 billion dollars. And it now turns out Birmingham is only the first of countless local governments and pension funds that were convinced to invest in baroque, highly leveraged investments they didn't understand by their greedy, dishonest or merely foolish financial advisors.

Again, the point of this litany of local and regional sleaze is that these are not the actions of a few bad actors. The ones who are caught are just the unlucky or the most blatantly hubristic. A remarkably dynamic strain of corruption, bottom-feeding con artistry and predatory financial behavior at all levels, some technically legal, some borderline, some blatantly criminal, is an integral aspect of American life, central to the evolution of our economic system. It's not a disease. It's long been a core attribute of the organism itself.

The Golden Revolving Doors:

Let's move from the municipal level to the national stage. At the moment we are in the midst of a major economic crisis-the bursting of the U.S.' housing bubble, the accompanying credit crunch, the risk of a global depression. Talk of enhanced (though still feeble) government scrutiny of financial markets fills the Congress. There is a long history of government rescuing capitalism from its own excesses over and over again (for a while, until a new, more creative form of business-as-usual sets in). The two Roosevelts in the first half of the 20th Century are the archetypal figures in those sorts of reform endeavors. In recent years the pace of that scandal-reform cycle has accelerated. After the revelations of Enron's sociopathic manipulation of energy markets and its wildly surrealistic accounting practices, WorldCom's fraud (the largest to that point in U.S. history) and so on back in '02 (all undetected by the increasingly highly suspect major auditing firms), Congress passed the Sarbanes-Oxley Act, the most aggressive attempt at regulation of financial markets in decades.

A mere three years later, by 2005, the markets had stabilized and armies of business lobbyists had managed to radically weaken or undermine governmental scrutiny of the financial world. Giant loopholes in business bankruptcy laws, permitting all sorts of corporate shenanigans, were introduced (and this as personal bankruptcy laws for individuals had on the contrary been viciously tightened as a result of fierce lobbying by credit card companies

and banks). Shareholders' rights to question corporate governance were seriously curtailed; regulatory agencies were under-funded and hamstrung. Two
years after that, this current, far more massive financial crisis resulting from
insanely complicated leveraged speculation on mortgages by investment
banks and hedge funds no one had been regulating and almost no one really understood was upon us, and talk of new regulations is again in fashion.
Given the severity of the crisis, though, it's astonishing how timid that talk
has been and how feeble the response so far. The U.S. Treasury, forced to bail
out the banks, was resistant to actually having a say in running them or in
forcing them to provide liquidity to the financial markets, ostensibly the very
reason for their bailout. The epochal, historical magnitude of this crisis will
almost certainly force the federal government to tighten the regulatory system, but, while these will be vast improvements over the laissez-faire madness of the Clinton and Bush eras, the odds are that after a few years new
forms of speculative mania will creep back, and it is unlikely the current
power elites will really have their dominance challenged. They will most
likely only have to do a mild pruning of their ranks and to offer up a few
scapegoats to satisfy the public's rage.

Until this crisis the power of corporate interests, the major player in
American life for 150 years, had never been more dominant nor countervailing forces as weak. The government is the only entity powerful enough to
occasionally rein in excesses by some business sectors, but, by and large, it
serves the interests of the most powerful economic players. In most cases
scandals and crises are little interruptions that sometimes require some usually minor recalibration, but amnesia rapidly sets in, and the ruling elites
return to their looting of the spoils. Lax oversight of the powerful is the
default setting or our politico-economic life. As long as the courts continue
to view the donation of money in politics as protected "free speech," that is
not likely to change radically enough to make a lasting difference. Corporate
tax rates are lower than anytime since WWII. Oil companies were until just
recently making vertiginous profits. Congress, however, has so far been
unwilling to even close the "Bermuda loophole" in the tax code that permits many U.S. corporations to shield large swaths of their income in tax
havens. It did, however, in 2004, pass a one-shot law to allow 840 of the
biggest U.S. corporations to reap a collective $265 billion dollar windfall by
allowing them to repatriate profits held overseas and be taxed a tad over 5%
rather than the normal 35%. And Congress hasn't so far even modestly raised

taxes on fossil fuels or on oil companies (or even rescinded their lavish sub-sidies) to invest in alternative energy research, even as the planet continues to warm alarmingly fast.

The new administration and a new less reactionary Congress should at least change the tone on these matters, but we will have to see whether sub-stantive changes that really challenge corporate dominance of American life are in the cards. The odds are against it. Even the much talked about "green jobs" programs are likely to, above all, profit big companies such as GE or major venture capitalists who are investing in alternative energy (T Boone Pickens, Vinod Khosla, et al).

One of money's great strengths as a stimulator of productivity and a booster of innovation is its fluidity, but that very trait permits it to penetrate into every node of power unless the most vigorous safeguards are put in place and vigorously defended. This has rarely been the case in human his-tory, and it is very far from the case today. The combination of extreme con-centrations of wealth and power, ever more complex information technolo-gies and financial instruments, and less and less transparent institutions and mechanisms of governance guarantee abuse on a massive scale. We may see slightly improved transparence for a brief while, but where money and power concentrate opacity quickly returns.

At the level of the federal government, one the main problems is the famous "revolving door" that sees a continuous flow between the world of big business and that of high-level public service. The governing elites of the apparatus of the state and those of the largest private enterprises are almost indistinguishable at this point. This has long been a prominent feature of American life, but it has gotten more and more extreme in recent years, and lobbyists, very often former politicians who know how to work the system, have evolved into astonishingly powerful players as well. The argument is made that those with the top specialized managerial skills can generally only be found at the highest echelons of the corporate world, and that they take huge pay cuts to come into public service. This is true to some degree, but it means that even the most honest of these people come into government with deeply ingrained pro-business attitudes. And the less honest may take a pay cut for a year or two or three but they make up for it with a vengeance later on when they rejoin the private sector, greatly aided by the connections they made and the favors they delivered while in public office.

This justification of the recruitment of business executives for top gov-

ernment posts omits a crucial point: government is in fact the biggest gen-
erator of wealth for the private sector. How governments tax, set interest
rates, lend, subsidize and legislate to a large extent dictates who gets rich and
who gets screwed. Just as large farmers' most lucrative crop is usually government subsidies, wealth in many sectors often has far more to do with who
you know than what you do. We have been seeing more and more people
in positions of political power who were instrumental in pushing through
legislation or regulations highly favorable to a firm or industry get a lucrative job in just that firm or industry once they leave politics. A particularly
blatant example is that of Congressman Billy Tauzin, who, the same day he
left Congress, began work as the head of the Pharmaceutical Research and
Manufacturers of America, one of the main pharmaceutical industry trade
groups, for, reportedly, over 2.5 million dollars per annum. Just two months
earlier, Tauzin had played a key role in bending every rule to shepherd the
highly controversial Medicare Prescription Drug Bill through Congress (at
3am!), a bill that was exceedingly generous to the pharmaceutical industry
and was probably written by pharmaceutical company lobbyists. But Tauzin
was not alone. Several other politicians who worked on the bill are now lobbyists for the pharmaceutical industry. In any case, while Tauzin's naked
chutzpah was indeed memorable, examples of such obvious payoffs for political favors are just too numerous to even begin to list. It's astonishing this is
not considered bribery, when some unlucky politicians have gone to prison
for accepting tickets to sporting events.

But all this is well known, so I'll just focus on one or two specific examples to drive home the extent of the problem. Here is a list of some of the
main people in the Department of the Interior during the first term of the
just departing Bush administration. That department is in charge of a big
share of the U.S.' public lands, including all our national forests. The
Secretary of the Interior was Gale Ann Norton, a long-time, major lobbyist
for oil, gas, mining and logging interests. The Deputy Secretary, J. Stephen
Griles, was the former Vice President of the United Mining Company and
also worked as a top lobbyist representing coal, oil and mining concerns. The
Solicitor of the department was a former lobbyist for the cattle industry. The
manager of Alaskan public lands was the former Director of Arctic Power, an
organization that lobbies for aggressive oil drilling throughout the Arctic.
The Assistant Secretary for Land and Minerals Management was a former
lawyer for the gas, timber and petroleum industries. I could go on and on.

Griles was one of the few actually caught in blatant violations (in the infamous Jack Abramoff affair) and sentenced to just under a year in prison in 2007.

It would be fair to argue that the Bush/Cheney administration, with its roots in the oil business, was perhaps the most blatant and shameless of all recent U.S. ruling cliques in its ties to industry and the most openly hostile to environmentalism or social equity, but it would also be a mistake to think its behavior is that total a departure from the norm. The Clinton administration was rife with former Monsanto executives and major figures on Wall Street. It was certainly a vastly more competent and less brazen management team (as was Bush Sr.'s), but it has long been viewed as totally normal in Washington to fill the highest echelons in government by borrowing from the top ranks of the corporate world.

The Enron affair is another extraordinary episode that spectacularly exposed the incestuous bonds that tie political and financial elites. I realize Enron received a great deal of attention, but there are a few key points that didn't receive the systematic scrutiny they deserve. First, Enron's management was most likely the most influential shaper of Dick Cheney's energy policy when the Bush administration first came to power, and arguably the most influential business enterprise in Bush's inner circle in his early period in office. Enron's ties to the Bush team and to some segments of the Republican Party were incredibly close. Bush himself and Karl Rove and Cheney were close friends with Ken Lay, Enron's CEO. Bush's private lawyer and later Attorney General, Alberto Gonzales, worked at the Houston law firm that represented Enron and signed off on its accounting schemes. Then very influential Senator Phil Gramm pushed through legislation shielding Enron from scrutiny while his wife, Wendy Gramm, served on the company's board. Former Montana Governor Marc Racicot became head of the Republican National Committee while still actively working for a lobbying firm that represented Enron. Robert Zoellick, former U.S. Trade Representative then Deputy Secretary of State (and now head of the World Bank!), served on Enron's advisory board. Christian Coalition and Republican strategist Ralph Reed lobbied for Enron, as did Ed Gillespie, Bush's campaign manager in 2000. I could list many more major government figures with substantive ties to Enron.

Again I realize that Enron was an exceptional case, but I would argue that it's only the scope of its ambition and recklessness and collapse that was unusual, not its close ties to political figures. A few of those political figures had to discreetly disappear from public view for a while, but most suffered no really serious after-effects from the Enron flameout itself. The most extraordinary example is Phil Gramm, who resurfaced as a key economic adviser to 2008 Republican presidential candidate John McCain. Gramm's past political and lobbying record, his current tie to the Swiss bank UBS and some verbal gaffes raised a few eyebrows, but the mainstream media did not focus on his astonishing role in creating the current financial crisis. They did berate him for one clumsy comment during the campaign, and that forced him to slip into the shadows once again. One man cannot single-handedly create a financial meltdown, but Gramm has certainly done more to facilitate it than anyone else. A darling of the financial sector, he was the leading politician pushing for the deregulation of that industry in the 1990s. He worked to cripple and defund such regulatory bodies as the SEC (Securities and Exchange Commission) and slipped in such laws as the Commodity Futures Modernization Act that no members of Congress actually read and none understood (perhaps not even Gramm himself; it was most likely written by lobbyists), which essentially prevented the oversight of newfangled financial instruments such as derivatives and the now infamous "Credit Default Swaps," those very highly leveraged, exotic, incredibly complicated speculative investments that constitute an opaque market of perhaps some 60 trillion (!) dollars in nearly completely unregulated gambles that came close to unraveling the entire planet's fiscal architecture. The novelist Tom Wolfe, borrowing a phrase from the economist Joseph Schumpeter, recently commented: "People lose touch of the underlying assets. It's all paper—these esoteric devices. It has become evaporated property squared. I call it evaporated property cubed." In any case, it's hard to believe Phil Gramm's economic ideas are taken seriously by anyone, or that he's not incarcerated for our collective economic safety.

The Democrats have not been all that willing to probe too deeply into Washington's ties to corporate America because they too are far from immune to that disease. People who live in glass houses hesitate to throw stones, even if their glass houses are not as opulent as the other party's. The former Democratic Senate majority leader, Tom Daschle, one of the main architects of Barack Obama's political ascent, is a case in point. He worked in a highly connected Washington law firm after his exit from the Senate and advised countless corporate clients on how to get what they wanted from

Congress, while his wife Linda, a former deputy administrator and then acting administrator of the Federal Aviation Administration, parlayed her connections to become one of the most successful lobbyists for airlines and military contractors. Now that the new President-elect (who yearns for a squeaky clean, scandal-free administration) would like to bring his dear friend and early supporter Mr. Daschle into the White House inner circle, these potential conflicts of interest are causing a few ripples. The odds are they'll find a way to finesse it. There really are almost no knowledgeable, experienced, credible national political figures with clout from either party who are not compromised in some way. It's the way the system works.

So the fact that Enron was not used more prominently by the Democrats in the '04 election and that they failed to communicate just how close the ties were between the Bush administration and one of the most spectacular corporate scams in history is revelatory of: their own fear of scrutiny; the media's failure to convey the depth of those ties; and the fact that the public is so understandably cynical that mere corruption fails to excite its sustained ire most of the time, though this current global crisis may prove to be an exception given the likelihood of its extreme severity and duration.

If there is an ideal candidate to illustrate most perfectly the revolving door phenomenon, Edward C. Aldridge just might take the cake. His saga offers a quintessential, archetypal model of how things work for the top echelons of DC inside players. This fellow was a Secretary of the Air Force in the Reagan administration, then President of the huge defense contractor McDonnell Douglas, then head of the Aerospace Corporation, then back in public service as a member of the top security clearance Defense Science Board and as a member of a top panel on new weapons buying and as Under Secretary for Acquisition, Technology and Logistics at the Defense Department (01-03), then he was named head of President Bush's Commission on Space Exploration, even though he was a member of the board of Lockheed Martin, the giant military contractor that stood potentially to profit heavily from his decisions in that role, and he's been on numerous corporate boards on and off. Essentially this quintessential player kept alternating between deciding which weapons systems the military would purchase and working for the firms that would then sell those weapons to the government.

And Aldridge (who retired when, finally, he fell under a bit of scrutiny at the end of Bush's first term) is far from alone: a 2004 report by the non-profit Project on Government Oversight found that 288 senior government officials got jobs with the 20 biggest military contractors between 1997 and 2004 after leaving their posts. In the other direction, Bush Jr.'s first term saw over 30 executives or major shareholders or consultants to big defense contractors named to top-level government jobs with policymaking authority in military affairs. And the boards of the biggest military suppliers are teeming with retired generals. It's hard to know which hackneyed animal metaphors to choose-the foxes guarding the henhouse or the pigs at the trough.

The rampant fad of ever-more privatization of tasks formerly handled by government agencies ("outsourcing") has exacerbated all these shenanigans, and the Iraq War has seen almost incomprehensibly extravagant levels of plunder, from the no-bid contracts awarded in construction, transport and supply to firms such as KBR, the former Halliburton subsidiary, and in "security" and intelligence work to mercenary firms such as the notorious Blackwater and CACI International (which supplied the worst Abu Ghraib torturers). Roughly 70% of U.S. intelligence work (some $42 billions' worth) is currently outsourced according to Tim Shorrock's revelatory book, *Spies for Hire: The Secret World of Intelligence Outsourcing*, which also details the revolving door phenomenon in the intelligence world that sees firms such as Booz Allen Hamilton and Science Applications International, largely staffed by former government spies, revel in extraordinarily lucrative contracts. To add insult to injury, in a recent exposé the New York Times revealed that a slew of retired generals who worked for TV channels as supposedly objective, expert commentators on military affairs, were being routinely coached by the Pentagon and paid by defense contractors, so not only are taxpayers being fleeced, they are being fed more and more sophisticated, covert propaganda disguised as objective analysis.

But while the Pentagon has the biggest budget to loot from, it would be wrong to think these sorts of practices are limited to the military or intelligence spheres. It recently came to light that the U.S. Justice Department had a cozy little set-up in which it negotiated settlements with large companies it accused of wrongdoing that would permit these firms to avoid criminal prosecution if they paid fines and changed their ways ("deferred prosecutions"). The catch is that the department appointed a corporate monitor in each case to make sure the company was complying properly. And what a lucrative gig that turns out to be. It just so happened former Attorney General (i.e. head of the Justice Department) John Ashcroft was assigned such a task (another no-bid selection process) to monitor a medical supply company. His consulting fee? Approximately 52 million dollars! When this news got around, it raised some eyebrows, but it turns out it's a routine practice. There may have been close to 100 such arrangements made in the last few years, and at least 30 former government officials, including 23 ex-prosecutors, got the juiciest plums. And it's probably all technically legal.

Another amusing news story, reminiscent by its theatricality of the Abscam sting that saw FBI agents impersonating Arab sheiks a few decades back, just broke as I was working on this chapter. It offers us yet another insight into how things work in our elite political circles. A Times of London investigative team tricked a high-level Houston-based lobbyist (and friend of President Bush and Vice President Cheney), Stephen Payne, by posing as representatives of a former ruthless President of Kyrgyzstan who wanted to meet with top-level U.S. government officials to help rehabilitate his reputation. Mr. Payne was surreptitiously filmed promising high-level access if a donation of a few hundred thousand dollars were made to the Bush Presidential Library being (not without controversy) built at Southern Methodist University. And, to be fair, that is probably a totally routine approach to raising money for presidential libraries (ridiculous monuments to vanity, the equivalent of modern pyramids, with far less architectural merit) and campaign funds.

Sadly, I could go on for thousands of pages, but I'm just trying to illustrate the syndrome. I'm not trying to be exhaustive. And lest anyone think I'm only beating up on the U.S., let's move on and take a look at the broader, global scope of corruption.

Global Shenanigans:

If one takes a look around the world, it's pretty clear that the countries whose economic and legal systems and political decision-making processes are fairly transparent and widely viewed as being at least mostly "clean" are quite few in number. Transparency International (TI), a highly respected international NGO think tank on corruption, puts out a range of reports, most famously its yearly Corruption Perceptions Index (CPI) that looks at perceptions of public sector corruption in 180 countries and territories. Unsurprisingly it finds a strong correlation between corruption and poverty. It's certainly no surprise to find the likes of Somalia and Myanmar sharing the lowest (worst) scores while Finland, New Zealand and Denmark rank highest. Most of the "cleanest" countries are in Northern Europe, and the likes of Canada, Costa Rica, Japan, Singapore, Australia, and sometimes Chile tend to also do well.

It does very solid, important work, but its CPI only looks at the public sector and is based on perception, and is therefore far from exhaustive. Closer scrutiny reveals that even nearly all of the "clean" countries have powerful "old boys'" networks that still call many of the shots and certainly are not immune from occasional tawdry scandals involving political parties' slush funds, bribes, and so on. Even perhaps the most efficiently run country on Earth, Switzerland, gains much of its wealth from the ethically suspect sheltering of money. And countries and firms might be more or less "clean" at home but ruthless in their global competitions. Just recently, a series of bribery scandals have rocked major EU companies. Investigators are looking at 2.1 billion dollars in suspicious payments made to get contracts all over the world by Siemens, the engineering giant. BAE, the British military contactor, was caught in highly suspect tactics to get a Saudi arms deal. Alstom, the French engineering firm, was found to have made hundreds of millions of dollars in bribe payments to get Asian and South American deals. In fact, until quite recently, most European countries allowed companies to deduct "commissions" (i.e. bribes) to get foreign contracts from their tax bills. This was only outlawed in France in 2000 and in Germany in 2003. The UK doesn't yet have any such anticorruption statutes. 37 countries signed a 1997 OECD anti-bribery convention, but very few do much to enforce it. Transparency International concludes in its most recent Bribe Payers Index, the most comprehensive survey of its kind, that overseas bribery by companies from the world's export giants is still common, despite the existence of the international anti-bribery laws criminalizing the practice.

And, again, these are the cleanest. Beyond these countries, it gets really, really dicey. The levels of corruption in countries such as Russia and China and Mexico and Brazil and Nigeria and India and Pakistan and Indonesia and Southeast Asia and throughout Central Asia and most of Africa and a lot of the Caribbean and Central and South America are so widely acknowledged and discussed and joked about by locals that there's no point in dwelling on them. And I just listed nations that house the vast bulk of the world's population.

Then there's another tier of countries or regions where completely illicit enterprise dominates large swaths of the society, where it is either the main source of income or close to it. These include drug producers such as Afghanistan, Columbia and some other regions of the Andes and of Mexico and Central America and the Caribbean (and even some specific parts of far northern California and of British Columbia dominated by the pot trade), and the Golden Triangle region in Thailand and Burma, and Lebanon's northern Bekaa Valley, to name only a few. I personally witnessed a shipment of hashish pass through a checkpoint near Baalbek manned by rival warring factions during the height of the Lebanese Civil War, as men put down their weapons and waved it through. Every faction got a piece of the action. War is war, but business must go on. "Pay us off, let the trucks through, and then we can resume killing each other…". How hard that sort of commerce is to stop is made starkly evident by the fact that Afghanistan, now occupied by U.S. and NATO forces, with a U.S. puppet regime in place, is producing as much opium as ever, the only real export crop the country has. The U.S. would have to have a lot of chutzpah to complain that other nations aren't controlling drug production or smuggling after this episode, but, of course, the U.S., despite its enormous budget and trade deficits, does have endless supplies of chutzpah.

Other regions defined by their black markets have different specialties. Transnistria in Moldova, for example, floods the world's hot spots with unmonitored Soviet era as well as newly minted weapons. South Ossetia is known for its counterfeiting rings that do a pretty good $100 bill, something the North Koreans used to be quite good at as well. Many border towns and ports around the globe are defined by smuggling of goods or people. In any event, the scale of the illegal and barely legal economy is rarely honestly tackled, but it's not a footnote to the world economy; it's one of its pillars, and it's almost impossible to draw a clear line between "legitimate" and illicit activity because they are almost completely intertwined, and there are so many grey areas.

I'll offer up a couple of anecdotes to illustrate first, how great fortunes are usually acquired in most societies, and second, just how deeply corruption penetrates into every nook and cranny of life in some poor countries. The first tale is of the tortilla empire of Mexico's "Tortilla King," Roberto Gonzales Barrera in Mexico. I only pick this story because I'm very fond of tortillas, and I've always been horrified that this gentleman became a billionaire selling inferior tortillas (his company, Maseca, uses dehydrated corn instead of fresh dough). His success had nothing to do with his product and everything to do with his close, lifelong friendship with the family of the one-time President of Mexico, the notorious Carlos Salinas de Gortari (and his even more notorious brother Raul), which gave him a monopoly of sorts and completely rigged the market in his favor. And Barrera was far from alone: the banker Roberto Hernandez, and the phone company magnate Carlos "Slim" Helu (now perhaps the richest man in the world), and many of Mexico's super-rich made their money at taxpayers' expense almost completely because of their connections to powerful political figures. And Mexico is no worse than a lot of other places. It's positively Scandinavian compared to, say, Nigeria.

The second surreal tale is an example of how hefty profits from illicit enterprise can, in poor countries, cause corruption so systemic and profound that it penetrates into every institution. In February 2007, three Salvadoran Congressmen were ambushed and shot to death on a rural road in Guatemala. This is a fairly violent part of the world, but the prestige of the victims made it newsworthy. Then it got more newsworthy. It quickly became apparent the perpetrators were in fact Guatemalan policemen, who when caught said that they had thought they were robbing drug dealers and didn't realize they had murdered foreign dignitaries. Rogue cops are routine in Central America, but these weren't low level cops. One was the head of the National Police organized crime unit! Four cops were charged and jailed though many more than four had obviously been involved. Then the saga got truly bizarre. Four days after their arrest and incarceration, the authorities say a riot broke out in the prison, and the rioters stabbed the four cops to death, but inmate witnesses said, and the evidence supported them, that a large, well organized unit of heavily armed men in uniforms and ski masks marched into the maximum security prison through seven locked doors and murdered the cops with no interference whatsoever from the prison guards. Clearly, any chance the prisoners could finger higher ranking officials had to be eliminated. The inmates say they rioted after the murders occurred, as they quite justifiably feared they would be made into scapegoats.

Everyone knew police corruption was rampant in this part of the world, which has a long history of civil wars and still active police and military death squads, but the extent to which drug money (Guatemala is a major transit point for U.S.-bound cocaine) had corrupted the society was vividly highlighted by the incident. Even more bizarre, some of the police death squads, it turns out, are composed of officers who are members of some fundamentalist Protestant churches and think of themselves as performing sacred work by cleansing the society of criminals. But what interests me in the context of this book's theme is that when the U.S. administration urges Congress to sign trade treaties with these nations (e.g. CAFTA), one hears the usual talk of prosperity and economic growth and so on. A few left-leaning members of Congress usually raise the issue of human and labor rights, but by and large it is glossed over by the media. These are still societies in which "free trade" helps only a tiny elite: some very wealthy landowning families, some multinational banana, coffee and maquiladora-style clothing factory companies, and the politicians and armed men and other officials in their pockets, but Guatemala, El Salvador and Honduras at least, are very close to failed, lawless states, in large part because of a lethal cocktail of our making: our very long term support of the privileged few in these regions and their brutal suppression of any challenges to their rule, and our insatiable hunger for drugs.

So, in general, when we hear "experts" constantly toss around terms such as "the economy" or 'global markets," we should realize these terms mask far more than they reveal. Outside of very occasional stories and specialized conferences and publications, the scope of the immense illicit and "unofficial" components of that world economy are rarely commented upon by the hordes of chattering financial analysts on cable TV or by the business press. And the vast "black" and "grey" markets and the worldwide networks of offshore money havens turn out not to be outlying phenomena, but crucial components of the international financial architecture that global elites not only have no real interest in abolishing, but depend on.

First of all, the very large economic sector that is blatantly criminal is only one small part of an immense "underground" or "informal" economy (i.e. operating outside of legal and tax structures) that represents, in many parts of the world, by far the biggest share of economic activity. According to World Bank estimates from 2007, as many as 50% of Latin Americans and 78% of Africans probably work in this "grey market" sector. The figures for Asia are very hard to figure out, but one 2002 estimate was that 90% of India's labor force was "informal." Now, for the most part, these people are not immorally flouting the law; they are simply trying to survive by selling their labor and/or running tiny enterprises in very low-income areas that are very poorly served by larger enterprises or by government agencies. But the scope of this unofficial market makes economists' babbling about India's, or

Indonesia's, or Mexico's GDP ludicrous. No one has any precise idea what
the real figures are. And, as is spelled out in Princeton professors Miguel
Centeno and Alejandro Portes' *The Informal Economy in the Shadow of the State*
and Sudhir Venkatesh's *The Underground Economy of the Urban Poor*, the informal market is far from insignificant even in the most developed countries.
Some credible estimates say as many as 30% of working age people in the
U.S. and 25% in Europe are most likely involved to some extent in "grey"
and "black" markets, so bear that in mind when you hear TV anchors pon-
tificating about how "the economy" is doing. Which economy are they talking about, the official one or its large shadow?

Some estimates have placed it at perhaps 20% of the global economy, but
no one really knows the scale of the underground economy or exactly how
to define its parameters precisely, and governments and most economists
don't like to talk about it. In a 2000 piece in the Journal of International
Affairs, "The Shadow Economy," three economists (Matthew Fleming, John
Roman, and Graham Farrell) explored this taboo topic and dared ask: "To
what extent does the exclusion of (underground) economic activity distort
official estimates of macroeconomic variables, including output, employment
and inflation?" Unimpeachable hard data doesn't exist, but the answer seems
to be: quite a lot. One revelatory indicator is what happens when governments switch currencies. Cash real estate transactions and purchases of luxu-
ry items frantically drove up prices throughout Europe as the conversion to
the Euro approached and people desperately sought to launder their hoards
of unreported cash. As the U.S. introduced new $20 dollar bills a few years
ago, a massive spike in sales taxes filled government coffers, as those who had
piles of undeclared cash rapidly sought to launder their loot, worried the old
bills would be phased out. But these phenomena don't include the lion's
share of actual crime-derived money from drugs, prostitution, and other illegal businesses, which is laundered in very sophisticated ways, within the
international banking system.

Around the world, there are a number of small countries or city-states
that have prospered by filling a shadowy but invaluable niche in the global
economic architecture: they have become "offshore" banking centers and tax
havens by creating local laws that aggressively protect their clients' financial
privacy and anonymity. In Europe we find the giant of the genre,
Switzerland, as well as Luxemburg, Liechtenstein, Monaco, Malta, Cyprus,
Gibraltar, the Isle of Man, Jersey, Guernesey, Sark, Alderney, and of course the

Vatican. Those surprised by that last name are probably too young to remember that in the late 1970s and 80s one of the most bizarre, sordid and convoluted banking scandals in history involved the Vatican bank (the "Institute for Religious Works") under the leadership of Archbishop Marcinkus. The saga included two bankers' mysterious murders, a covert Masonic lodge, political slush funds, the Mafia and the CIA-it would be impossible to make this stuff up.

But I digress. In the Americas these havens include: Bermuda, Barbados, the Turks and Caicos and Caiman Islands, Aruba, Belize, and Panama. In the Pacific region, Hong Kong, the Philippines, Hainan, Labuan, Vanuatu, Fiji, Tonga, Vanuatu, Samoa, Nauru, the Marshall Islands; and in the Middle East, new players, such as Dubai, with Beirut banks still going strong despite Lebanon's instability. The quantities of capital that are parked and traverse through these centers are enormous. Around one third of the world's capital invested in foreign accounts is in Swiss banks, for example. We're talking about millions of accounts, as well as tens of thousands of front companies in these havens. There are more dummy companies registered in Gibraltar or Jersey or some of the Virgin Islands than there are inhabitants in each of those places. The loss of taxes (which has to be made up by poor schmucks like us) is incalculable, but it is without question massive. German economists have come up with annual lost revenue of close to 50 billion dollars for Germany alone, but, again, no one really knows.

These havens specialize in different aspects of fiscal discretion, and they vary in their degrees of shamelessness. Some, such as Bermuda, are ideal places for large corporations to base their "headquarters" (not infrequently a post-office box), so they can escape much higher taxes at home. Others specialize in services such as very lax ship registries (e.g. Panama or Liberia, even landlocked Switzerland!), or the setting up of series of dummy companies and bogus foundations, while the biggest (Switzerland, Liechtenstein, Hong Kong) also offer elaborate money management services to the well to do. And the most sophisticated players use these havens in combinations to make their fiscal trail truly impenetrable. Try tracing a Panamanian-registered enterprise's accounts in Luxemburg managed by a Swiss money management firm-not that uncommon a species.

Every once in a while, a scandal breaks out. A particularly bad dictator is ousted but absconds with a fortune and his country tries (usually unsuccessfully) to trace the money and recuperate the plundered billions (e.g. Abacha,

Mobutu, the Salinas brothers, Baby Doc, Suharto, the Marcos'…), or drug cartels or terrorist groups are found to have accounts in one of these locales, or a particularly large-scale tax avoidance scam comes to light, as has been happening recently in Liechtenstein. Noises are made, and often the haven in question accepts a few minor concessions if the countries complaining are powerful enough, but the "sanctity" of client privacy invariably remains strongly in place. A slew of tax avoidance instances have been uncovered this past year. A mole at a bank in Liechtenstein leaked a list of rich Germans sheltering funds to the German tax authorities and caused a high degree of embarrassment (and some resignations of officials caught with their fiscal pants down). And an ex top UBS banker was charged with helping an American developer avoid $200 million dollars in taxes by using accounts in Switzerland and Liechtenstein.

Though this is, in fact, totally routine, these cumulative embarrassing revelations have drawn enough attention that they have forced European tax authorities and the U.S.' IRS to exert pressure on their governments to tighten laws regarding foreign accounts and enforcement. As I write this, UBS, under considerable pressure from several public trials in which sordid details are being aired, is considering releasing the names of 20,000 very wealthy American clients who may have shielded as much as $20 billion dollars from taxation to the IRS. This would be very unusual for a Swiss bank, and a sign of changing mores in that world if it occurred. But, I suspect that once the dust settles and a few people have been made examples of, it is unlikely much will have changed. The world's wealthiest will continue to find welcoming places to surreptitiously park hefty portions of their money.

The truth of the matter is that the world's financial elites and major powers have no real desire to seriously curtail this activity. If the U.S. and the EU and Japan put their collective feet down, they could radically reduce the size of this parallel, shadowy financial universe rather quickly. But most of the planet's biggest players make use of these services, either individually or in their enterprises or governments. Corporations seek every possible mechanism to keep their taxes as low as possible; wealthy families and individuals the same; and governments' clandestine intelligence services make extensive use of these institutions to move money around. Some of their foes do too, but the system is too valuable to global insiders to jeopardize on account of a few dictators, organized crime syndicates, drug kingpins or even terrorists, who, government propaganda notwithstanding, do not at present even remotely constitute an existential threat to world business. World financial markets have recently been far more of a threat to themselves (and to us) than any terrorists.

Routinely Irrational:

So far I've been discussing the large structural forces that govern our monetary lives to show that the way "the economy" is discussed almost always glosses over its seamier aspects, and that those sordid components are not sideshows but integral parts of the system, but what about our personal relationships to fiscal life? How sane and centered are we in our financial dealings?

A tenet of classical economic theory is that markets work efficiently to determine the true price of things because large numbers of "rational actors" make economic decisions that are logical and in their best interests. This idea has long been hard to take seriously; and is now, in light of the current global panic, viewed as laughable by nearly everyone. Even before this crisis hit, several influential books had challenged its core premises. A recent bestseller, *Predictably Irrational* by MIT professor Dan Ariely, to name only one, makes the very obvious argument that emotions and social norms play a large, even preponderant role in our behavior. There is, in fact, a long history of such refutations of this dubious doctrine of rational economic actors. As we are now vividly reminded, one obvious phenomenon that dramatically undermines the theory of rational actors is the predictable, periodic emergence and implosion of speculative "bubbles." In the last decade alone we've seen a slew of books on that topic, including: Mike Dash's *Tulipomania: the story of the world's most coveted flower and the extraordinary passions it aroused*; Malcolm Balen's *A Very English Deceit: the secret history of the South Sea Bubble and the first great financial scandal*; Edward Chancellor's *Devil Take the Hindmost: a history of financial speculation*; Charles Kindleberger's *Manias, Panics, and Crashes: a history of financial crises*; and Robert J. Shillers' *Irrational Exuberance*. Of course more important than the books has been reality: the Savings and Loan debacle of the 80s, the tech bubble collapse in 2000, and the current global meltdown.

Far from rational economic actors, our financial behavior seems every bit as prone to being swayed by our emotions and fantasies as our sex lives. It is well known in the world of professional market analysts that the direction the masses of small investors are going in is almost invariably the wrong direction. They buy in late, close to the top, as stocks are ending a prolonged rally, and sell in a panic when buying opportunities are in fact best. Many large firms use small investors' behavior as one of their key indicators. When small investors rush into the market, it's one pretty good sign it's time to sell. In a sense all serious money managers are inside traders. They know far more than the rest of us rubes; they're spending their entire working lives swimming in a world of information they and their hordes of analysts (usually!) know how to decipher far better than the small investor getting dregs of denatured advice from shrieking cable television "financial experts." The entire system is rigged to benefit the big players, whether they are technically violating insider-trading rules or not.

In fact, insider-trading rules, on close examination, seem to be, to put it mildly, very selectively enforced. As with political bribery the top players are rarely snagged. Despite an occasional Martha Stewart-caliber celebrity indictment, it's mostly overly ambitious young brokers and their friends and relatives, or even further down the food chain, guys in the mailroom who overheard something who get charged. But, in fact, all of high-level Wall Street deals are based on inside information. The biggest actors just have clever ways of being massively remunerated that are not usually precisely, technically illegal. Quite a few studies have shown that officers and directors of companies routinely generate abnormally high returns in the markets. A 2004 study by Alan Ziobrowski at Georgia State University found that U.S. Senators with stock portfolios on average beat the markets by 12% a year, almost certainly based on information about businesses they are privy to as a result of their work in the corridors of power, which is not technically illegal, but if that's not inside information, what is? As R. Foster Winans, the author of *Trading Secrets: Seduction and Scandal at the Wall Street Journal*, points out: "Wall Street brokerages have made billions in recent years by using complex software to foretell what their large customers…will be doing before they do it, based on their knowledge of the customers' past behavior…If the authorities turn a blind eye to public officials who profit from non-public information and corporate insiders who make money based on what they learn behind the boardroom doors, and if it is legal for big trading houses to take advantage of their customers' trading habits, what is the value of the insider-trading law?"

But, as we've seen, even these money professionals who scorn the herd mentality of the peons are themselves far from immune to other-than-rational attitudes regarding money. I've on occasion had dealings with circles of Wall Street folks, and have been quite surprised at how many of them discreetly or covertly subscribed to a range of esoteric theories about investing, ranging from almost cult-like obsessions with arcane mathematical formulae such as the Fibonacci series or the Kondratieff curve or elaborate astrological systems, or to other offbeat cultural indicators (hemlines, Super Bowl results...). I'm in no position to judge the validity of any of these ideas, but they are, by mainstream standards, wacky. And any look at these trillion dollar risks inherent in some of the most leveraged derivatives, or at the practices at banks that have allowed a number of junior traders the last few years to run up losses in the billions in mere days, have to raise questions about the core sanity of the worlds of high finance. If nothing else, it's pretty clear dealing in huge amounts of money has an intoxicating effect that often clouds judgments. It's also true that the ever-increasing speeds of transactions and capital flows that send trillions galloping around the world create a highly unstable system so complex it's beyond anyone's ultimate control. Like a very powerful, fast car racing at top speed for which a small error or piece of debris on the road can easily lead to disaster, the global economic system itself is at best manic, at worst totally delusional.

But let's get back to the micro level: individuals. My observations of my own behavior and of the people I have known lead me to conclude that most of us have deeply problematic relationships to money. I have seen among my friends and acquaintances as many couples broken apart by their radically different attitudes toward and behaviors involving money as by infidelity or drinking and drug use. Arguments about money, far from being rational, often quickly lead to rage. They trigger our deepest insecurities. Part of that response is in some sense quite rational, in that poverty is a highly undesirable outcome with dire, even terrifying consequences, and the realization that one's aspirations will never be realized due to financial limitations can also be a crushing blow, but the level of rage and violence personal conflicts about money engender seem to come from deep in the Id and to unleash some of our darkest demons.

Debt:

A number of social trends highlight not only our problems handling money but also how the nature of our relationship to it is rapidly changing. Our relationship to debt is one prime example. Till the late Renaissance Christians were forbidden from charging interest (as Muslims still are today). Until fairly recently being in debt was considered highly undesirable, even

shameful, and there were debtors' prisons. Today, however, the entire economy is completely based on debt at all levels: governmental, corporate and
personal. The size of the government's debt is so astronomical it defies comprehension. And ever more complex markets in all sorts of debt instruments
and derivatives of bundled debt involve trillions of dollars (and, as we've seen
recently, apparently can go seriously awry...).

To be completely free of debt is now abnormal. Most Americans have
mortgages. 40% of American families spend more than they earn. As the
nation reeled from the 9/11 attacks, the President famously urged everyone
to go shopping to help the economy, and presumably to charge it all on their
credit cards, which is how nearly everyone shops these days, even for formerly cash transactions such as fast food: U.S. consumers purchased $51 billion
worth of fast food on their credit and debit cards in 2006, compared to $33.2
billion just a year earlier. According to the Federal Reserve Bank, total U.S.
consumer debt (not including the much vaster mortgage debt) reached $2.46
trillion in June 2007. In 1968, consumers' total credit card debt was $8 bil-
lion (in current dollars), while today it exceeds $880 billion. The median
U.S. household income is currently $43,200 and the typical family's credit
card balance represents almost 5 percent of their annual income. On average,
today's consumer has a total of 13 credit obligations. A few prescient business
observers had long warned that increasing debt at all levels was unsustain-
able. The business community finally started reaching the same conclusion,
albeit far too late. A summer 2008 survey conducted by the National
Association for Business Economics among business leaders had found that
the combined threat of mortgage defaults and excessive indebtedness had
overtaken terrorism as the biggest short-term perceived threat to the U.S.
economy. By then of course, it was getting painfully obvious.

According to a 2008 study by Bankrate, Inc.: 64% of people polled who
carry debt admitted it is a cause of worry (and that was before the crash).
People live in terror of what their secret credit rating scores hidden in the
"vaults" of the big three credit bureaus are (you can get yours, but you have
to pay!). The amount of late payments on credit card debt has been rising
fast. One in six families with credit cards pays only the minimum due every
month, and approximately half don't pay the full amount of charges each
month. And all these figures are sure to rise dramatically as the current recession deepens and credit card debt is likely to emerge as yet another bubble.
And a noteworthy aspect of that is that the interest rates on credit cards are

astronomical and rising: the average interest rate for standard bank credit cards topped 19% in 2007, rising from 16.5% in 2003. And there are all sorts of other hidden fees. In another time, this would have been more honestly called what it is-usury, or, in more recent vernacular, loan sharking. To borrow heavily on one's credit cards is completely irrational financial behavior. The interest rates are higher than any other type of (legal) loan. The entire system is of course set up to make their use easy and fast so the desperate and the lazy (and to be fair just about everyone else) take the path of least resistance. And attempts at regulation have floundered in Congress as the banking industry lobbyists have far deeper pockets and therefore far more access than consumer advocates.

I haven't focused on mortgage debt because the current sub-prime mortgage and credit liquidity crisis is being so widely discussed that anything I say would be redundant, but while sleazy lending institutions and bankers' packaging of dementedly leveraged credit instruments and lax government regulations are the prime culprits in that mess, a great deal of irrational or just stupid behavior by individuals was also manifest. To be fair, though, many of them were fair game because they were not fiscally educated and were too busy working multiple low paying jobs to desperately try to enter the middle class to pay close attention to fine print, and, apparently, the world of money has gotten too complicated for anyone to be able to make sane decisions, especially the "experts."

Gambling:

Another even more troubling sign of our collective financial irrationality is the exponential growth of gambling in the last two decades. Once mostly the province of organized crime it has been appropriated by large corporations and state governments and radically expanded. Today, 42 states have lotteries and 37 have commercial, Indian or racetrack casinos. Only 2 (Utah and Hawaii) don't allow any form of gambling. An estimated two-thirds of the adult population placed some sort of wager last year.

According to the American Gaming Association casino gambling revenue doubled between 1995 and 2006. Here are the industry figures for "gross gambling revenue" (GGR)-the amount wagered minus the winnings returned to players-in 2006: Commercial Casinos-$34.11 billion; Indian Casinos-$25.08 billion; Lotteries-$24.63 billion; Pari-mutuel Wagering-$3.58 billion; Charitable Games and Bingo-$2.24 billion; Card Rooms-

$1.10 billion; Legal Bookmaking-$191.0 million. The grand total came to $90.93 billion dollars-by some calculations more than films, sports, theme parks, cruise ships and recorded music combined. And that doesn't count Internet gambling, that some estimate at $7 to $8 billion dollars but no one really knows the full scope of because the companies are based offshore. Internet gambling has been under legal pressure from the U.S., but it had been growing by leaps and bounds and luring more and more young people. And of course the immense amount gambled on stock and bond and commodity and real estate markets is not included in those figures though some people's relationships to those investments obviously share quite a few characteristics with pure gambling.

Gambling revenues have been down a tad with the current recession, but this is so far a small downward blip in an otherwise incredible multi-decade expansion. From 1974 to 1994 the amount Americans legally bet rose 2,800 percent, from $17 billion to $482 billion. Gambling, once considered a vice, is now viewed as a normal part of American entertainment. According to a 1996 survey by the U.S. Travel Industry Association, close to 40% of U.S. residents had been to Las Vegas in their lifetimes, and almost 90% of them gambled during their visit. There are some people on the left who are deeply concerned about gambling's many social harms and who rightly view the use of lotteries to raise state revenues as a covert tax on the poor, but they are few and far between and politically marginal. For the most part the only significant groups of any size still opposing gambling's expansion are linked to Evangelical Christian organizations, and they have been fighting a losing battle. The gaming industry is a powerful political player that spends millions on lobbyists, especially at the state level. In Virginia's 1995 legislative session, gambling interests had 48 lobbyists working bills. In Texas, they hired 74, more than two for every state senator and one for every two House members. No wonder we went from only two states that had legal gambling in the mid 80s to only two that don't have any today.

There is no doubt that gambling on its current scale causes immense social harm. A lot of the money from lotteries goes to the advertising firms that run campaigns to encourage people to buy tickets and to the bureaucracies that run the lotteries. Official propaganda notwithstanding, lotteries have not raised money for education in any serious way. The extra income just allows states to help plug their deficits. And there is no doubt it is one of the most regressive forms of taxation: people with household incomes under $10,000 bet nearly three times as much on lotteries as those with incomes over $50,000. I strongly suspect that every dollar of income a community or state government gets from gambling probably winds up costing several dollars in addressing the resulting indirect social harms (prison, court, foreclosure, protective child custody, hospital, and morgue costs).

Casinos are even worse than lotteries. After casinos re-opened in Atlantic City, the crime-rate in a thirty-mile radius doubled. Counties with legalized gambling have, on average, double the rate of personal bankruptcies than those without. The estimates for the number of people who are seriously, pathologically addicted to gambling range from 1.5% to 5% of the population, depending on whether you tend to accept the industry's own figures or those of its critics. While this is a small percentage of all those who gamble, it still represents millions of people, and this small group may account for up to a quarter of all casino and lottery profits. A comprehensive study of problem gamblers in California found that 3.7% of the state's population has a lifetime pathological gambling problem. That translates to 750,000 to 1 million Californians with serious gambling issues. The average debt incurred by a male compulsive gambler is between $55,000 and $90,000 and around $15,000 for a female gambler. Problem gamblers divorce at twice the rate of non-gamblers and are twenty times as likely to commit suicide. Some estimates say sixty-five percent of them commit crimes to support their habit.

And, of course, other than for a handful of genuinely skillful professional poker players or sports bettors for whom it's a career, gambling is by definition a losing proposition for almost everyone. Everyone knows the odds are very scientifically designed to make consistent winning impossible. That's why casinos are such a profitable business. In fact, in those rare instances someone figures out how to beat or even the odds, as card counters did in blackjack, through memory and skill, the casinos make that illegal, and the law supports them. In any sport, that would be called fixing the match, but the gambling "industry" just changes the rules of the game and bans anyone who can figure out a way to beat it.

To gamble might make some sort of emotional sense, but it's fiscally a demonstrably completely irrational behavior, and it encourages extraordinarily ridiculous superstitions even in people who should know better. The fact that a large swath of the population engages in it is yet another nail in the coffin of the "rational economic actor" fairytale. To add insult to injury, the majority of people who gamble do so by playing slot machines, which are sort of diabolical, hypnotic devices that stimulate the most primitive parts of the brain with ringing bells and whirling graphics and involve no skill whatsoever. Playing them for too long reduces a person to the mental state of one of Pavlov's dogs.

Gambling has always existed and most likely always will, but not long ago it was viewed as a fringe, unsavory pastime or a stage for young men to go through. Today it's a mainstream, widely advertised "recreation" option, and a major industry invested in by the biggest and most respected pension funds and university endowments. The neighborhood illegal numbers-running operations of yore seem positively quaint compared to this massive money extracting, dream crushing juggernaut. This is an instance of big "legitimate" business and government muscling out criminals when they saw gambling was a lucrative racket and ultimately creating something far bigger and far more destructive.

I am largely a libertarian regarding social life, and prohibitions of behaviors that are so persistent almost never work (and I gambled quite a bit in my youth), but I have to wonder if there can't be a middle ground between outlawing something and allowing it to grow to a degree that not only causes major collateral damage but does so largely at the expense of the poorest and most desperate among us. I don't know what gambling's explosion in popularity and acceptance tells us about the current state of our society, but my few visits to large casinos made me question whether our civilization deserves to survive.

Shop-Apocalypse:

Another behavior that may better than any other help us see the core problems money poses on the individual level is compulsive shopping. A 1992 study estimated its prevalence in the population at 2 to 8%, but most specialists believe it has risen dramatically since then and most likely includes at least twenty million people. Most analysts of this phenomenon say some 90% of those who suffer from it are women, but others point out men can get away with behaviors that are more socially acceptable ("collecting," frequent upgrading of electronic equipment, and so on) but often mask compulsive acquisitiveness, so, once again, no one really knows how many victims of this disorder there are.

We live in a culture in which we are aggressively exhorted to consume and acquire nearly every moment of our waking lives, and in which we nearly all routinely purchase enormous quantities of unnecessary products. Our whole economy is based on, in Ivan Illich's term, "the creation of needs," so how do therapists decide who among us is truly a shopaholic when the entire society could easily be viewed as insanely materialistic? As with alcohol consumption or sexual paraphilias, the usual measure is that it has to seriously limit or disrupt one's life. New York psychologist April Benson, author of *I Shop Therefore I Am: Compulsive Buying and the Search for Self*, writes: "One patient of mine got fired because she was compulsively shopping on the Internet all day. There are other people who neglect their children and park them in the mall constantly because that is what they need to feed their habit. Lots of marriages break up over compulsive buying. In fact, we don't call it compulsive buying unless there is some significant impairment in some aspect of your life."

The stated inner motivations of those compulsive shoppers who have spoken about it vary: loneliness, a hunt for thrills, to fill an inner need, to boost self-esteem or fend off depression. So far it seems very hard to treat. Serotonin uptake inhibitors (Prozac, Zoloft, Paxil, et al) do no better than placebos. A few pioneers, such as the aforementioned Ms. Benson, are trying to develop effective group therapeutic approaches, but there has been very little large-scale research done and there are no standards for treatment. According to most of the specialists this is above all a disorder of self-image as expressed in a hyper-materialistic culture, which explains why clothing is so frequently the item of choice for chronic shoppers-because fashion is so closely associated with self-image. The constant bombardment of advertising drives home that you are not perfect as you are and need some "fixing," but have no fear-a fix is just a purchase away. My observations of people I know lead me to believe that some form or another of "over-shopping" is extremely widespread. It's actually surprising more people don't succumb to chronic shopping, as it requires great self-discipline to resist the siren call of consumerism.

April Benson notes that chronic shoppers overspend not just on things but on services as well: "I had one patient who had her hair blown dry maybe two or three times a week…She was spending at least $200 if not $250 a week on her hair, and that didn't include all the hair products," she recounts. This leads me to think that the compulsive pursuit of aesthetic surgery-a $13 to $15 billion dollar industry and growing by leaps and bounds, according to investigative journalist Alex Kuczynski's eye-opening book,

Beauty Junkies-is a closely related phenomenon. Both of them seem to stem from a similar crisis of self-image. Advertising does everything it can to heighten our feelings of inadequacy and our sense that we're not living up to social ideals, and it offers us magical products and procedures as shortcuts to that promised land. When clothes, cosmetics and spa visits don't deliver, surgery is the logical next step.

On some level aesthetic surgery is rational. Looking more youthful can confer real advantages in the world of work and in enhancing one's sexual desirability, though, as Kuczynski recounts in her book, there are many social milieus in which the frighteningly obsessive pursuit of the hot new procedure and nearly annual surgeries or at least botox treatments are the norm. There are combination aesthetic surgery/sightseeing trips abroad to countries where the procedures are cheaper. There are more and more urban neighborhoods and suburbs in which the "nipped and tucked," collagened, liposuctioned, implanted and botoxed in the over-40 set outnumber the unaltered in that age cohort, despite some of the very real risks associated with such operations, and the occasional stories of grotesque disfigurements and even deaths. This is now a totally accepted part of middle class American life with giant shows in the nation's biggest convention centers. According to the American Society for Aesthetic Plastic Surgery, nearly 11.7 million cosmetic surgical and non-surgical procedures were performed in the U.S. in 2007 (91% on women, 9% on men). Since 1997 the overall number of cosmetic procedures has increased 457 percent. This is an extreme form of compulsive shopping, in which one is not acquiring things but a new appearance. If soul upgrades or trade-ins became available, there would undoubtedly be chains of "Doctor Faust Clinics" in malls across the land.

A Nation of Petty Thieves:

A final behavior worth looking at is employee theft. I find it interesting, because unlike pure robbery or a blatant theft of cash, which most of us would most likely not participate in, it's extremely widespread. Statistics on the phenomenon include all theft from employers, but what I'm interested in, in this context anyway, is petty theft. Those at the highest levels of an enterprise who design elaborate frauds and steal hefty amounts do by far the most damage to businesses, and this form of white-collar crime has grown by leaps and bounds starting in the 90s. Fraud investigation ("Certified Fraud Examiners") is a booming business, and workplace surveillance technology is now widely deployed. Some business analysts point to the greed engendered or at least exacerbated by the incredible profits top hedge-fund managers made (at least until just recently), the end of loyalty to companies as firms are more and more bought and sold and merged, and so on, as precipitating factors in this surge in scamming by executives, but while this increase in white-collar greed is another indicator of our money neuroses and the prevalence of corruption, I find petty theft from employers a more interesting social phenomenon.

The U.S. Chamber of Commerce estimates that 75% of employees steal from the workplace and that most do so repeatedly, and that one third of all U.S. corporate bankruptcies are directly caused by employee theft. The American Society of Employers estimates that 20% of every dollar earned by a U.S. company is lost to employee theft. Of course when one hears such statistics and sees headlines such as "U.S. companies lose nearly $400 Billion per year in lost productivity due to "time theft" or loafing," one has to take it with a grain of salt. These phrases are loaded with assumptions. From an employee's angle, a job can be seen as "time theft" of his or her time on a grand scale. As an antidote I highly recommend essayist Michael Ventura's classic piece on work from the employee's perspective "Someone is Stealing Your Life" or Bob Black's little anarchist gem *The Abolition of Work* that begins by paraphrasing and tweaking Marx: "Workers of the world, relax."

And those rebellious attitudes I just expressed highlight precisely why employee theft is so widespread: deep down most of us are either resentful or at least ambivalent about being forced to work for what we often perceive as someone else's unfair profit, which may be true or not, depending on the specific situation. We are, of course, filled with contradictions. Someone might both be thankful for a job and still steal office supplies. Most workers are not as coherently, ideologically rebellious as I am, but they are most often profoundly conflicted. They might feel exploited, resentful and bored but still feel tinges of team spirit or loyalty to their employer. We are complex beings. I think most people take stuff because our culture is so materialistic that getting something for free may make us feel a tad guilty, but it is profoundly tempting and empowering. We rationalize petty theft from our workplaces, consciously or unconsciously, as a form of justifiable wage adjustment. We feel underpaid and undervalued and taking stuff makes us feel we are evening the score just a little bit. And our society's more and more extreme disparities of wealth and power and the prevalent winning at all costs mentality make us all feel like suckers if we cling to old-fashioned moral strictures, especially when we assume, usually quite correctly, that "everyone else is doing it."

Commentators have mentioned that people are far more willing to pinch stuff at work that seems plentiful and won't be missed than to actually snag cash, and point to this as an example of human irrationality, in that theft is theft, but I would dispute that. Context is everything. When a Brinks truck overturns on a highway and cash spills out, very few people return the money. When they do, it makes the news, because it's so unusual. Such examples and the nearly universal workplace poaching we've been discussing may seem like petty matters, but these predictable and seemingly trivial behaviors reveal just how weak and damaged social solidarity is in our culture. They highlight our deep mistrust and loathing for those institutions with economic power that govern much of our lives. Class awareness in a classic Marxist sense has never been that strong in the U.S., and appeals to populist "class warfare" are taboos in mainstream political discourse, but a very widespread muddled rage and resentment with strong class overtones is most certainly a powerful undertow.

The sheer prevalence of workplace poaching is what is so revelatory. According to nearly all studies a majority of the population engage or have engaged in it. If one adds in all those who are not 100% forthright in their income tax declarations, I think I am on very firm ground declaring that only a small minority of the population could believably claim to be rigorously, impeccably honest by society's official yardsticks. And that lack of forthrightness apparently applies to our most intimate relationships: according to Psychology Today, more than 70% of married men and women keep stashes of money their partner does not know about. So, being totally "honest" in that conventional sense is not the norm in our society, and it is less normal than it ever was. No surprise, then, that, according to sociologist Robert Putnam (in his groundbreaking Bowling Alone), in 1950 more than half of all Americans surveyed felt that most people were "moral and honest." By 2000, that percentage had fallen to a tad over 25%. It takes one to know one, and this is one domain in which people know the painful truth about themselves and their neighbors.

What is most striking to me about all the money-related behaviors I have been discussing (gambling, debt, "shopaholism," and petty employee larceny) is that while they have all long existed in one form or another, their growth in the last few decades has been extraordinary. Our attitudes toward money have changed nearly as much as our sexual norms, and our financial behaviors are as radically novel as our sexual mores. While some view new sexual attitudes as liberating and others see them as degenerate, it's hard to see anything clearly positive about these trends in our economic lives. We are in new territory. Old moral strictures are dissolving, but nothing too solid has yet replaced them. Most people are not compulsive gamblers or dangerously indebted or out of control compulsive shoppers, but if you add all those folks up, it's far from an insignificant number, and a whole bunch of others have problems in those areas that wouldn't quite qualify them as pathological but that are nonetheless borderline or at least potentially worrisome. Throw in all those for whom bitter fights about money are common in their families or relationships and factor in our nearly universal at least mild dishonesty and petty larceny, and one could be justified in concluding that a majority of us have some aspect of our relationship to money that is at best unhealthy, at worst deeply problematic.

But it would be grossly unfair in my view to lay the bulk of the blame on individual moral failings when money itself is such a treacherous, corrupting substance, and our entire society's relationship to it is so toxic. It would be like blaming children for mishandling plutonium. How can we be blamed if our sense of self-worth and our self-image is tied to how much money we have when without sufficient money we are in fact powerless and subject to constant indignities, when money can in fact get one out of many jams and open many doors, when our media incessantly carpet-bomb us with reminders that money is the key to happiness, and when we are in fact treated with respect when we have plenty and like dirt when we have none? Being obsessed with money and terrified of not having enough is a perfectly logical response when lack of money hampers one's every move. Insolvency is, objectively, a terrifying fate. I would argue that we should rather be deeply impressed when someone is able to arrive at some sort of more or less reasonably balanced relationship with money, because everything in our social environment works against such an outcome, and, in my experience, such people are exceedingly rare.

Notes:

-The widely used Balzac quote is actually a paraphrase from a line in his *Le Père Goriot*. In the original French, it's: *"Le secret des grandes fortunes sans cause apparente est un crime oublié, parce qu' il a été proprement fait."* Here's my own rough English translation: "The secret behind great fortunes for which there is no obvious explanation is a crime that has been forgotten because it was well pulled off."

The Legal System:

on the 2007 Stanford Law Review investigation of immigration asylum cases:
-"On the Verge of Expulsion And the Fringe of Justice" by Adam Liptak in the NY Times, Apr 15, 2008

on New York State's judicial system and fair legal representation:
-"Lawsuit Says State Failing Poor Criminal Defendants" in New York Civil Liberty Union News, Winter 2008

on federal judges accepting free vacations:
-"Golf Anyone? The Movable Feast Called "Judicial Education" by Dorothy Samuels in the NY Times, April 24, 2004

on the conflict of interest scandal involving the Chief Justice of West Virginia's Supreme Court, Elliott Maynard:
-"West Virginia's Top Judge Loses His Re-election Bid" by Ian Urbina in the NY Times, May 15th, 2008

-The Santa Clara County v. Southern Pacific Railroad Company of 1886 was a convoluted U.S. Supreme Court case that wound up indirectly entitling corporations to protection under the Fourteenth Amendment.

Medicine:

On the lobbying of doctors by pharmaceutical and medical equipment firms and on the cost of MRI and other imaging technologies:
-"Many Doctors, Many Tests, No Rhyme or Reason" by Dr. Sanjay Jauhar in the Science Times, March 11th, 2008

on new drug studies covertly written by Merck:
-"Merck Wrote Studies For Doctors" by Stephanie Saul in the NY Times, April 16th, 2008

on the financial dealings of the American Psychiatric Association:
-"Psychiatric Association Faces Senate Scrutiny Over Drug Industry Ties" by Benedict Carey and Gardiner Harris in the NY Times, July 12th, 2008
on the Dartmouth study on racial disparities in medical care:

-"Research Finds Wide Disparities in Health Care by Race and Region" by Kevin Sack in the NY Times, June 5, 2008

on the cost and inferior results of the U.S. health system, as found by a Commonwealth Fund study:
-"While the U.S. Spends Heavily on Health Care, a Study Faults the Quality" by Reed Abelson in the NY Times, July 17th, 2008

Corruption:

on the temptations of border agents:
-"Border Agents, Lured by the Other Side: As Enforcement Grows, Corruption Cases Increase" by Randal C. Archibold and Andrew Becker in the NY Times, May 27th, 2008

-*Perfectly Legal: The Covert Campaign to Rig Our Tax System to Benefit the Super-Rich-and Cheat Everybody Else* (Portfolio, 2005); and *Free Lunch: How the Wealthiest Americans Enrich Themselves at Government Expense and Stick You With The Bill* (Portfolio, 2007), both by David Cay Johnston.

on the railroad scams of the 1870s and the "robber baron" era:
-the great old classic: *The Robber Barons* by Matthew Josephson (1934)

on Rockefeller and the founding and predations of Standard Oil, the great classic by the mother of investigative journalism:
-*The History of the Standard Oil Company* by Ida Tarbell (McClure, Phillips, 1904)

on the CIA's historical relationships to the drug trade:
-another great classic: *The Politics of Heroin in Southeast Asia* by Alfred W. McCoy (Harper Colophon Books, 1973)

on Enron's incredibly close ties to the Bush Administration:
-"Enron's Tangled Web" on the Public Citizen website at: www.citizen.org

on corruption in China:
-Philip Pan's *Out of Mao's Shadow* by Philip P. Pan (Simon & Shuster, 2008)

New York Grime:

on NY City and metro area corruption, a few random articles (out of hundreds) mostly from a brief period of a few months in the spring and summer of 2008:
-"Tales of Incompetence and Corruption Haunt Crane Work in City" by William K. Rashbaum in the NY Times, July 16th, 2008
-"Agency With a History of Graft and Corruption" by Alan Feuer in the NY Times, April 23rd, 2008
-"7 Plead Guilty to Rigging Property Auctions" by Katherine A. Finkelstein in the NY

Times, June 12, 1999
-"Cuomo Sees Fraud in Some Lawyers' Pensions" by Nicholas Confessore in the NY Times, May 9, 2008
-"School Bus Safety Officials Are Accused of Soliciting Bribes" by Steven Greenhouse in the NY Times, May 14, 2008
-"Home Alone-With Medicaid Fraudsters: In a $30 million home health-care scam, some well-connected names" by Tom Robbins in the Village Voice, May 13, 2008
-"Company With Big City Contracts Is Tied to Mob Schemes in Affidavit" by William K. Rashbaum in the NY Times, July 2nd, 2008
-"Connecticut Trash Hauler Pleads Guilty in Mob Case" in NY Times, (AP) June 4, 2008
-"Officials Accused of Taking Agency Money in Fake Adoptions" by Benjamin Weiser in the NY Times, July 17, 2008

on John McNamara, the car dealer who conned GM:
-"Car Dealer Gets 5 Years for Bilking G.M. of More than $400 Million" by Linda Richardson in the NY Times, August 10, 1996

-A fairly accurate portrayal of corrupt politics in the NYC borough of Queens can be found in the fictional film *The Yards* (James Gray, 2000)-with Mark Wahlberg, James Caan, Joaquin Phoenix, Faye Dunaway, Ellen Burstyn and Charlize Theron

on the financial fiasco in Birmingham, Alabama:
-"High Finance Backfires on Alabama County" by Kyle Whitmire and Mary Williams Walsh in the NY Times, March 12th, 2008

Golden Revolving Doors (National Corruption):

on the push to undermine governmental scrutiny of the financial world in 2005:
-"A New Mood in Congress to Forgo Corporate Scrutiny" by Stephen Labaton in the NY Times, March 10th, 2005

on obscene corporate tax loopholes:
-"G.O.P. is Moving to Slow Action on Tax Loophole" by David Cay Johnston in the NY Times, June 18th, 2002
-"A One-Time Tax Break Saved 843 U.S. Corporations $265 Billion" by Lynnley Browning in the NY Times, June 24th, 2008

on the Department of the Interior during the first term of the Bush administration:
-"The United States Department of the Interior or Norton & Company, Inc.???" from Defenders of Wildlife (www.defenders.org)

on Enron's incredible machinations:
-"Officials Got a Windfall Before Enron's Collapse" by David Barboza in the NY Times, June 18th, 2002

on the remarkable carnage wrought by Phil Gramm to the financial markets:

-"Foreclosure Phil: Would you trust the man who broke America's financial system to fix it? John McCain does" by David Corn in Mother Jones magazine, July/August 2008

on the amazing saga of the ultimate revolving door, business/government insider profiteer, Edward C. Aldridge:
-"Pentagon Brass and Military Contractors' Gold Mine" by Leslie Wane in the NY Times, June 29th, 2004

-Tom Wolfe quoted by Andrew Ross Sorkin in the NY Times in "Legacy of "Bonfire" Like a Long Heartburn," June 24, 2008

on intelligence outsourcing:
-*Spies for Hire: The Secret World of Intelligence Outsourcing* by Tim Shorrock (Simon & Shuster, 2008)

on the retired generals posing as objective commentators on military affairs under the control of the Pentagon:
-"2 Inquiries Set on Pentagon Publicity Effort" by David Bastow in the NY Times, May 24, 2008

on the doling out of incredibly lucrative Justice Department "corporate monitor" jobs to former government officials:
-"30 Ex-Government Officials Got Lucrative Posts as Corporate Monitors" by Eric Lichtblau and Kitty Bennett in the NY Times, May 23rd, 2008

on Tom Daschle's possible conflicts of interest:
-"Obama Pick May Test Conflict-of-Interest Pledge" by David D. Kirkpatrick in the NY Times, November 20th, 2008

Global (fiscal) Shenanigans:

-Transparency International (www.transparency.org) publishes an annual Corruption Perceptions Index (CPI) that ranks the world's countries
on bribery scandals that have rocked major EU companies:
-"Ex-Manager Tells of Bribery at Siemens" by Carter Dougherty in the NY Times, May 27, 2008
-"In Europe, Sharper Scrutiny of Ethical Standards" by Nicola Clark in the NY Times, May 7, 2008

on black markets, corrupt regions and organized international criminal networks:
-*Wages of Crime: Black Markets, Illegal Finance, and the Underworld Economy* by R.T. Naylor (Cornell University Press, 2002)
-*McMafia: A Journey Through the Global Underworld* by Misha Glenny (Alfred A. Knopf, 2008)
on the dubiously acquired tortilla empire of Roberto Gonzales Barrera:

-"How a Tortilla Empire Was Built on Favoritism" by Anthony DePalma in the NY Times, February 15th, 1996

on the truly bizarre case of the February 2007 murder of three Salvadoran Congressmen in Guatemala:
-"In Guatemala, Officers' Killings Echo Dirty War" by James McKinley Jr. in the NY Times, March 5th, 2007

on the bloody drug wars in Mexico:
-"Mexico's War Against Drugs Kills Its Police" by James C. McKinley Jr. in the NY Times, May 26, 2008

on the global "grey"/ "informal" markets:
-*The Informal Economy in the Shadow of the State* by Miguel Centeno and Alejandro Portes (Princeton University Press, 2003)
-*The Underground Economy of the Urban Poor* by Sudhir Venkatesh (Harvard University Press, 2006)
-"Underground Industries Flourish Worldwide" by Heide B. Malhotra in the Epoch Times, September 20-26, 2007

on the real size of the underground economy:
-"The Shadow Economy" by Matthew Fleming, John Roman, and Graham Farrell in the Journal of International Affairs, Volume 53, No. 2., Spring 2000

on "offshore" banking centers, tax havens, money laundering, etc.:
-"Dans L'Archipel Planètaire De La Criminalité Financière" in Le Monde Diplomatique, April 2000
-"Inquiry Into a Guarded World: Wealthy Americans Undergo Scrutiny Over Offshore Accounts" by Lynnley Browning in the NY Times, June 6, 2008
-"UBS used "cloak of bank secrecy" to help clients avoid U.S. taxes" by Stephanie Kirchgaessner and Joanna Chung in The Financial Times, Jul 17, 2008
- "U.S. Asks Court to Force UBS to Provide Names: Bank Clients Suspected of Evading Taxes" by Lynnley Browning in the NY Times, July 1, 2008
-"Tax Havens Face Pressure From Europe" by Stephen Castle in the NY Times, May 15, 2008
-"Senate Report Examines Role of Banks in Tax Evasion" by Lynnley Browning in the NY Times, July 17, 2008

on the Vatican bank scandal:
-*The Moneychangers: How the Vatican Bank Enabled Roberto Calvi to Steal 250 Million Dollars for the Heads of the P2 Masonic Lodge* by Charles Raw (Harvill Press, 1992)
-"Archbishop Marcinkus, 84, Banker at the Vatican, Dies" by Margalit Fox in the NY Times, February 22nd, 2006

Routinely Irrational:
some books on the irrational in economic behavior and bubbles:
-*Predictably Irrational* by Dan Ariely (Harper Collins, 2008)
- *Tulipomania: the story of the world's most coveted flower and the extraordinary passions it aroused* by Mike Dash (Three Rivers Press, 2000)
-*A Very English Deceit: the secret history of the South Sea Bubble and the first great financial scandal* by Malcolm Balen (London: Fourth Estate 2003).
-*Devil Take the Hindmost: a history of financial speculation* by Edward Chancellor (Farrar, Straus & Giroux, 1999)
-*Manias, Panics, and Crashes: a history of financial crises* by Charles Kindleberger (John Wiley & Sons, 1978; now it its 5th edition)
-*Irrational Exuberance* by Robert J. Shillers (Princeton University Press, 2000)
-*Famous First Bubbles:The Fundamentals of Early Manias* by Peter M. Garber (MIT Press, 2000)
-And of course, the granddaddy of them all, the 19th Century classic, *Extraordinary Popular Delusions and the Madness of Crowds* by Charles MacKay (1841; Harmony Books, 1980)

on the 2004 study by Alan Ziobrowski at Georgia State University about U.S. Senators' stock portfolios:
- "In stock market, US senators beat averages-A report showing outsize portfolio gains for US senators is raising new questions about ethics and conflicts of interest for Capitol Hill power brokers" by Gail Russell Chaddock in the Christian Science Monitor, March 9th, 2004
- *Trading Secrets: Seduction and Scandal at the Wall Street Journal* by R. Foster Winans (St. Martin's Press, 1986)

Debt:
-National Association for Business Economics (www.nabe.com)

-Bankrate, Inc, stats on debt, etc. at: www.bankrate.com
Gambling:
-*Gambling in America* by Earl L. Grinols (Cambridge University Press, 2004)
-Statistics from the American Gaming Association at: www.americangaming.org
-Gambling stats on the PBS/Frontline site:
www.pbs.org/wgbh/pages/frontline/shows/gamble/etc/facts.html
Shopping:
-Ivan Illich, the late great radical social critic, analyzed "the creation of needs" in his 1978 *Toward a History of Needs* (Random House).

on compulsive shopping:
-"A New Look at Compulsive Shopping" by Helga Dittmar (senior lecturer in psychology at the University of Sussex in Brighton, U.K) in the Journal of Social and Clinical Psychology, 2005, 24 (6), pp. 832-859
-"Family History and Psychiatric Comorbidity in Persons With Compulsive Buying:

Preliminary Findings" by Donald W. Black, M.D., Susan Repertinger, M.D., Gary R. Gaffney, M.D., and Janelle Gabel, R.N in the American Journal of Psychiatry (155:960-963, July 1998)
-*I Shop Therefore I Am: Compulsive Buying and the Search for Self* by April Benson (Jason Aronson, 2000)

on the $13 to $15 billion dollar aesthetic surgery industry:
-*Beauty Junkies* by Alex Kuczynski (Doubleday, 2006)
-A huge "Body Beautiful" ("The Ultimate Cosmetic Surgery Expo") event was held at the Javits Convention Center in New York City in September 2007. Here is a line from one of its (full page) ads in local newspapers: "Win Thousands of $$$$ In The Ultimate Cosmetic Surgery Giveaway!! Including a Two Day Cosmetic Makeover Vacation Package In Beautiful San Jose, Costa Rica."

A Nation of Petty Thieves:

on the profession of "certified fraud examiners" and workplace surveillance technology:
-Association of Certified Fraud Examiners (www.acfe.org/)

on employee theft:
-"Taking at the Office: Employee Larceny Is Bigger and Bolder" by Greg Winter in the NY Times, July 12th, 2000

-Michael Ventura's classic essay on work from the worker's point of view: "Someone is Stealing Your Life" by Michael Ventura in the L. A. Weekly, January 26th, 1990

-Bob Black's little anarchist gem of an essay "The Abolition of Work" originally appeared in 1985 in his anthology *The Abolition of Work and Other Essays*, published (but intentionally not copyrighted) by Loompanics Unlimited.

on spouses concealing money from their partners:
-"Typically Twisted" by Kathleen McGowan in Psychology Today, August, 2008

-Robert Putnam's groundbreaking classic study of the breakdown of American social solidarity is: *Bowling Alone: The Collapse and Revival of American Community* (Simon & Schuster, 2000).

BELIEFS

"People are strange when you're a stranger…" —The Doors

I have, in my life, had the opportunity to travel fairly extensively. In the course of those peregrinations and in my routine comings and goings here in my hometown I've had, besides the thousands of normal quick communications we all engage in during the course of daily life with strangers, shopkeepers and neighbors, hundreds of more involved conversations with a wide range of people. One of the things that I've been most surprised by over the years is how unpredictable people can be. People's outward appearance definitely has not, in my experience, been that good a predictor of their behaviors or ideologies, for example. I realize they're atypical, but I've met anti-drug, straight arrow types with long, scraggly hair, wearing torn jeans; and very experienced acidheads in three-piece suits; soft-spoken young women in flowery dresses who were staunch conservatives; and big, tough blue collar guys who were vegans. At the very least I have learned not to assume too much based on people's external presentation. Beyond that though, I have been even more shocked by how many of the people I have met in random circumstances turned out to have some extremely unconventional ideas.

Americans, in my experience, seem, on average, to be particularly zany in some aspects of their worldviews. I began to expect that if I spoke with a random American long enough some very surprising beliefs would eventually pop out. Perhaps this is due to the relative youth of the country, the weird mix of restless settlers, con men, and dreamers who found their way here, and the myth of endless possibilities that is an important element of the national identity. To be fair, though, other cultures also produce a lot of weirdness. We Americans have good reason to stare, mouth-agape at, say, the Eurovision Song Contest or Norwegian Satanic death-metal rock bands.

There is no disputing that other countries have birthed countless offbeat subcultures and puzzling phenomena. To pick just a few random examples: there's long been a sizeable sub-group of Germans and Czechs obsessed with faithfully re-enacting Native American rituals (triggered by the late 19th Century novels of Karl May); Brazil has an extraordinary variety of wild spiritual groups based on mixtures of African, indigenous, 19th Century European esoteric, and modern UFO cult ideas; India has its mind-boggling array of gurus; Chinese martial arts and esoteric healing schools often make very far-fetched claims about supra-normal feats and immortality; and so on. In fact, every nation and region is replete with many traditions and ideas that seem outlandish to outsiders.

And when we look at religion, one of the key cornerstones of nearly all cultures' worldviews, we see that the central tenets of any faith almost always seem very weird to those from other traditions. Religions' foundational ideas are based on extraordinary, paranormal revelations, miracles, mysteries and mythic elements in the lives of their founders. They are based on faith and emotional commitment, not rational analysis. Indeed, their proponents invariably present them as lying above and beyond rationality. To outsiders who are not raised in their folds, however, their ideas simply seem bizarre, but because we live in a pluralistic society in which a wide range of religious traditions have to co-exist, we tend not, these days, to encourage widespread public debates about the minutiae of theology.

Given the West's long history of religious wars, pogroms and persecutions, this is probably very wise. If one person believes Padma Sambhava literally chased the demons from Tibet and hid secret teachings in lakes and clouds and another that Jesus walked on water and reanimated Lazarus, that's fine as long as they don't forcefully try to impose their beliefs on each other or the rest of us. This relative tolerance has recently become a widespread, majority social phenomenon according to a 2008 Pew Forum on Religion and Public Life report, the U.S. Religious Landscape Survey. Even half-hearted tolerance certainly represents a vast improvement on our past practices.

And of course, in every tradition there is a wide spectrum of believers-from the most sophisticated who interpret their faith's teachings as more mytho-poetic wisdom than literal fact, to those fundamentalists who see them as literal truths, to a bunch of folks somewhere in between these poles. Most people accept their ancestors' religion as a given but just don't think too much about its theological underpinnings and don't worry too much when they violate some of their faith's inconvenient strictures. We are obviously still fighting heatedly over the role of religion in the public sphere, but, mercifully, in the industrialized world at least, it's been nothing like the carnage of the Thirty Years' War, even in the very religious U.S., at least so far. Some might point to the long "Troubles" in Ulster or the wars in Bosnia and Kosovo to dispute that, but those conflicts were more rooted in ethnic, cultural, political, and economic factors than in purely religious divisions.

One result of this mostly admirable pluralism and tolerance, though, is that, in terms of public discourse, we sweep these mythic, a-rational spiritual beliefs that are so central to so many people's cultural identities under the rug. We acknowledge or celebrate diversity by safely sticking to the surface of things. During the holidays, the media gush about how wonderful it is that we can celebrate Christmas, Chanukah, Kwanzaa, and respect each other's beliefs. It's really bad manners (and maybe dangerous) to needle your Christian in-laws during Christmas dinner about whether they really literally believe in Jesus' miracles, or to mock your Orthodox Jewish acquaintances' dietary and Sabbath restrictions, or to ask your African American neighbors lighting Kwanzaa candles if they know about the gun battles in Southern California between the Black Panthers and followers of Ron Karenga (the inventor of Kwanzaa) back in the 60s; or to ridicule Hindus' or Jains' ideas about reincarnation; or to needle Mormons about the Mountain Meadows massacre...

Again, this is progress. We should respect others' beliefs. I am not at all in favor of rekindling rabid battles between Protestants and "Papists," or to see the rebirth of witch burnings. The tensions between the West and some strains of militant Islam are bad enough. I'm all in favor of letting sleeping dogs lie, and religion may be one of those areas in which staying distantly polite and on the surface of things in public is indeed the wisest course, but I can't help but notice that this creates a big discrepancy between the tone in much of our media regarding assumptions about our collective beliefs and the actual ideas that animate real people. It permits us to pretend that our worldviews are much tidier and rational than they are in reality. Religion is not at all the only domain involved in this chasm between our public discourse mostly anchored in secular rationality and the far less rational inner life of most human beings, but it is one of the most glaringly obvious, so it's a good place to start.

In the U.S. Christian conservatives strongly feel that secular "leftists" control the communications' media, which, in a technological mass society, form the equivalent of the public square. On one level this is obviously grotesquely laughable, as the large media conglomerates are intimately tied to the highest levels of corporate capitalism, but from these Christians' perspective this paranoia is not entirely off base. The media do by and large try to maintain the neutral, civil tone regarding religion I discussed above, and these Evangelicals often view themselves as the norm, the "real" Americans, so a neutral tone that treats "exotic" faiths such as Islam or Buddhism (or worse secular humanism) as equally deserving of deference strikes them as a form of usurpation.

Meanwhile, atheists and agnostics also have every reason to feel like a beleaguered minority in the U.S. Researchers at the University of Minnesota polled 2,000 U.S. households in 2006 and found that atheists were the most distrusted minority group, ranking below Muslims, recent immigrants, and gays. An atheist could not currently overtly, successfully run for President or for public office in most regions of the U.S. Religious faith is at the moment a requirement for nearly any elected office outside of a few progressive enclaves.

The truth is that mainstream media empires are above all profit-driven enterprises by and large run by business executives with the de-facto center-right worldviews of their social class and staffed at the journalistic level by probably mostly centrist to slightly liberal folks (with notable exceptions in both cases, of course). These enterprises seek to maximize their profits and therefore to offend as few large groups of people as possible, and not to attract the wrath of any powerful entities, be they of the governmental, corporate or mobilized-populace variety, so they tend to seek to reflect what status quo consensus they can discern. This has changed a bit as first talk-radio, then cable television and the Internet have increasingly made possible more precisely targeted, specialized programs or networks or websites that can aggressively cater to groups with specific ideologies. The most powerful and influential of these are, predictably, on the right, such as the FOX Network and all Rupert Murdoch's print publications, and all those rabid radio provocateurs in the Rush Limbaugh template. The cable TV network MSNBC has recently emerged as a liberal competitor to FOX, and a new universe of bloggers on the center left has also become a dynamic political force, though these are still smaller and less powerful than the media of the right. But even these partisan voices, outside of the most rabid on the right, whose profession is to shock, have to tread very carefully where religious tolerance is concerned. The largest conglomerates still hate any hard-to-control ideological controversies that could hamper profits. The ménage à trois of capitalism, hyper-consumerism and scientific advertising still seeks as much as possible to erase any jagged ideological differences that could upset our appetites, hamper our gluttony, and slow the wheels of consumption and commerce.

In any case there are far deeper paradoxes regarding the rationality of our beliefs lurking here. It's been a banal cliché ever since Freud (and long, long before-it's a key theme in much mythology) that human beings are internally conflicted creatures who have to contend with powerful instinctual drives and impulses that don't dovetail too well with civilized behavior or the rules of logic. Depending on our ideological bents we use different terms to describe this condition and disagree on its origins and on the best approaches to negotiating these dueling inner forces. Historically, staunch moralists have preached the negation and containment of our "baser" urges through willpower, asceticism, and outright suppression, while more Dionysian traditions have experimented with expressive safety valves. Stern Christians trace these conflicts back to the eviction from Eden; followers of Hobbes and Burke on the right have put the onus on human nature; those on the left following in Rousseau's footsteps have tended to blame social forces and inequalities for perverting humanity's central innocence. But, whatever we call it and however we think it should be addressed, the basic situation is news to no one.

Given how fragile the veneer of rationality is in the human make-up, perhaps what should surprise us most is that reason is as valued as it is. We humans are such a tormented species, we seem to require powerful mythic ideologies to contain and canalize our myriad contradictions. Even ideologies that purport to be purely rational, such as Marxism, often wind up resembling messianic religious movements. A scientific/rationalist approach to understanding the world is a very recent phenomenon in the human trajectory, and it has never succeeded in displacing the mytho-poetic realms in our psyches, and probably never will, despite its impressive successes. In fact, as David Noble argues persuasively in *The Religion of Technology*, most of the founding ancestors of the modern scientific perspective in the late Middle Ages in the West, such as Roger Bacon, were themselves totally bathed in millenarian religious ideas. And a certain messianic, cult-like flavor persisted well into the 19th Century with such central figures as Auguste Comte, who viewed the scientific elite as a sort of secular monastic brotherhood. Engineers, too, have been far from immune: the fathers of electric power, to cite a striking example, were a strange pair. Nikola Tesla at one point thought he had received communications from Mars, and Thomas Edison was obsessed with paranormal phenomena and communicating with the dead. Quite a few of the major figures in militant Islam have been engineers. Some of NASA's scientists and quite a few robotics and cyber researchers and biologists hold outlandish techno-utopian ideas. So science itself, while its methods (at their best) are uniquely rigorous and verifiable, has mythic/a-rational elements in its very DNA, and these continue to find expression. And some overly zealous advocates of science fall into "scientism"-a sort of religion in its own right, one that tolerates no competing worldviews and is closed-minded to any evidence that might challenge its presuppositions.

These contradictions were evident from the earliest onset of the tradition: those astonishingly lucid Greek philosophers who laid the groundwork for the scientific approach in the West probably nearly all believed in the literal existence of Zeus and Athena and Hermes, and the rest of the pantheon. And even more than two millennia later, Newton, the very archetype of the scientific genius, was obsessed with "heretical" theology and was a very active practicing alchemist and esotericist. If Newton couldn't live only on the rational side of the street, what hope is there for the rest of us? It may simply be that rationality will always be just one style of cognition within the exceedingly complex ecosystem of human consciousness, and that even science and scientists can never escape the other-than-rational dimensions of the mind. But these long-lived paradoxes become far more potentially dangerous in a climatically destabilized, overpopulated world with collapsing ecosystems, major geopolitical realignments, a wobbly global financial architecture, and nuclear and biological weapons, genetic manipulation, robotics, and nanotechnology.

Once we look beyond id/super-ego battles at the micro level within individuals' psyches, and examine contradictions between rational and other-than-rational tendencies in our larger collective ideologies and beliefs, more complex and troubling questions come up, and these, in my opinion, are rarely looked at unflinchingly in our public discourse. And, again, this is not only true in the religious sphere. Our political ideas too are usually far from rationally arrived at-they are very likely colored by our age, region, social class, ethnic group, milieu, and so on. Most of us inherit a great deal of our political ideology from our families and surroundings, just as we do with religion-that is one of the core definitions of culture. Some of us do question the ideas that have been transmitted to us and change our political orientations, just as some of us, more than in previous generations, convert to new faiths or abandon our ancestral one (these days, some 25% of us change or drop our original religious affiliations, according to that Pew report), but, by and large, despite that increased politico-religious fluidity, most people still inherit their political and religious traditions and accept them as a given and don't feel compelled to scrutinize them too closely. This is one key reason political choices are often far more knee-jerk and emotional (and therefore more readily prone to manipulation) than they are rational, to the great chagrin of many political intellectuals who have recently produced a slew of books on aspects of the topic, including: Al Gore's *The Assault on Reason*; Susan Jacoby's *The Age of American Unreason*; Damian Thompson's *Counterknowledge: How We Surrendered to Conspiracy Theories, Quack Medicine, Bogus Science and Fake History*; and Christopher Hitchens' and Daniel Dennett's atheistic polemics. Another very popular recent genre offers analyses of our propensity for irrationality drawn from neuroscience, from the aforementioned *Predictably Irrational* to *Welcome to Your Brain* by Sam Wang and Sandra Aamodt, to Ori and Rom Brafman's *Sway: The Irresistible Pull of Irrational Behavior*.

Neuroscience and evolutionary psychology can certainly produce interesting insights into our propensity for other-than-rational worldviews and choices and behaviors, but it is important not to neglect political and sociocultural factors, especially the increasingly overwhelming scale and complexity of our technologies and the institutions that govern our lives, and our resulting growing sense of insignificance and powerlessness. For one thing, given the sad history of ever more sophisticated propaganda, deceptions, cover-ups and lies that have emanated from governments and ruling elites for over a century, it is hard to blame people for distrusting authoritative discourse and for being susceptible to accepting even outlandish conspiracy theories. From Hearst's (and now Murdoch's) "yellow" journalism to Goebbels' and Stalin's propaganda machines to the CIA's covert coups and ambitious manipulation of the arts and literature in the 1950s and 60s (exposed in Frances Stonor Saunders' *The Cultural Cold War: The CIA and the*

World of Arts and Letters and Hugh Wilford's *The Mighty Wurlitzer: How the CIA Played America*), from Nixon's and tobacco executives' blatant lies to the Iran-Contra scandal, to the recent distortions of intelligence leading to the Iraq War, most people, whatever their ideological perspective, now seem to contain within their political brains a strange mix of reflexive patriotism on the one hand and a very understandable willingness to believe the most convoluted *X-Files* type conspiracy theories about their leaders on the other.

A relatively new but very important wrinkle in human belief systems is that in the far less rooted, far more mobile, insanely complex, vertiginously changing, bafflingly diverse technological societies created by modernity, people still cling (sometimes desperately) to old belief structures (or, more often, mutating variants of them), but they also can't help, consciously and unconsciously, tacking on whole new layers of usually poorly digested ideas from a wide range of disparate sources. These ideological layer-cake collages can on occasion produce very sophisticated and productive cross pollinations, as we see in such phenomena as, say, research on Buddhist meditative techniques by neuroscientists, or in figures such as Thomas Merton or Teilhard de Chardin who could draw from Eastern philosophy or science (respectively) to enrich their own Christian traditions. They are more likely to be a bit more haphazard: someone may view himself as a conventional Episcopalian and moderate Republican but also believe, say, that there are aliens in Area 51; or we find "straight edge" high school kids with piercings and tattoos who are in punk/metal Christian bands and take vows of premarital celibacy; or a prim conservative who consults astrologers (Nancy Reagan).

If we do a rigorous self-audit of our beliefs, nearly all of us will discover that we contain a not very coherent mix of some traditional ideas we've unconsciously inherited from our social milieus; widespread, mainstream views we accept without much reflection; and a whole range of other more idiosyncratic and less conventional ideas in some domains we've accumulated along the way from a variety of sources. If we're honest, we'll have to admit that this inner brain-stew is rife with contradictions and incompatible ideas, and that our responses are far more emotional and instinctive than rational in most areas of life. Probably one of the greatest illusions perpetrated by our media is the myth that we (their audience) are predominantly rational readers-listeners-interlocutors-citizens. This is especially galling when all the advertisements aimed at us are designed by diabolical specialists to bypass our feeble rationality to appeal to the far more potent instinctual parts of the brain, but that's another matter.

Modern, industrial society is defined by its reliance on technology, its machines and its massive infrastructure. Engineering rules our world. And while it's possible to be a software or automotive designer or nuclear or hydraulic engineer and to be devoutly religious, engineering is a stepchild of scientific culture, and scientists are, as a group, the least religious profession-al category-not surprisingly, given the history of the battles between organized religion and science that have so marked our civilization from the late Middle Ages on. The percentage of non-believers among scientists is much higher than in the general population, and in the most prestigious, top rungs of the scientific world, higher still. The U.S. is clearly the most religious of the major industrialized nations. A 2005 AP/Ipsos poll in ten countries found only 2% of atheists and 4% of agnostics here, compared to the least religious nation polled, France, which had 19% of atheists and 16% of agnostics (still a minority-even France still sees hordes visit Lourdes). A 2004 Pew Research poll had very similar results for the U.S.: 12% of those under 30 and 6% over 30 were "non-religious." But scientists have long been radically different in that regard, and have remained consistently skeptical. A study done in 1914 by one James H. Leuba found that 58% of 1,000 randomly selected U.S. natural scientists expressed "disbelief or doubt in the existence of God." A 1996 poll with similar questions found that 60.7% of the scientists were skeptics. When one polls the highest echelons of the scientific establishment, the numbers are significantly higher. A recent poll found that 93% of the members of the National Academy of Sciences were atheists or agnostics. It's certainly pretty difficult to reconcile a Biblically based funda-mentalist view of the Earth as being only a few thousand years old and to be a credible geologist or radio astronomer or geneticist or botanist or anthro-pologist.

The language of science is the lingua franca of the engineers whose works define our world. Science may arrogantly overstep its bounds when it claims to have ultimate answers, when it expresses confidence it will even-tually unravel all the mysteries of consciousness, and when it represents itself as the only legitimate approach to knowledge and cognition, and, as I point-ed out earlier, it's not nearly as tidily rational a tradition as it purports to be, but, all that said, it is, justifiably, the most privileged form of knowledge, unique in its universal applicability and the replicability of its results. It's hard not to applaud science's triumph over medieval superstition, but its dominance has come at a very high price. The "de-sacralization" of the world many have bemoaned has indeed had some dire consequences in our relationship to nature, but, for better or worse, the scientific method is without question the most potent, reliable, universal system of mass knowing and doing we have developed, and while intuition has been a factor in many great scientific discoveries, science officially aims to be, above all, a supremely rational domain.

It was inevitable that after some resistance the scientific worldview would earn a privileged role in the corridors of power. Nothing else delivers such reliably potent technologies and effective methods of social control. Even in a strangely archaic political culture such as the U.S. in which our just departing President can articulate skepticism about evolution, ignore nearly universal scientific consensus on climate change, and actively seek to suppress studies by the government's own professional scientists that arrive at conclusions his oil company backers and Evangelical supporters disapprove of, nearly all the actions the government undertakes are still based on scientific data or at the very least on scientific methodology. The President may be a fundamentalist Christian, but the nuclear weapons that define his nation's power were designed and are maintained and upgraded by mostly atheist or skeptical physicists, and the microbiologists who would be the ones called upon in case of a pandemic or biological weapons attack are probably also nearly all secular rationalists, and even when they're not, scientific rationality rules their discipline and has colonized their minds. As we look at the political elites that rule nations around the globe, we see that there are quite a few imbeciles, religious fanatics, zany dictators, vicious autocrats, kleptocrats, plutocrats, and even a few complete madmen among them, but that, despite it all, scientific rationality is the only universally accepted worldview among the managerial classes that actually keep all the industrial and transportation and infrastructure systems running.

This fundamental divide between the beliefs of the masses around the world and those of the technical elites that actually run everything has a bizarre effect in the language and tone used in our media. The language of science and its offspring, technology, is, as I mentioned, the de facto lingua franca of the planet, the only worldview universally accepted by the globe's hands-on managers, but the overwhelming majority of the population, even in highly industrialized countries, don't understand most of it, and don't in fact share many of its core assumptions. Religious conservatives, who are so numerous in the U.S., certainly don't, and even most highly educated people in non-scientific fields have, at best, very fuzzy ideas about even the most fundamental concepts of physics or chemistry or mathematics or astronomy or biology and genetics, or about how electricity or most of our key technologies actually work. Still more rare are people who actually understand something as central as, say, photosynthesis, the basis of nearly all life on Earth. This makes it very hard for even sophisticated, educated people to be able to reliably differentiate between propaganda, pseudo-science and reliable data, or to be able to look at statistics or studies or corporate claims with a sufficiently critical eye.

To be fair, as I alluded to above, many in the scientific/technical elites are themselves prone to all sorts of conscious or unconscious other-than-rational behaviors and ideas, just as Newton and Aristotle were. Not much has changed on that score, so the divides I'm discussing exist not only between worldviews and groups but within our own individual psyches as well. But, nonetheless, this discrepancy between a scientific outlook and so many of our actual beliefs is real, and it is papered over in our society's "official" discourse by an unexamined pretense of universally accepted ideas, of a shared normality. This impression of a consensus may be largely true at the level of daily life: most people want a violent crime-free environment, clean air and water, good schools, less congested highways, and so on. But in the realm of ideology and beliefs, there is only consensus if one restricts oneself to broad, hollow words: "democracy," fairness, efficiency. If one begins to poke a bit at the fragile linguistic membrane covering our supposed shared values, irreconcilable contradictions spill out all over the place. So the mainstream media walk on eggshells to, consciously and unconsciously, avoid stirring up these hornets' nests.

According to a November 2007 Harris Online survey of close to 2500 respondents, 79% of adult Americans believe in miracles, 70% in heaven and angels, 60% in hell and the devil, a third in witches. 42% did say they subscribed to Darwin's theory of evolution, but nearly as many, 39%, were strict creationists-believers in a literal reading of Genesis. Roughly one third espoused beliefs in UFOs, and about that many in the validity of astrology. Now I'm not taking sides in these debates. I'm not here to ridicule belief in UFOs or angels or devils or astrology or to stake out a hardcore skeptical, rationalist position. My own belief systems are as riddled with contradictions as most everyone else's, and I hold a fair share of very exotic, other-than-rational ideas. The only reason I bring these matters up is that topics such as miracles, UFOs, astrology, and angels are archetypes-poster children of irrationality and flakiness, as far as a scientific-rationalistic worldview is concerned. Their very mention elicits snickers at just about any serious scientific gathering. When political candidates have on rare occasions mentioned having sighted a UFO at some point in their lives, for example, the jokes on late night TV have been relentless and enduring. No matter how many people subscribe to these beliefs, and despite occasional sympathetic coverage on specific media outlets (CNN's Larry King seems to have a soft-spot for UFOs and the paranormal, for example), they remain not only marginalized, but the butt of jokes.

Beliefs that are held by either substantial majorities of the population (miracles, angels) or sizeable minorities (UFOs, astrology) are viewed as the height of idiocy by the scientific and technical elites whose worldview is the privileged perspective of modernity and of technological power, and the media, largely unconsciously, tiptoe around these gaping chasms in the weltanschauung. Differences between the beliefs of uneducated masses and those of ruling elites are obviously nothing new, but the contradictions I'm describing are not only a classic divide between the sophisticated and the semi-literate. The dizzying speed of change and the ever-increasing technological and social complexity of our lives can at times result in a great deal of angst and a pervasive sense of deracination and instability for nearly all of us, no matter how well educated we may be. Human beings have always relied on a mix of the practical and the mythic, the objective and the subjective in their judgments, and that remains true, except today everything is speeded up, and any sense of vestigial rootedness is fading fast.

None of us are immune to the ideological confusion that roils our culture. The strange bouillabaisse of overheated ideas of all stripes we now all swim in and the discrepancies and chasms I described (as well as a slew of others) can lead to bizarre ideological hybrids, some of which can turn out to be creatively novel and highly productive, some zanily amusing, some ridiculous, and some dangerously destructive and potentially lethal (besides the contemporary terrorists we're obsessed about, let's not forget Jim Jones, Tim McVeigh, the Solar Temple, Heaven's Gate, Aum Shinrikyo...). It's not often discussed in mainstream media, but the wide range of millenarian ideas and conspiracy theories that percolate in nearly every social milieu and fascinate so many of us are far more than fringe phenomena in our culture-they are far more widespread than usually acknowledged, and they are one of the most telling symptoms of the precariousness of our civilization.

Before I plunge into a look at conspiracy and apocalypse fixations, I'd like to clarify what, in my view, distinguishes reasonable suspicions of conspiracies from fanciful and ideologically pathological ones. We are a conspiratorial species. Wherever there is power to contend over and resources to be allocated (or seized), individuals and cliques in every society have invariably sought to devise covert strategies to acquire as much as possible. As a rule more than an exception, corporations collude, manipulate markets, and corrupt politicians; and governments lie. There are plenty of conspiracies going on all the time, from high school classes to city councils to parliaments and ministries to boardrooms to the highest levels of the world's intelligence services. One of the main functions of good investigative journalists is to constantly try to find out about the most important of these schemes and to expose them. Some of these conspiracies have major implications-lies or distorted stories that can lead to war, such as the "sinking" of the battleship Maine used to help start the Spanish-American War or the Gulf of Tonkin "incident" in Vietnam; or the manipulation of markets that can pass on enormous burdens to society, as was the case with Enron's deliberate sabotage of the energy supply to California. We can be sure many conspiracies are never exposed, and on occasion the seemingly wildest, most paranoid suspicions prove true as the evidence finally comes out years later-even most hippies back in the 60s (who had no problem taking that trickster Carlos Castaneda at face value) didn't give much serious credence to rumors that the CIA had extensively experimented on people with LSD, but it certainly had. Extreme wariness about official government or corporate pronouncements is not paranoia-it's wisdom.

But, that said, when one is convinced that some all-powerful, or nearly all-powerful cabal is behind much of human affairs, we are leaving the zone of informed skepticism and entering that of delusional paranoia. That sense that one's secret enemies are nigh omnipotent and can continuously and systematically manipulate events on a massive scale and deceive the entire world for very long stretches of time is one key sign that we are dealing with a mythic construct, not a reasoned analysis. And this tendency is very widespread in our culture, from Christians who see Satanic forces at work in every development they don't approve of, to those on the grassroots left who have convinced themselves the astonishingly incompetent Bush administration could somehow have planned and carried out the 9/11 attacks and pinned it on Islamic militants without any leaks, to the whole subculture of UFO enthusiasts who have elaborate beliefs about long term secret U.S. military-alien alliances (headquartered in Area 51) to control humanity, to a whole slew of sub-groups who have picked this or that bogeyman-the Trilateral Commission, or Rockefellers, or Rothschilds, or the British Royal Family (à la Lyndon LaRouche), or Jewish bankers, or the UN or EU, and so on ad nauseam, to focus on as the secret force behind much that is wrong with the world.

This type of demonization and scapegoating loses sight of the fact that most conspiracies fail or are only partially successful; most plots involve one clique in a ruling elite working against another; and all these possible conspirators are human beings just like us. Lobbyists and gangsters and politicians and corporate raiders are as likely to have heart attacks and strokes and get cancer and be depressed and have indigestion and migraines and hemorrhoids and problem children and substance addictions and heartbreaks as the rest of us. We may be justified in wanting to imprison some of them, but we are all just highly fallible human beings.

The aforementioned constellation of conspiracy mythologies that has sprung up surrounding 9/11, starting among some sectors of the left and then spreading, is an instructive example. Because the event was so dramatic and novel and it wound up, in the short term, serving the political agenda of the jingoistic right, many on the left simply could not accept that the Bush administration was not behind it, especially coming on the heels of the disputed 2000 presidential election (which really did have its fair share of actual conspiracies and dirty tricks by the right). To some extent this paranoia is a result of the profound ideological chasm between the values and beliefs of modern, "hip" urbanites and those of Evangelical Christians and the bellicose right. It was hard for the more "modern" parts of the population to accept being governed at the federal level by what feel like archaic, aggressive Puritans, when these "moderns" felt the culture wars of the 60s and 70s should have settled the matter and that progressive, open-minded pluralism would now be universally accepted. The divisions between social classes and between the business right and the labor and lumpen left have certainly been dramatic in our history, but the cultural divide between the "Bible Belt" and reasonably sophisticated circles in New York or San Francisco or Seattle (or

Austin or Ann Arbor or Madison or Santa Fe) is so enormous that there is almost no basis for conversation, let alone agreement. This is not in fact a nation with a shared ideology. Neither of the two overarching tendencies can accept the worldview or the legitimacy of the other.

This was apparent in the rabid attacks on Bill Clinton by the far right that included preposterous accusations of murder plots and every slander imaginable. Even though Clinton was in many ways a center right politician who passed key pro-business legislation, such as NAFTA, and far from progressive welfare "reform," with Republican support and only a minority of Democratic votes, something probably only a Democratic president could have done (in the same way only a lifelong anti-Communist such as Nixon could make peace with China), the far right had become habituated since the Reagan "revolution" (in fact a counter-revolution) to a Republican president who would at least further some of their agenda. They had, in their minds, taken back the reins from the communist pagan hedonists. They could absolutely not accept the legitimacy of a "modern" cultural pluralist as the head of the government, even if he was in fact more of a moderate Republican than a liberal Democrat by historical standards. This represented to them a nightmarish return to the horrors of the 1960s, and they were therefore willing to resort to nearly anything (short of violence, mercifully) to destroy or undermine him.

This 9/11 conspiracy syndrome is the biggest such phenomenon (at least on the left) since the Kennedy assassination obsession, which launched the modern genre, but the Kennedy assassination was far murkier in many respects as so many subsidiary plots (CIA attempts to kill Castro; Oswald's very strange connections on the left and right; the incomprehensible role of Jack Ruby; the lack of transparency of the investigations...) occulted the issue and couldn't help but raise slews of legitimate questions. That is far less the case this time, but the paranoia has been very "sticky." According to a 2006 Scripps Howard poll 36% of adult Americans think the government was either hiding facts about the events or even somehow behind the attack; 16% thought bombs planted in the buildings brought the towers down, and 12% felt that a missile, not a plane, struck the Pentagon. There are books (*Towers of Deception, The Big Wedding, The Shell Game...*), countless websites and blogs, and now films (*Able Danger, The Reflecting Pool*) that argue for this or that alternative theory. Other polls have found other results. The most conservative result was in a more recent Zogby poll that found only a tad under

5% who thought the U.S. government was directly behind the attacks. Once again polls are all over the place. I guess a lot depends on how the question is asked. Other polls have been somewhere between the 5% and the 36%. Whatever the exact numbers are, it's a very lively subculture.

The content of these conspiracy narratives ranges from obsessive technical discussions about the melting point of steel and the purported impossibility that planes could have brought down the buildings to Byzantine plots involving Islamists, Nazis, and Republican pedophiles. I don't know how accurate that Scripps poll is. It seems like an astonishingly high number, because if it's even remotely true, these beliefs must have extended far, far beyond the "left," in that the "progressive" left (as opposed to milquetoast liberals) can't be more than 3% to 8% (at very best; liberals are not much more than 20%) of the electorate depending on how rigorously one defines "progressive," but I seem to run into many, many people who share these 9/11 conspiracy beliefs, so perhaps that poll is in the ballpark. Again, here is a belief not often discussed by the media, or, when it is, that is treated (not completely unjustifiably) as the province of a lunatic fringe, but that is, whatever the exact figures, far more widespread among the population than usually acknowledged.

All that said, however, by far the biggest and most influential segments of the U.S. public prone to extreme "conspiracy thinking" are to be found among swaths of the Evangelical Christian population and among a number of groups on the populist far right. There certainly is a great deal of discussion in the media about the political importance of conservative Christians, and occasional exposés about some of the more extreme tendencies in that world as well, but just how radically the worldviews of many Evangelicals depart from global secular rational norms is rarely probed. Part of this is due to their sheer numbers, political influence (roughly 20% of the voting electorate are hardcore Evangelicals) and economic clout (according to one credible 2006 estimate 69.5 million American adults were active Evangelicals, and their household income was $2.1 trillion that year, 28% of the total of all U.S. families) and part of it is due to that taboo I mentioned earlier-the fear of probing too deeply and triggering quakes along the immense religio-ideological fault-lines that crisscross the national psychic landscape. In my view, apocalyptic Christians get way too much of a pass from most media, given how consequential their far-from-rational beliefs can be.

How differently do these Christians interpret world events than, say, a State Department analyst? Well, a CNN poll during the first Gulf War found that 14% of Americans thought it marked the beginning of Armageddon. A 1993 poll tallied 20% of respondents who felt Christ's second coming would come to pass in the year 2000. Either alarmingly or reassuringly, though, this is very far from something new. Apocalypticism and conspiracy paranoia are not synonymous-one can be an apocalypticist who expects some sort of dramatic end to the human project without being fixated on cosmic or political conspiracies, or conversely one can be obsessed by political conspiracies but not subscribe to any particular "End Times" mythos, but one also very often finds, especially among some strains of Evangelicals, that these two belief orientations come together. This apocalypse/conspiracy dyad has a remarkably long pedigree, and, despite new wrinkles, it's actually surprising how little its core content has changed over the centuries and how many times the same plotlines are recycled with only minor tweaks.

Apocalyptic visions and prophecies can be found in many of the world's most ancient creation myths and in nearly all its religious traditions. They seem to be a deeply ingrained template in the human psyche, probably because regional (floods, droughts, earthquakes) and even global (ice ages) cataclysms have occurred (and continue to occur) and the deep cultural memories of some of the most dramatic remain embedded in the collective unconscious. But the formats for most of the most widespread apocalyptic conspiracy theories that roil our culture in the West have more recent roots-Christian eschatology. Most of us know at least the major plotlines of that very odd text penned around 95 AD, the *Book of Revelation*: authentic Christians will be deceived and betrayed by a false leader (the Antichrist) secretly in league with Satan, but God will intervene as the "End Times" produce so much sin and degradation that he has to send in the cavalry, i.e. the Four Horsemen of the Apocalypse, to shake everything up during a particularly rough stretch (the "Tribulations"), and then it will all come to a head in the final cataclysmic battle in the Middle East (Armageddon). The good Christians win and a thousand years of just Christian rule (the millennium) ensue.

Now a lot of folks in Western history have focused on this action-packed narrative (and a smattering of other scriptural tidbits in *Ezekiel*, *Daniel*, and *Matthew*) to build the core of their worldviews. There has long been a subset of Christians who feel, at any given point, that this divinely ordained apocalypse is very close at hand. They are not only fundamentalists who consider scripture to be literally, unfailingly true, but they view these texts as filled with secret codes (another strange human obsession) that reveal future events, and they are constantly searching for likely suspects for the Antichrist role and for signs of the End Times-just about any disaster: earthquake, flood, war, viral outbreak, or even such trivial matters as new currency or bar codes on packaged goods trigger speculation about how they may be signs of the beginning of the end. The most popular conspiracy scenarios vary somewhat over time. In the first few centuries CE Satan and the Antichrist were usually viewed as the same figure, then somehow they became separate characters in the drama. The Devil really didn't become a figure of major obsession till roughly the 8th and 9th Centuries, but then paranoia about him went through the roof till at least the end of the 1500s, and ebbed a bit after the Renaissance but never completely went away.

Jews got linked to the Satanic early on in the Christian era and were routinely accused of the most hideous crimes throughout the Middle Ages and beyond-Martin Luther saw Jews as linked to the Antichrist, but he also felt the same about Turks and Catholics, and a lot of other folks. As the great scholar of religion, Elaine Pagels, put it: "Satan has, after all, made a kind of profession out of being the `other'." The demonizing of Jews later flourished into a wide range of wildly extravagant forms on into the 20th Century when they were featured as protagonists in extraordinarily imaginative political and economic plots to grab global domination. Highlighting just how much mileage one dubious text can have, the notorious *The Protocols of the Learned Elders of Zion*, that malevolent forgery/hoax drawing from earlier works and rumors going back centuries, published by the Czarist secret police in various forms from 1905 to 1917, has had a very long and pernicious shelf life. This utterly ridiculous text was presented as a record of secret meetings of Jewish ruling elites planning to take over the world, but it found an extraordinary resonance with other anti-enlightenment, anti-Masonic, anti-intellectual, and anti-modern narratives on the paranoid right. It is still published to this day by a range of anti-Semitic conspiracy enthusiasts, even including a few old-school Russian nationalists, the spiritual heirs of the original forgers.

In the last few decades, however, the Jews, after so many centuries, have finally faded as the bad guys in most Western right wing conspiracy scenarios. In fact, in an exceedingly bizarre shift, hard line West Bank settlers and bellicose, uncompromising Israeli politicians have, in the last few years, been increasingly viewed as crucial allies by a whole movement of "Christian Zionists" such as the now infamous Reverend John Charles Hagee, whose support John McCain had sought in his presidential bid but had to renounce when Hagee's rabid diatribes about Muslims, gays, Catholics, and Hurricane Katrina victims surfaced on the Web. The founder of Cornerstone Church in San Antonio, Texas, with over 19,000 members, Hagee telecasts his ministry on 160 TV and 50 radio stations, available weekly in almost 100 million homes in the U.S. and some abroad as well. He helped found Christians United for Israel in 2006. This new and very dynamic and politically influential wing of evangelicals (if they weren't so numerous and motivated McCain would not have made overtures to Hagee to begin with) interprets the *Book of Revelation* in such a way that the unification of all of the "Holy Land" under Jewish rule is a necessary precondition for the End Times to begin, so they have become the Israeli right's most aggressive foreign supporters.

Of course once all hell breaks loose and the Final Judgment comes around, those Jews who fail to convert will be eternally damned. We all know politics makes strange bedfellows, but it is a bit mind-boggling nonetheless to see those sectors of the far right, who not too many decades earlier were rabidly anti-Semitic, anti-Catholic and overt segregationists, now forge alliances with armed West Bank Jewish settlers and right wing apocalyptic Marianist Catholics (in their mutual anti abortion struggle) and to borrow language from the Civil Rights Movement. The new alliance between right wing Protestants and extreme conservative Catholics, some in the lineage of the infamous Father Coughlin (whose immensely popular syndicated radio addresses in the 1930s were rabid, highly divisive, xenophobic fascist rants) is as striking and bizarre as that between Jews and Evangelical apocalypse enthusiasts. These Marianists are not a huge movement but they are a driving force in the most radical parts of the anti-abortion movement and they have a lot of support among less radical but sympathetic conservative Catholics. Their views on End Times and Satanic conspiracies are very close to their new Protestant Evangelical allies. A very tangible indication of this new de facto alliance is the fact that Protestant Evangelicals, who were once terrified at the prospect of a Catholic President when Kennedy was elected, are today great fans of Roberts and Alito, the two new conservative Catholic Supreme Court justices.

Jews have been far from the only targets of conspiracy paranoia over the centuries. Here in the U.S. witch hunts roiled New England in the 1600s, rumors of Masonic and Catholic conspiracies were a staple in the 1800s, anarchist and communist immigrant workers were pariahs in the 19th and early 20th centuries, and "reds" in the intelligentsia were hounded by Joe McCarthy and the blacklist in the late 1940s and 1950s. A frequent refrain in these paranoid movements in the U.S. has been that America is a Christian (and white and capitalist) nation that is now threatened by very powerful, covert anti-Christian cabals that have infiltrated the highest levels of power. In Europe 18th Century Freemasons and a Bavarian group in the same style, Adam Weishaupt's Illuminati Society, were perfect attractors for this sort of paranoid mythology: they were after all secret societies associated with the Enlightenment and the spread of secular ideas. It's not surprising the old theocratic and monarchist order sought to resist by slander since all else seemed to be failing, and a few books appeared in the late 1700s in Europe to begin this case against these new groups of cosmopolitan intellectuals. The first may have been one by an Englishman, John Robison, with an unwieldy but unambiguous title: *Proofs of a Conspiracy Against All the Religions and Governments of Europe, carried on in the secret meetings of Free Masons, Illuminati, and Reading Societies, collected from good authorities*. It's remarkable how many of these anti-Masonic, anti-modern ideas have survived to the present day in the U.S., if often in slightly tweaked forms, among sectors of Christians and others on the far right. The Evangelical media baron Pat Robertson is still obsessed with Freemasonry, for example.

A very different, far less political type of fascination with secret societies swept artistic avant-garde circles in Paris and London in the late 19th and early 20th centuries as colorful esotericists-figures such as Aleister Crowley and Dion Fortune and Madame Blavatsky-founded a slew of esoteric spiritual groups such as the Golden Dawn, Theosophy Society, and the Ordo Templi Orientis. Echoes of this fascination, though now tinged with playful irony, extend even to more recent avant-garde or countercultural figures such as Thomas Pynchon (in *The Crying of Lot 49*) and Robert Anton Wilson. Some of the late Victorian spiritual ebullience was ultimately quite influential, introducing many Westerners to Eastern spiritual ideas for example, and acting as one of the antecedents to current "new age" movements, some circles of which are quite prone to believing fanciful myths of all types, especially those involving extra-terrestrials. But the more potently paranoid conspiracies remained by and large the province of the right.

For those on the right, quite a few of the values unleashed by the Enlightenment and the French and American revolutions–universalism, deism, secular humanism, scientific curiosity, open-mindedness and toler-ance, and Kant's arguments for international cooperation (in *Perpetual Peace and Other Essays*)–are suspect, and at their core reek of treason. For the most extreme, only an apocalypse can cleanse the world of these scourges that inexorably lead to moral relativism and ultimate perdition, and return us to a predictable, static, simple moral universe. The paranoia about the secret societies of the Enlightenment later morphed as it combined with anti-socialist and anti-liberal reactionary movements to produce new hybrid con-spiracy themes that began blending in more secular elements or even some-times abandoned the religious angle as some groups of conservatives became more obsessed with Communism than with Satan.

There is a whole forgotten universe of then very influential conspirato-rial literature in the English-speaking world that set the template for much conspiracy writing into the present. A woman named Nesta Webster, who co-wrote a series of articles in the London Morning Post which brought the aforementioned *Protocols of the Elders of Zion* to the attention of the English audience for the first time, penned a series of "classics" in the 1920s, includ-ing: *World Revolution: The Plot Against Civilization* and *Secret Societies and Subversive Movements.* In the 1930s a Father Denis Fahey wrote the fiercely anti-Semitic *The Mystical Body of Christ in the Modern World* and one Gertrude Coogan wrote *Money Creators*, which claimed the Federal Reserve Bank was covertly set up by the Rothschilds and the Illuminati. As the right went after Roosevelt during the New Deal, one Elizabeth Dilling (perhaps an Ann Coulter of her day) wrote such works as *The Roosevelt Red Record and its Background*, which linked the President to commie Jews.

The Cold War saw the emergence of a very lively ecosystem of populist far right groups, some of which still exist in vestigial form (John Birch Society, Liberty Lobby, etc.). Some frequent targets of their conspiracy the-ories were, among others, the Rockefellers, the Council on Foreign Relations, the United Nations, later the Trilateral Commission and Bilderberger meetings on banking policy, whom they all saw as linked to secret Communist cabals that covertly ruled the world. William G. Carr's 1950s tracts *Pawns in the Game* and *Red Fog over America*, jumbled together old tropes–Illuminati/Jewish/Satanic banking conspiracies with new tech

angles-he accused them of using radio-transmissions as mind control devices
to achieve the dreaded "one world" government. Another period piece is a
rant by a former Communist turned white supremacist, Kenneth Goff's *One
World a Red World*, which posited Stalin as the Antichrist (to be fair he did
make an excellent candidate). Getting a bit more mainstream, Phyllis
Schlafly's early 1960s tome, *A Choice not an Echo*, a pro Goldwater campaign
screed, denounced the internationalists who secretly controlled both political parties. Another noteworthy work was Gary Allen's 1971 *None Dare Call
it Conspiracy*, which sold upwards of 5 million books.

One could go on and on. I'm only scratching the surface and citing a
few works out of hundreds because I'm not writing a comprehensive history, but to do justice to how widespread conspiracy thinking is in our contemporary culture, it's necessary to at least have a sense of its intellectual
roots. It's during the New Deal era but especially the Cold War period that
the idea that the government was evil and secretly controlled by covert cabals
took root and that catchphrases such as the "New World Order" begin to
appear. This view of government and Wall Street has long been mirrored
on the left by the sense that powerful capitalists control all the levers of
power, and often the same financial institutions attacked by the populist right
are targets of the left as well, though for very different reasons. By and large
though, while there have certainly been and continue to be plenty of leftists
with silly conspiracy theories, as we saw with the 9/11 variant, most leftists,
influenced by Marxism, tend historically to have sought to erect analyses
more anchored in the reality of power relationships and less extravagantly
fanciful and mythic than those of the extreme right.

It is notable how resilient some of the key themes of these right wing
conspiracy scenarios have been. In recent decades we've seen some shifts, as
Jews have often been replaced by Muslims as bogey men, and as various core
constituencies on the far right-apocalypse obsessed Evangelicals, new rural
"Christian Identity" extremists, strict moral conservatives, more secular radical libertarian free market absolutists, and new generations of white
supremacists or xenophobes-generate new variants of some of the old classic conspiracy templates, but that ultimate source, *The Book of Revelation*, may
very well be more popular than at any point since the Middle Ages. There
are occasional other groups besides American Evangelicals who get obsessed
with that text-Rastafarians for example (it's mentioned in several Bob
Marley songs and a slew of other reggae tunes), though the Rastas obvious-

ly have a radically different interpretation of who the heroes and villains are in the narrative. *Revelation* seems to be an ideal Rorschach blot onto which different aggrieved groups can all project a lot of repressed psychic material and utopian yearnings. Still it's U.S. Evangelicals who form the lion's share of those for whom that text holds such sway, and whose resulting worldviews are so consequential for American (and therefore global) politics.

It's important to bear in mind that Evangelicals are far from a monolithic group. They tend to be politically conservative, but one subset is fairly liberal on many issues. Let's not forget religious Christians were on the front lines of Abolitionism and the Civil Rights struggle in the U.S., and that Jimmy Carter, the most progressive president since the end of the Second World War, is a passionate Evangelical. Also, even among the most conservative, there are major theological divisions that have significant political ramifications. To oversimplify a pretty complex picture, one divide that separates Evangelicals is that between pre and post-millennialist factions (there are also much smaller groups of a-millennialists). The pre-millennialists believe that Christ will return to usher in the thousand-year period of utopian Christian rule, while the post-millennialists believe Christ will only return after that millennium of rule by Christians. This is an important point, because it tends to make the post-millennialists far more politically aggressive. Quite a few pre-millennialist folks figure Jesus' return is pre-ordained anyway so devoting oneself to living a moral life and ignoring politics as one awaits the period of tribulations can seem sufficient. The post-millennialist believers feel that to create the conditions propitious for the prophecies to unfold and Jesus to return they have a moral obligation to take over and establish that thousand-year rule of the good Christians.

For fifty years, starting from the end of the 1925 Scopes "Monkey" Trial (which most older people know about through the 1960 Stanley Kramer film with Spencer Tracy and Frederic March, *Inherit the Wind*, based on an earlier play) which the anti-evolutionists won but that humiliated them in the national and international media and caused them to withdraw from public battles, fundamentalist Christians were not an aggressive political force. Most of them were passive pre-millennialists and stayed out of active politics. That changed a bit with the rabid anti-Communism of the 50s and the increasing public role of figures such as Reverend Billy Graham and groups such as Moral Rearmament, but it wasn't till the 1976 Presidential election when Carter, himself an Evangelical, ran, that, ironically in retrospect, much larger numbers began to participate politically. The groundwork had already been laid by a revival of apocalyptic writing in the early 1970s. Hal Lindsey's enormously influential *The Late Great Planet Earth* had sold 10 million copies. A 1974 book during the "oil shock"- *Armageddon, Oil, and the Middle East Crisis* also sold quite well. The Republican Party worked hard with great success to incorporate this powerful emerging force into its ranks (after all a far more logical political alignment) as Carter hit hard times, and especially during the Reagan years. The Evangelicals turned out to be the key missing ingredient conservative activists had needed to cement the very effective coalition they were building that also included the big business center right, small business owners, Southern whites, rural voters, neo-conservative anti-Communist and "muscular" foreign policy advocates, and pissed-off white blue collar men.

Most fundamentalists today are still pre-millennialists but the post-millennialist movement made gains starting in the 1970s, and, more significantly, a new sort of far more politically militant Evangelical Protestantism-Reconstructionism- began to coalesce due to the work of a few key activists, especially R.J. Rushdoony, Greg Bahnsen, and Gary North, who saw the U.S. as a "Christian redeemer" nation at its core. These very influential thinkers, essentially hard-line Calvinist theocrats, managed to convince a wide range of key Protestant leaders that, whatever their views of the end times and Armageddon, they could all agree that Christians were called upon by God to exercise dominion over the nation's political life and social institutions-this ideology of "Dominionism" became (and remains) very popular across Evangelical America and even in some more mainline denominations and among some very conservative Catholics groups. An even more radical ideological tendency, the particularly militant wing of Pentecostalism known as "spiritual warfare" came to public attention in the recent Presidential campaign because the Republican Vice Presidential candidate, Sarah Palin, apparently shares its tenets, though she refused to discuss it with the press. This is a movement that bears watching in that it views its struggles against its political opponents as akin to fighting demons, something that could lead to big, big trouble down the line.

With the end of the Cold War, the current *bêtes noires* of right wing religious conspiracists have shifted and usually include: Islam, the "homosexual agenda," "pagan" environmentalists, feminists, globalists, immigrants, the European Union and UN, and so on. For Dominionist leaders such as Pat

Robertson, James Dobson, and Reverend Tim LaHaye (co-author of the insanely popular *Left Behind* series about the Rapture and the End Times-well over 60 million books sold) and their ilk, "the secular humanist conspiracy" is the new Communist menace, so the battle to reintroduce their brand of Christianity into school curricula and to challenge the teaching of Darwinian evolutionary theory, in their view one of the cornerstones of secular rationalism, are among their key objectives. The "culture wars" obsess them. A leading Evangelical conspiracist, David Noebel of Summit Ministries in Colorado, authored some books a few years back, and my favorite of his titles tells us a great deal about these folks' mindset: *Communism, Hypnotism and the Beatles.*

Right wing conspiracism also includes a wide range of other hybrid groups that have created their own idiosyncratic collages of apocalyptic material and their own styles. The "militia movement" which was so active in the 80s and 90s and reached its apotheosis in the Oklahoma City bombing, is less prominent now but far from entirely gone. At one time in the early 90s millions of people in rural America were at least tangentially involved or related to people in such militias. Earlier in the 80s, far smaller groups of extreme far right armed insurrectionists born of the farm and rust belt economic crises emerged-The Covenant, The Sword and the Arm of the Lord; Posse Comitatus, and others. Some of them robbed banks and committed murders. A lively ecosystem of far right groups, often armed, that includes out and out Nazi/Aryan Nation types, racist skinheads, Southern heirs of the Ku Klux Klan, extreme libertarian survivalists, the Christian "Identity" movement, the aforementioned "spiritual warriors" and a range of other related subcultures, continues to percolate under the mainstream's radar. The newest variant that is potentially most alarming is the anti-immigrant armed group, the most well known of which is the Minuteman Project, which hasn't been really violent to date, but which may be a template for much uglier groups to come as immigration is likely to remain an increasingly dangerous flashpoint in our politics for the foreseeable future.

This landscape of rural and exurban, mostly apocalyptic Christian gun enthusiasts with strange notions is a reservoir of potentially alarming movements. These folks went into a frenzy when then President Bush (senior) used the words "new world order" in a speech on foreign policy. This loaded term, so pregnant with meaning in these circles, became for many of them a sure sign that a traitorous, malevolent government was involved in a global conspiracy to take over their counties. Paranoia about sightings of mysterious black helicopters with UN troops (very structurally similar to the "Men in Black" paranoid rumors about aliens a few years before) swept the heartland. Secessionist movements advocating forms of local governance in which the county sheriff would become the highest authority and federal laws and taxation would be declared illegitimate became popular in a few places, and some even tried to set up their own "constitutionalist" courts. Federal officials such as park rangers were attacked and threatened, most aggressively in northern Nevada. And the tragic mishandling of the arrest of the far right figure Randy Weaver in Idaho and then the catastrophically clumsy, tragic (perhaps criminal) government siege and attack on David Koresh's Branch Davidian compound in Waco, Texas, radically exacerbated anti-government feelings in these milieus (including in Tim McVeigh-it was his rage about Waco that finally pushed him to act).

For the moment these groups of seething, armed, paranoid, conspiracy obsessed citizens are not in the news nearly as often in the 80s and 90s. The Oklahoma City bombing made many of them take stock and back down from their most extreme positions and their support fell off drastically. Then the nation's fears understandably focused almost exclusively on radical Islamic extremists after 9/11, but these other folks have not gone away. There is no way to estimate their numbers, as it's a constantly shifting land-scape. There may only be a few tens or perhaps a hundred thousand of the most militant and a few million sympathizers, but they are only the tip of the iceberg of a large swath of our population that is receptive to Evangelical apocalyptic narratives and that instinctively shares quite a few of these militants' beliefs. Under the right (or wrong) set of circumstances, especially an economic crisis that hit the white working class hard accompanied by other events that triggered their paranoia (say, a black President they thought was a secret Muslim…), this reservoir of confused, paranoid populist rage has the potential to erupt in very frightening ways, and it's mostly ignored by the media unless a violent incident occurs.

It is too easy, though, for urban sophisticates to mock these seemingly unhinged folks in the hinterlands. People's insecurities and rage tend to get canalized into the path of least resistance-the pre-existing cultural channels in their milieus. An inner city African American youth might get drawn to groups with Afrocentric esoteric belief systems (far more common in the black community than most non blacks realize), a down-on-his-luck small farmer in Kansas to the "Christian Identity" movement, and a young lefty radical to those who are convinced the Bush team orchestrated 9/11. The instability at the very core of our civilization makes us all, these days, prone to ideological instability.

The massive disruptions engendered by the forces of globalization and by mega-technologies generate a vast collision of centripetal and centrifugal dynamics: the centralizing and "flattening" forces of fluid global capital on the one hand, and the resistance of those who defend their specific cultural identities and regional autonomy on the other. This gives rise to a wide swath of political and cultural reactions. On one end of the spectrum one finds various forms of rejections of modernity. The most obvious are fundamentalist religious movements of all stripes, from the Amish to the Hasidim to hard-core Christian Evangelicals to Wahabbist Islamists to the recently in the news old-school Mormon polygamist sects of the U.S.' Southwest. Politically, this resistance is often expressed in ultra-nationalist, populist, nativist and "tribal," ethnically based autonomy movements often associated with the right, but it takes other forms on the left, in for example indigenous groups defending their lands and cultures, such institutions as the World Social Forum and the Via Campesina, and even "Slow Food." In fact, none of us are immune to feeling rendered insignificant and powerless by the impersonality, sterility, and crushing scale of contemporary economic and social systems, and our reactions to this alienation are also expressed in our personal behaviors, as seen in the increasing popularity of organic and locally grown foods in a subset of the consuming public, gardening and forms of "natural" medicine, and even some extreme outdoor sports–all efforts to reclaim some ancestral connection to the natural world and to carve out some tiny measure of individuality and autonomy vis à vis "the system."

At the other end of the spectrum we find the complete embrace of the modern, of a techno-utopian future, usually accompanied by enthusiasm for unfettered capitalism. Some proponents of genetic, robotic and cyber technologies, many of them prominent figures in their fields, tout a new world in which technological breakthroughs solve most of our problems, or at least launch us into a "post-human" era. Princeton biology professor Lee Silver, author of *Remaking Eden: How Genetic Engineering and Cloning Will Transform the American Family*, and more recently of *Challenging Nature: The Clash of Science and Spirituality at the New Frontiers of Life*, is an enthusiastic proponent of human cloning, genetic "enhancement," designer babies, and an era in which the altered "gen rich" will become a new, superior species to the unimproved "gen poor." He is perhaps the most outspoken, but his neo-eugenic views are surprisingly not as fringe as they should be in the world of genetic researchers. Others, such as robotics pioneer Marvin Minsky and Hans Moravec of the Robotics Institute at Carnegie Mellon, author of *Robot: Mere Machine to Transcendent Mind,* advocate trans-humanism, the desirability (and inevitability) of a new species of robots superior to humans. This transhumanist movement had for a while as its flagship the Extropy Institute (closed in 2006) and its publication, Extropy: The Journal of Transhumanist Thought, which popularized the idea that scientific and tech-nological progress (advances in computational power, life-extension, cryon-ics, nanotech, and other fields) would some day soon permit humans to have unlimited life spans. Affiliated or like-minded groups include: the World Transhumanist Association, the Singularity Institute for Artificial Intelligence, the Alcor Life Extension Foundation, the Foresight Institute, the Immortality Institute, Betterhumans, TransVision, and the Institute for Ethics and Emerging Technologies.

These Transhumanist-Extropian ideas sound, at best, overly exuberant, but many researchers in the exploding field of "anti-aging medicine," while less extravagant in their claims, basically share very similar outlooks and get a lot of positive media attention. Let's be realistic: these will most likely turn out to have been megalomaniacally simplistic fantasies that failed to account for all the unintended consequences that inevitably transpire when one attempts to alter incredibly complex, living systems, but they tend to get favorable mainstream media coverage with hardly any substantive critique of their claims. I wonder if these somewhat adolescent fantasies will peter out as America's hyper-dominance in the world abates, or if, conversely, they will balloon as a form of compensation.

One of the key concepts that excites these utopians the most is a term coined by mathematician and sci-fi writer Vernor Vinge, "the Singularity"-the arrival within the next few decades of a threshold moment when expo-nentially increasing technological progress finally leads to the creation of superhuman machines more intelligent than we are that can replicate and improve themselves without our help, which pushes history into the end of the purely human era into a new "post-human" future whose contours are impossible to predict. The most well known current enthusiastic exponent of this future is the inventor and bestselling writer Ray Kurzweil, author of

The Age of Intelligent Machines, *The Age of Spiritual Machines*, and *The Singularity Is Near* (currently being made into a movie). Kurzweil is without question a genius with countless important inventions to his credit, but his belief that we humans will soon transcend our biological condition and his quest to resurrect his late father's consciousness by using artificial intelligence do place him outside the mainstream, but not as far as one might suspect, given the likely naïveté of his vision. He is not treated as a fringe figure but is widely read and treated deferentially by the media.

The unfettered techno-utopian imagination, with its aversion to the very idea of limits, is a powerful strain in Western, and especially American culture. Potent archetypes-the pioneering profiteer, the technological entrepreneur, the visionary engineer-combine with grassroots subcultures of backyard inventors, pseudoscience enthusiasts, and sci-fi geeks with distant roots in Jules Verne and H.G. Wells, to produce a large (if mostly male) audience that is extremely receptive to visions of a technologically engendered paradise. There are, however, powerful countervailing forces to these rosy, cornucopian scenarios. The reality of limits-to the planet's climatic stability and ecosystems' resilience, to land's carrying capacity, to resources, to the U.S.'s omnipotence, to predictability when manipulating discrete pieces of highly complex systems, to financial speculation-are much harder to ignore today than they were in the past, so resistance to a sanitized technological future has, not surprisingly, also become a deeply resonant theme in our culture. And this battle between techno-utopianism's siren call and our deep desires to re-establish a balance with the natural world and to rediscover the joys and stability of small scale community life is not only being played out by opposing ideological tendencies but within our own minds-most of us hold an unexamined mix of aspects of both of these impulses within our own personal "belief portfolio."

It is true that these conflicts go back a long way. We can see the antecedents to our own wrestling with modernity's collateral damage in the earliest resistance to enclosures then to industrialization with the Luddites in England and the purported "saboteurs" in Lyons' sewing factories, William Blake's cursing of the "Satanic mills," and the dueling pulls of Romanticism and Positivism in the 19th Century, but the scope of our globalized economy and the crushing scale of our architecture, institutions and engineering feats, as well as the potent seduction of material abundance have beaten a lot of the resistance to modernity out of us or driven it into unconscious or less direct modes of expression. The ever increasing speed and scope of change have, though, without question radically exacerbated the contradictions, so that the reaction against unfettered "progress" which had been mostly dormant for two decades after World War II, has once again arisen, and the battle between the plunge into the postmodern and the yearning for a return to authentic roots and traditions has intensified.

This can be seen in a wide range of trends. We are building more and more gigantic, oddly shaped, "futuristic" skyscrapers, but also more planned, "new urbanism" communities that mimic old style village life. We are eating more and more strange synthetic supplements in pills and taking more and more mood altering prescription drugs but also paying top dollar for organic, heirloom foods from small farmers. Many of the young dance to robotic, electronic techno beats, but acoustic folk music is once again popular, and so on. Our conflicted reactions to modernity find their most pointed expression in science fiction. It must mean something that most of the most popular and consequential sci-fi films of the last 2 decades have involved battles between humans and a race of robots or androids they have created that then try to enslave or destroy or at least resist their makers-the *Terminator* and *Matrix* series, *Blade Runner*, *I Robot*, *A.I.*, and by far the most sophisticated and profound of the lot, the TV show *Battlestar Galactica* (the current one, not the abysmal original).

The potential menace of modernity's excesses is a very old theme in sci-fi. It takes a wide range of forms: in such artifacts as the films *THX 1138* and *Farenheit 451* and *2001* (with the eerie, demented, murderous computer, HAL); and in all the countless books and films and TV shows with familiar plots about genetic mutants and germ weapons run amok or about the abuse of information technology by totalitarian regimes. These cautionary tales about technology are in fact every bit as popular a theme as the marvels of technological progress in the history of sci-fi, with roots that go back to such early dystopian classics as *Brave New World* and *1984*, and further back to Mary Shelley. Some writers fall clearly in the techno-utopian camp (Verne, Wells, Asimov, Heinlein, Clarke), some in the cautionary camp (Huxley, Orwell, John Brunner, to some extent P. K. Dick and Norman Spinrad), but many are as ambivalent as the culture as a whole. The "cyberpunk" movement, for example, was as romantically infatuated with the possibilities of cool new tech as a James Bond film. Those novels are filled with exciting prosthetic weapons, jacks that connect human brains directly to the Web, new "smart" drugs, genetic enhancements-but are darkly pessimistic about the shape of future societies, portraying a world with rampant decay, poverty and corruption controlled by amoral *zaibatsus* and gangsters. Another typical example of the pull between the modern and the ancient is the hugely popular sci-fi novel *Dune*, which celebrates the moral fiber of an archaic Bedouin-like culture but also features really cool space travel technology.

The split in our attitudes vis à vis modernity are expressed very vividly in the "counterculture" that coalesced in the 1960s. That social phenomenon was (is) so exuberant and multi-faceted that it's hard to define precisely or to fully wrap one's brain around, but it's had a profound and lasting effect on our culture that doesn't get its due. The silly fashions, naïve utopianism and extraordinary excesses of the 60s and early 70s make that period the butt of jokes, but the forces unleashed in those years radically and lastingly shook up our politics, arts, attitudes, social mores, and technologies (the birth of the personal computer is awash in LSD, as was Nobel Prize winner Kary Mullis, credited with developing the polymerase chain reaction technique; even Francis Crick was an acid enthusiast, though most likely long after his co-discovery of DNA). It may not be widely acknowledged, but to this day, in many of the most influential cultural milieus (the arts, music, literature, theater) and in Silicon Valley and larger cyber circles, either a majority or a sizeable minority of the noteworthy figures have dabbled in or seriously explored the use of psychedelics, yet another example of a behavior almost never mentioned in other than a pejorative or comic context and legally proscribed, but that actually covertly continues to play a significant role in the nation's cultural, and to a lesser extent, scientific, production. The counterculture has mutated and evolved, but it is far from dead. Its impacts and the reactions against it have been deeply consequential and continue to define our political landscape and many of our most contentious socio-political struggles. A variety of the movements and approaches that reached critical mass in the wake of the counterculture have become permanent features of our social geography.

And one aspect of this vast phenomenon that's rarely discussed is its split personality vis à vis technology and progress. On the one hand, there was a powerful longing in the 60s for a return to a simpler life, to re-connecting with nature and its cycles and to escape from the soulless sterility of suburbs and urban canyons, something beautifully expressed in the "Moloch" section of Allen Ginsberg's *Howl*. This initially took the form of easy-to-ridicule "back to the land" communes, very few of which endured, but it birthed the immense natural-organic-heirloom-heritage-slow food movement, the widespread acceptance of alternative-holistic-complementary medical approaches, a rekindled interest in indigenous worldviews and nature-based religions and philosophies, and much of modern environmental awareness.

On the other hand, a sort of techno-utopian psychedelic futurism with strong Gnostic strains that dreamt of space colonies and worshipped sci-fi and liked electronic music was also a very strong flavor in the counterculture, and the aforementioned "extropians" and the most exuberant early hackers, as popularized in artifacts such as Mondo 2000 or even the early Wired, were (are) very much heirs of this tradition. This dichotomy took and continues to take all sorts of forms. While folk and countless world "root" musical forms were being rediscovered, new multi track recording studios permitted futuristic aural collages à la *Sergeant Pepper* or *Satanic Majesties'*. Today a Williamsburg hipster might enjoy both Bluegrass and a weird Theremin orchestra, a West African griot and a German "industrial noise" band. The LSD apostle Timothy Leary advised us to drop out of the rat race in the 1960s, but wound up aspiring to download his consciousness into software and/or to be cryogenically frozen as he approached death. The influential countercultural thinker, Terence McKenna, was, before his untimely death in 2000, a proponent of an "archaic revival" (of shamanic wisdom), but he also described visions of both a techno-utopian future in which cyber technology was so sophisticated it would be invisible and we could live as pre-lapsarian naked apes with tiny super computers implanted in our neural circuitry, or, alternately, an Armageddon-like eco-collapse end to the human trajectory with a transformation into some sort of Gnostic pure consciousness, a vision with some similarities to Arthur Clarke's *Childhood's End*. Terence, brilliant as he was, was far from consistent in his prognostications, but his seemingly contradictory archaic, utopian, and apocalyptic visions merely reflected (in admittedly wildly expressive and brilliantly creative ways) the confoundingly conflicting impulses regarding modernity we all wrestle with.

The split even finds expression in the types of psychedelics various countercultural factions prefer. Many of the techno-utopians embrace synthetics, such as LSD and the new generations of designer drugs in the phenethylamine family (2C-B, 2CT-2, 2C-T-7, 2C-E, etc.) created by the genius chemist Sasha Shulgin, and they hunt for any new substance that might enhance their cognitive powers ("smart" drugs). The neo-shamanic circles (currently more culturally influential and dynamic) make pilgrimages to Amazonian shamans or syncretic Brazilian churches or even Gabon and only use plant-based "entheogens" with long histories of indigenous human use, such as ayahuasca, peyote, San Pedro cactus, iboga, and psilocybin mushrooms. Both of these tendencies are utopian, but one embraces technology and impatiently looks forward to transcending the messy and perishable world of flesh to enter a new age in which pure consciousness can live eternally encased in flawless machine bodies, the other harks back to an Earth-honoring ethos and seeks to establish a sustainable society rooted in ecological wisdom informed by indigenous worldviews. In fact, most countercultural hipster types combine elements of both these seemingly diametrically opposed ideologies in their worldviews, as Terence McKenna so strikingly did. Buckminster Fuller is another fascinating figure in that he was (and is) widely admired by intellectuals in both these camps, for his optimistic cornucopian techno-utopianism by the "futurists" and for his profound love of nature and his emulation of nature's designs in his own work by the more Earth-honoring.

A fascinating mythic meme that has gained widespread underground popularity in countercultural milieus and beyond is one that José Arguelles, the creator of the "Harmonic Convergence" in 1987, and later Terence McKenna, helped boost: a fixation with the ancient Mayan calendar as a predictor of extraordinary historical events that are about to unfold and transform our civilization (or destroy it). These prognostications usually focus on the year 2012, a purported end-point of the Mayan calendar, as a watershed moment, at which point a shift to a new era will begin. Of course, as I discussed earlier, end-of-the-world (or of the world as we know it) predictions are nothing new, but not all these millenarian movements are classically Christian. Interest in apocalyptic predictions took some new forms in the 20th Century-fascination with the oracular trance readings of psychics, especially Edgar Cayce, and in the interpretation of various Native American (Hopi, Iroquois), and other (Nostradamus) prophecies. Millenarian impulses seem to be a strong and permanent feature of the human imagination, and this contemporary hipster-countercultural version, while far less vast or politically consequential than the Christian Right's embrace of Armageddon, is interesting because it is widespread in milieus that include highly influential figures in the worlds of art and culture and in progressive and environmental activism. Among those edgy artistic hipsters for whom the now widely known Burning Man festival in the Nevada desert is the high point of their annual calendar, for example, the 2012 obsession is almost the "official" religion.

This year 2012 fixation has cross-pollinated with the aforementioned Singularity concept to become a very heady mythos. It's no surprise it has developed a substantial following (even in mutated forms on the Christian right). It combines a (not unreasonable given climate change, plummeting biodiversity, unstable geopolitics and nuclear arsenals) fear of catastrophe, wisdom from a sexy/exotic ancient Mesoamerican culture, esoteric mathematics and paleo-astronomy, and extremely appealing techno-utopian fantasies. Like most millenarian packages, it has both dire catastrophe as a cleansing punishment for our sins and failings, and some sort of subsequent utopia, either actually embodied on Earth, or in pure spirit form if the world of matter is truly doomed. The specific predictions tend to be a bit vague. The various exponents tend to hedge their bets, something I suspect they'll do more and more as the date approaches (unless, of course, they're right, and won't I feel like an idiot as I'm vaporized…or enlightened…). My own bet is that if nothing too Earth-shattering happens, many will feel disillusioned like the Millerites in 1844 when the Second Coming failed to arrive as advertised, and they will then gravitate to new belief constellations. Others will point to some major political event or technological development (they happen all the time) or other and claim that it indicates that the dawn of the new era has in fact arrived. Some Harmonic Convergence boosters claimed the fall of the Berlin Wall was linked to their mass meditation efforts in 1987.

I have to admit that the apocalyptic mindset is one I am not unfamiliar with. I too have great qualms about the sustainability of our civilization, and a variety of catastrophes wouldn't surprise me. It's just that I am less willing to believe their exact dates are predictable, or that they will invariably be global and simultaneous. Minor and regional cataclysms occur all the time, and we are each destined to endure our own personal, terminal cataclysm-death. I live two miles or so from where the Twin Towers stood, but, besides very toxic air for a few days after 9/11, my life was largely unaffected, at least in the immediate, by that event While there is a disaster in one place, another, even nearby, may be tranquil or prospering. Global Armageddon is certainly not impossible at some point (nukes? asteroid impact? eventually of course the heat death of the Sun), and a radically hotter and impoverished biosphere with a large amount of resulting starvation and unrest and warfare seems like a certainty at this point, but one doesn't need a Mayan calendar to figure that out. I also can't dispute that some branches of science, especially genetics and computing, are indeed taking us into unknown territory. What I resist is the pat mindset that enthusiastically and uncritically embraces a worldview that encompasses and explains everything, that ties it all up into a neat little prophecy and provides the believer with an illusion of a form of control.

The most influential current exponent of a version of this 2012 "hypothesis" is author Daniel Pinchbeck, whose second book *2012: The Return of Quetzalcoatl*, postulates that we are experiencing a rapidly accelerating global transformation of consciousness (a wildly popular "new age" theme), and that this will result in new understandings of space-time and other mind-boggling paradigm shifts coming to a head in that fateful year. The book is a kitchen sink of esoteric speculations on topics as varied as ESP, crop circles, the author's own prophetic encounters with the spirit of Quetzalcoatl in the Amazon while on ayahuasca, and so on. He is a fairly good writer so he tells a good tale, but it's extraordinary how seriously his work is being taken by far more people than one would expect, among many young, grass-roots environmental activists for example. Granted, Pinchbeck's *2012* is not nearly as popular as the much sillier *Da Vinci Code*, or as the work of that fascinating trickster Carlos Castaneda was back in the 60s, but it, and Arguelles and McKenna's writings on this 2012 myth, while they have compelling aspects, are so far from cohesive intellectual structures and require such giant leaps of faith to take at face value that one has to see in this whole phenomenon another symptom of a society that is extremely confused and grasping at a wide range of mythic straws.

The Y2K phenomenon back in 2000 was a good indication of how easily very different segments of the population, from millenarian Christians to secular grassroots environmentalists to cyber geeks, can whip themselves into extraordinary levels of silly hysteria on the flimsiest of grounds. Y2K was a perfect foil for many Americans' paranoia because so many of those omnipresent sci-fi and millenarian themes I discussed earlier figured in the plot: here was a technologically induced catastrophe caused by human hubris and lack of foresight (an early version of the coming human-robot wars). For the cyber savvy it was a way to highlight their new social centrality, our dependence on them for our very survival and wellbeing; for the neo-

Luddites, it presented a great "we told you so" opportunity; for survivalists the chance to have their moment in the Sun as journalists visited their bunkers and reported on their preparations; and for Evangelical apocalypticists another hopeful sign of the End Times. For older Europeans who had survived the Blitz or the Blitzkrieg or carpet bombings or the Holocaust or the battle of Stalingrad or the fire bombing of Dresden, or for Cambodians who had survived first the American bombings then the Khmer Rouge, or Tutsis who survived the Rwandan genocide, to name only a few groups of survivors of real catastrophes, the thought that a few electronic devices going on the blink for a while might represent an existential crisis for an entire society must have seemed truly bizarre.

One of the strangest subcultures in recent years has been that of those who say they have been abducted and studied by aliens, and those who share the belief that this is happening on a wide scale. This is yet another movement that is not quite as dynamic as it was during its peak in the 80s and 90s (such a bizarre period, in retrospect) but that is far from extinct. It was not at its height nor is it now a tiny movement. It's very hard to know exactly how widespread a belief system it is, but syndicated radio programs that catered to this audience, especially Art Bell's (until his recent retirement), which was on over 500 stations nationwide, were immensely popular. Whitley Streiber's 1987 book, *Communion*, which launched this theme into the popular culture, sold several million copies, and some of the biggest conferences centering on abductees drew thousands of people. A 1991 Roper Poll, commissioned by some researchers into abductions, including Bud Hopkins, to estimate how many Americans might have been abductees quizzed some 6,000 people, and found 119 who so purported. This led Hopkins and company to estimate that 3.7 million Americans might have been abducted by extraterrestrials. Hopkins was not a neutral analyst: he was basically a believer in the tangible reality of the phenomenon, and the poll's methodology was severely criticized by skeptics, but even if it were way off and only half or even a third that many really believed they had had such an experience, that's still astonishing.

According to another more recent Roper poll done for cable TV's Sci-Fi Network, a majority of Americans believe UFOs are real and not just an illusory phenomenon and that the government is hiding information about this; 48% think that aliens have visited earth at some point; 21% believe some humans have been abducted by aliens. These numbers are higher than the

Harris poll I mentioned earlier, so it's hard to know the exact figures, but, either way, there is a fair amount of support for the abductee narratives. These are usually described as traumatic and often involving forced medical exams, especially of reproductive organs, but there is also a minority that reports transcendentally uplifting encounters with wise beings here to warn humanity about its nuclear weapons (as in the 1951 film *The Day the Earth Stood Still*) or about our pending eco catastrophe. There have been reports of alien abductions around the world, but the English-speaking world accounts for the overwhelming majority, and most of those are in the U.S. The phenomenon has not surprisingly led to the birth of an entire subculture of conferences, support groups, websites, radio shows, and publications. Many of the participants share a very specific, detailed picture of the different alien races that have, in their accounts, been active here on earth, some benign, some evil, some in between, from the benevolent "Nordics" to the famous, mysterious, emotionless "Greys" to the nasty Reptilians.

UFO fascination has been a permanent feature of our cultural landscape since the late 1940s when modern sightings of saucer-shaped objects began with pilot Kenneth Arnold's 1947 sighting, and Jung made the first serious efforts to grapple with the mythic elements involved in these sightings and beliefs. Some anthropologists, historians, and folklorists point out, however, that there is a very old and long history of reports of human encounters with alien beings. Jim Schnabel, a science writer and author (in 1984) of *Dark White: Aliens, Abductions and the UFO Obsession*, noted that abduction narratives share many common traits with reports about witchcraft and demonic possession from the Middle Ages and Renaissance. Carl Sagan, John Mack, and Jacques Vallee have also written about the kinship between contemporary alien encounter reports and those about interactions with fairies, demons, incubi, succubi, and other supernatural beings that were so common all around the world in earlier centuries, and are still a feature of contemporary shamanic experiences.

Even the archetypal modern extraterrestrial alien encounter stories go back quite a ways. There were quite a few sightings of "mystery airships" in the late 1800s. A Colonel H. G. Shaw's account in the Stockton Daily Mail in 1897 described three tall humanoids, who, upon emanating from such a ship, tried to kidnap him and his friend but from whom they were able to escape. And there were occasional weird accounts of alien encounters here and there around the world from the 1920s into the 1950s, but the first well-known alien abduction report was that of Barney and Betty Hill, which occurred in 1961 and eventually garnered widespread national coverage. Reports of abductions picked up a bit in the 70s, but were relatively rare until the early 80s when it really started to become a mass phenomenon and grew dramatically into the 1990s. Interestingly, this is roughly the same period during which the mass pedophilia and Satanism panics I described in Chapter 3 started to take off-the dark shadows of Reagan's "morning in America" perhaps. I am not the first to have noticed the juxtaposition of these two phenomena. The aforementioned Jim Schnabel, and Gwen Dean, a therapist who studied the matter, saw quite a few parallels between the paranoia about ritualized Satanic sexual abuse that swept the nation in that period and the abduction narratives. Dean tracked forty-four similar features, including the invasive sexual elements, the types of altered states described, the frequency of mysterious periods of "missing time" that couldn't be accounted for, the use of hypnosis to "retrieve" memories, and so on.

All this had already been preceded by disturbing reports of mysterious cattle mutilations going back to the 1970s, especially in the U.S.' Southwest, that some locals began attributing to aliens, and these then became associated with visits by the now famous, equally mysterious "men in black." These beliefs sound totally risible to a rational sophisticate, but when one probes them, things are not quite so pat. This is often the case with research into at least the most interesting odd or paranormal phenomena. An honest, open-minded analyst with no axe to grind often finds that irrefutably conclusive proof to support the claims always remains out of reach, but that outright dismissal is also usually not possible because too many bizarre loose ends and tantalizing bits of evidence just can't be readily explained. Most people I know who have tried to study these matters wind up feeling as though they have fallen into a black hole where all certainty has vanished and where one's paranoia and angst become dangerously inflated. I had friends who were serious local investigative journalists who covered the cattle mutilation stories in New Mexico and Colorado in the late 1970s and did a lot of field-work. They were skeptics at first but came away convinced something truly bizarre and very hard to explain was taking place. I also have personally known several people who were utterly convinced they had been abducted by aliens and had crystal clear memories of the experiences. I have also had some experience with people suffering from delusional psychiatric episodes, and there was no similarity whatsoever between the two groups. The purported abductees were lucid and perfectly functional, often socially success-ful individuals. And they had nothing to gain–they had not sought any pub-licity nor had they discussed it widely. The psychiatrists who have treated abductees, even those who are totally skeptical about aliens, tend to report the same thing: the overwhelming majority of these people feel somewhat traumatized by their perceived experiences, but they do not manifest any symptoms of classic delusional pathologies, and they seem to be a broad cross section of ordinary folks.

Of course the rationalist skeptics, such as Carl Sagan, feel the only pos-sible explanation to how widespread these stories have been and continue to be has to lie in some predisposition in the human brain's circuitry and chem-istry that can be activated under some circumstances in a subset of the pop-ulation. One of the more sophisticated of these neurological explanations was offered by Dr. Michael Persinger who says these experiences as well as most mystical states can be tied to specific electromagnetic patterns in the brain and can, in fact, be induced by stimulating those specific parts of the brain also linked to epilepsy. He argues that the experience of having a sense of the presence of another being in one's room as one is half asleep, for example, is quite common, as are the weird experiences some get in the hypnogogic, near-sleep state, including "night terrors" and sleep paralysis, and that cultural factors cause people to give the most vivid of these experiences different narratives and interpretations. Other hypotheses advanced by skep-tics range from hoaxes to unconscious absorption of science fiction plots (abduction plots were already common in sci-fi magazine short stories in the 1930s), to hallucinations induced by temporary schizophrenic attacks, to dis-torted repressed memories of childhood sexual abuse. The most serious of these theories may have some merit, but the phenomenon is a bit too broad, bizarre, messy, and multi-faceted to be so tidily explained, as there are just too many well-documented cases that defy each type of explanation, and I am certainly not going to try to settle these debates. There is no doubt that it is very hard for a reasonable person who does not have a memory of encountering extraterrestrials to believe in the literal existence of aliens here among us without incontrovertible proof. Because it is such a serious claim, the burden of proof falls on those who believe it's true, and such proof has never been marshaled in an irrefutable way. It's always rumors and accusa-tions of cover-ups and plots to hide the truth by omnipotent people in gov-ernment. One has to wonder why, for example, if such advanced races of

174 DELUSIONS OF NORMALITY

beings could so easily travel the extraordinary distances to get here and have been watching us so long, they didn't just subjugate us, since, as Jared Diamond points out in *Guns, Germs and Steel*, that is what more advanced technological societies have always done to less well equipped ones. To counter this and other questions, extraordinary theories about these aliens are proffered-they are described as everything from "trans-dimensional" beings who can phase in and out of our dimension to angels to time travelers, and on and on.

Also, while defenders of believers in abductions have pointed to the core consistency of the plotlines in many reports as an indication of their likely veracity, there is no doubt that such reports are far rarer in non-English speaking regions and far more numerous in the U.S. than anywhere else, and that the content of the stories tends to vary by location. There are far more reports of scary abductions in the U.S, while descriptions of benevolent interactions are more common abroad, and the types of aliens described are quite different outside of the U.S. than they are here. All this seems to argue for the presence of an important cultural filter on the experience, whatever it may be. But all that said it is still a deeply puzzling phenomenon. Serious investigators come away with many unanswered and seemingly unanswerable questions, and many of them give up for the sake of their sanity. The murkiness and mysteriousness of the field led some of the most open-minded but sophisticated researchers into the phenomenon, such as John Mack and Jacques Vallée, to come away with the sense that perhaps the abduction and UFO questions highlight to what extent our categories of "real" and "imaginary" may be lacking, and force us to admit we know much less than we think about the nature of reality.

I personally find it far more disconcerting if it's true that millions of people have vivid memories of a traumatic or powerfully benefic emotional experience that they are absolutely convinced was tangible and real, but that did not in fact take place in the three dimensional world of matter, than if there were actual physical aliens in tin cans who had used technology to get here. The latter would pose a major military problem, no doubt, and perhaps spell the end of our species, but it wouldn't undermine our fundamental sense of reality. The former scenario, in my view at least, throws into question the very notion of any reliability of human memory and experience, and any firm sense of a shared reality. In any case I'm not trying to prove or disprove anything. A great deal has been written about all this, and I'm not trying to contribute to UFO-logy. I'm mostly interested in determining how many people share far-from-mainstream beliefs and in looking for clues to try to decipher a bit of our culture's very confusing zeitgeist. The alien abduction phenomenon, whatever one thinks of it, is about as far from mainstream acceptability as one can imagine, so the fact that so many people believe such abductions have occurred (again, 21% if that poll is to be believed) and that so many otherwise seemingly reasonable people with nothing much to gain from confabulation claim to have been abducted and do show at least some signs of psychological trauma, is in and of itself quite remarkable.

I could go on and dig up countless, unusual subcultures with far-from-mainstream ideas, from the very numerous aficionados of a range of "new age" ideas to serious esotericists of all stripes to nudists to breatharians to Goths, and I could cheat and throw in all the individuals with this or that obsessive, erroneous fixation at the center of their worldview and all those with real psychiatric delusions, but I'm not trying to be exhaustive (I'm already exhausted). What I think I have managed to demonstrate in this chapter is that the conventional view of our belief landscape: that we are mostly reasonable people-a hefty majority in the sane center with a few whacky movements, groups, and individuals at the peripheries of our culture-is a fiction. If one adds up: those who believe in the literal truth of religious texts even when they contradict demonstrable physical realities; those who subscribe to the various Christian End Time and Armageddon scenarios or the countercultural ancient prophecy variants à la 2012; those on the right and left who see omnipotent conspiracies behind nearly all major socio-political events; those who are convinced by sci-fi derived, inflated techno-utopian predictions of our future; those who believe that there are aliens among us and that the government is covering it up; and a bunch of the other very offbeat belief systems floating around; and add in the fellow travelers of these tendencies who may be less fanatical but take one or another of these ideas at least somewhat seriously, and I'd bet you have, even accounting for some overlaps in these groups, a solid majority of the population.

The illusion of a sane center persists because none of the unconventional ideologies I described have achieved majority status, so, when taken one at a time, a majority can always be mustered to dismiss any one of them as preposterous, and the defenders of harmony and social order can breathe a sigh of relief each time, but they shouldn't, because that majority will always include a whole lot of people with other very strange minority views of their own. Furthermore, those with the most unconventional views are often far more culturally and politically dynamic than their more conventional fellow citizens. What passes for a sane, reasonable center may just be the least vital, most inert and staid part of the population, and that's always a fairly large group, but whether it can be counted upon to make sure the "center holds" in strange times (or for much of anything else) is an open question.

I clearly have my biases, but my goal here has not been to advocate anything or debunk anything or to bemoan irrationality or, conversely, an excessive reliance on rationality. My avowed purpose was to try to get us to see ourselves as we really are, and my diagnosis is that, by mainstream media standards, most of us are, ideologically speaking, zany (at best), or dangerous lunatics, and that the "mainstream" is in fact, the biggest mirage of all: almost no one really lives there full time.

But I have to admit that this surrealistic belief landscape I have described worries me deeply, and I really do understand and have sympathy for the urge to paper over the ugly truth and to pretend most of our fellow citizens are reasonable people. Maybe the media and the guardians of "official," received ideas are right to act as though unusual ideas were just the province of small groups of eccentrics. Perhaps this is a useful delusion that actually helps keep some sort of minimally sane, functional commons operating in such a massive, complex, increasingly wobbly and decaying pluralistic society. Perhaps the truth would be too frightening and disorienting and ultimately just too disruptive.

In the same way Saddam Hussein wanted the Iranians to think he still had "weapons of mass destruction" when he no longer did, perhaps we need to keep all the barbarians at bay by making them continue to believe there is a sane, rooted, centered majority. If they began to realize there were hardly any doctors and nurses left in the asylum, who knows what would happen? Even those of us who share far-from-mainstream ideas want to be protected from those who have different weird ideas than ours. This is one of the key arguments for maintaining a strict separation between religion and the state, between private pursuits and the public sphere. Secular, reasonable, logic-based public institutions may be the only glue that can hold this madhouse from even more rapid fragmentation. So, I feel some pangs of guilt in trying to expose the exuberant (and at times dangerous) lunacies of so many

Americans, but I also feel that at least some of us can benefit by having a more realistic sense of the actual contours of the disturbing mental landscape that surrounds us. I can accept that a delusion may be useful, but I'm also hopelessly addicted to lucidity.

Notes:

-The Eurovision Song Contest, held since 1956, is a televised annual pop music competition held among the countries of the European Broadcasting Union (mostly but not all in Europe). Viewers vote for the winner but can't vote for their own country's representative. It's one of the most-watched non-sporting events in the world (hundreds of millions of people watch it live every year). The acts can be incredibly cheesy or truly bizarre. Recent surreal winners have included an Israeli transvestite and an extravagantly costumed Finnish heavy metal band, and some nations with contested or divided linguistic allegiances, such as Belgium and Switzerland, have on occasion had entries sung in made-up languages.

-Karl Friedrich May (1842-1912), one of the best selling German writers of all time, is mostly known for books set in the American Old West with romantic Indian heroes even though May only came to the U.S. once and never made it west of Buffalo, NY. His work inspired a keen interest in Native American lore in a sizeable subculture in the German-speaking world. The East German film industry produced a series of films based on his novels in the 1960s.

-Brazil's remarkable, dynamic proliferation of offbeat spiritual groups and phenomena include the many variants of African-based religions such as Candomblé and Umbanda; various forms of spiritualism; 19th Century European esoteric imports, especially Kardecism; the new syncretic churches that use the psychoactive "hoasca" tea as a sacrament (Santo Daimé, Uniao do Vegetal and La Barca); many psychic healers with large followings such as "Doctor Fritz" and John of God; many UFO cults; and innumerable hybrids of these and other influences.

- Padma Sambhava is the mythic foundational figure said to have brought Tantric Buddhism to Tibet in the 8th century and to have "subdued the demons" there in the process.

-The U.S. Religious Landscape Survey, 2008 Pew Forum on Religion and Public Life, June 2008

-Maulana Karenga (born Ronald Everett), an author and political activist who later became Chairman of the black studies department at Cal. State, Long Beach (1989-2002), is best known as the founder of Kwanzaa in 1966. But in 1965 he had founded Us, a black nationalist group, and in 1969 Us and the Black Panthers disagreed over who should head the new Afro-American Studies Center at UCLA and two members of the Black Panthers were shot dead in a gun battle. Karenga subsequently served a few years in prison in the 1970s for a different incident but then resumed his academic career.

-The Mountain Meadows Massacre was a mass slaughter of a wagon train of civilians in the Utah Territory by the local Mormon militia in September 1857 during a period of tension ("The Utah War") between the U.S. Army and the Mormons. Everyone over the age of eight was killed in an attempt to cover up the perpetrators of the massacre.

on the distrust of atheists in the population:
- "Atheists identified as America's most distrusted minority, according to new U of M study"-University of Minnesota, 2006, at: www.ur.umn.edu/

-I am using the term "Dionysian" as many others have: to describe the wilder, more unrestrained sides of cultural expression. The Dionysia were orgiastic rites held in ancient Greece in honor of the fertility god Dionysus.

- Thomas Hobbes (1588-1679) was an English philosopher and political theorist, most famous for his 1651 work *Leviathan*. Hobbes was a pessimist about human nature and felt that strong governments and laws were the only barriers to our barbarism and selfishness.

-Edmund Burke (1729-1797) was an Anglo-Irish politician and political philosopher widely considered to be one of the defining ancestors of modern conservatism.

-Jean Jacques Rousseau (1712-1778) was a highly influential Enlightenment age philosopher (and composer and novelist and the inventor of modern autobiography) most well known for his analysis of the tension between society and human nature. In counterpoint to Hobbes, Rousseau believed that man was fundamentally good in the natural state but was corrupted by society.

- *The Religion of Technology* by David Noble (Alfred A. Knopf, 1997)

- Roger Bacon was a 13th Century Franciscan friar whom some cite as one of the earliest advocates of the modern scientific method in the West.

-Auguste Comte (1798-1857), the creator of the philosophy of "Positivism" and one of the fathers of sociology, was a French scientific thinker known for his advocacy of science and rationality as the only sound bases for all knowledge and decision-making.

-Nikola Tesla (1856-1943), one of the most consequential scientists and inventors of the modern era for his many revolutionary contributions in electricity and magnetism (especially alternating current electric power) and radio, was at one time the most famous inventor in the U.S., but his sometimes very extravagant experiments and claims eventually caused him to be widely regarded by many as the very archetype of the mad scientist. His more edgy, mysterious, offbeat research projects still elicit great interest among certain subcultures.

on Newton and the occult:
-A deeply researched PBS Documentary on Newton's work on alchemy and his other esoteric interests, Newton's Dark Secrets, aired in June 2008.
-*Isaac Newton: The Last Sorcerer* by Michael White (Da Capo Press, 1999)
-The Chymistry of Isaac Newton Project supported by the U.S. National Science Foundation (at: webapp1.dlib.indiana.edu/newton/index.jsp)

books bemoaning irrationality in the modern public:
-*The Assault on Reason* by Al Gore (Penguin Press, 2007)
-*The Age of American Unreason* by Susan Jacoby (Pantheon, 2008)
-*Counterknowledge: How We Surrendered to Conspiracy Theories, Quack Medicine, Bogus Science and Fake History* by Damian Thompson (Atlantic Books, 2008)
-*God Is Not Great: How Religion Poisons Everything* by Christopher Hitchens (Twelve Books, Hachette Book Group, 2007)

neuroscience-based analyses of our propensity for irrationality:
-*Predictably Irrational* by Dan Ariely (Harper Collins, 2008)
-*Welcome to Your Brain* by Sam Wang and Sandra Aamodt (Bloomsbury USA, 2008)
-*Sway: The Irresistible Pull of Irrational Behavior* by Ori and Rom Brafman (Doubleday, 2008)

on the CIA's manipulation of the arts and literature in the 1950s and 60s:
-*The Cultural Cold War: The CIA and the World of Arts and Letters* by Frances Stonor Saunders (The New Press, 1999)
-*The Mighty Wurlitzer: How the CIA Played America* by Hugh Wilford (Harvard University Press, 2007)

- Thomas Merton (1915-1968), a Trappist monk, social justice activist, and highly influential progressive Catholic intellectual, was a keen student of comparative religion and the author of many widely read books (over 60!) on spirituality. He was a great leader of inter-religious understanding, and had many dialogues with figures such as the Dalai Lama, Thich Nhat Hanh and D. T. Suzuki.

-Pierre Teilhard de Chardin (1881-1955) was a French philosopher, Jesuit priest, paleontologist and geologist. His theories about the cosmos' evolution toward greater complexity and about consciousness have deeply influenced many modern thinkers. Much of his work was viewed as doctrinally suspect and was denied publication during his lifetime by Vatican officials.

some polls on the numbers of non-believers in the population and among scientists:

-The 2005 AP/Ipsos Poll: "Religious Fervor In U.S. Surpasses Faith In Many Other Highly Industrial Countries" (at: www.ipsos-na.com/news/pressrelease.cfm?id=2694)
- "Leading scientists still reject God" by Edward Larson and Larry Witham in Nature, Vol. 394, No. 6691, 1998 (Macmillan Publishers Ltd.)
-2004 Pew Research poll on religion at: pewresearch.org and http//people-press.org/report/?pageid=757
-The 1914 Leuba study of the religious beliefs of scientists: Leuba, J. H. *The Belief in God and Immortality: A Psychological, Anthropological and Statistical Study* (Sherman, French & Co., 1916)

-November 2007 Harris Online survey on religion:
 Harris Poll #119, November 29, 2007: "The Religious and Other Beliefs of Americans: More People Believe in the Devil, Hell, and Angels Than Believe in Darwin's Theory of Evolution" (online at: www.harrisinteractive.com/harris_poll/index.asp?PID=838)

notable recent "terrorists," besides the Islamic militants we are so obsessed with nowadays, that I mention:
-Jim Jones, founder of the Peoples Temple cult, infamous for the mass forced suicide/murder in Guyana of 900 group members in 1978, among the largest mass "suicides" in history and the greatest loss of U.S. civilians in a human-caused disaster until 9/11/01
-Tim McVeigh, the far-right militant who was convicted and executed for bombing the Alfred P. Murrah Building in Oklahoma City on April 19th, 2005, killing 168 people, the deadliest act of terrorism in the U.S. before 9/11/01
-The Order of the Solar Temple, a bizarre secret society founded by Joseph Di Mambro and Luc Jouret in 1984 in Geneva, Switzerland that combined mythology about the medieval Knights Templar and new-age esoteric beliefs, and wound up imploding in a series of gruesome, ritualistic mass suicides and murders in Switzerland and Quebec in 1994
-The Heaven's Gate, another odd syncretic (apocalyptic Christian and "new-age") group led by Marshall Applewhite, that committed mass suicide (38 people) in Rancho Santa Fe, California, in 1997
-Aum Shinrikyo, a fairly extensive, secretive apocalyptic Japanese cult led by Shoko Asahara that carried out the sarin gas attack in the Tokyo subways in March 1995, killing 12 commuters, seriously injuring 54 others and affecting at least another thousand. The group had committed previous murders and crimes and had incredibly ambitious terrorist plans. (For a fascinating, in-depth look at the group and at the psychology of apocalypticism, see: *Destroying the World to Save It: Aum Shinrikyo, Apocalyptic Violence, and the New Global Terrorism* by Robert Jay Lifton (Metropolitan Books/Henry Holt, 1999).

The two examples I cite of false or uncertain information that were used to start or exacerbate wars:
-the "sinking" of the battleship Maine in Havana in 1898 helped precipitate the Spanish-American War because the rabid imperialist press of the day used it to whip up anti-Spanish sentiment, but the cause of the explosion that sank the ship remains a controversial mystery. The odds are the explosion was just an accident.
-the Gulf of Tonkin "incident" in August 1964 (actually two incidents), involved alleged

North Vietnamese attacks on a U.S. destroyer that were used to justify the large-scale involvement of U.S. troops in Vietnam and led to Congress' passage of the "Gulf of Tonkin Resolution" which basically granted President Johnson the authority to intervene militarily without a formal declaration of war (sound familiar?). It turned out at least one of the purported "attacks" never occurred and that the U.S. ship provoked the other minor skirmish.

- Carlos Castaneda (1925-1998) wrote 12 wildly popular books starting with the *Teachings of Don Juan* in 1968 that describe his supposed studies of shamanism with mysterious indigenous teachers. His accounts were widely believed to be factual (including by the anthropology department at UCLA, which awarded him a Ph.D. on the basis of this "research") until Richard de Mille systematically debunked them in the mid 1970s. In retrospect it's astonishing they were so uncritically accepted by not just the hippie subculture but by academics. The understanding of shamanism has become far more sophisticated since the 1960s, among specialists at least. Castaneda's work was certainly highly entertaining and even deeply insightful at times. There's no doubt he was a genius of sorts, but he was above all a genius of a con man. The strange circumstances surrounding his death and the disappearances (and likely suicides) of several of his closest female followers/lovers right after his death add a final mysterious (and creepy) addendum to his saga.

For an excellent history of the CIA's extensive involvement with LSD:
- *Acid Dreams: The CIA, LSD and the Sixties Rebellion* by Martin Lee and Bruce Shlain (Grove Press, 1986)

on the conspiracy theories that have sprung up surrounding 9/11 and their debunkers, there are too many books and websites and polls to even begin suggesting any. A quick look online will turn up thousands of sites and references.

on 2006 Scripps Howard/Ohio University poll on 9/11 conspiracy beliefs:
- "Third of Americans suspect 9-11 government conspiracy" by Thomas Hargrove, August 2006, in Scripps Howard News Service

-on Evangelicals as percentage of the electorate: www.pewresearch.org

-on Evangelicals' economic clout, see: Report Buyer's market analysis at:
www.reportbuyer.com/consumer_goods_retail/demographics/evangelical_christians_u_s.html

-one can find info on past CNN polls at: transcripts.cnn.com

-A good book on right wing populist ideology:
Right-wing Populism in America: Too Close for Comfort by Chip Berlet and Matthew Lyons (Guilford Press, 2000)

-Political Research Associates and their website (www.publiceye.org) and publications are invaluable resources for the study of the radical right

-see also: "How Apocalyptic and Millennialist Themes Influence Right Wing Scapegoating and Conspiracism" by Chip Berlet in The Public Eye magazine, Fall 1998

-Another very important group that tracks the far right is one founded in 1971 by Alabama civil rights attorney Morris Dees, The Southern Poverty Law Center, and its Intelligence Project (www.splcenter.org/intel/intpro)

a few scholarly books on U.S. apocalyptic millennialism:
-*Cosmos, Chaos and the World to Come: The Ancient Roots of Apocalyptic Faith* by Norman Cohn (Yale University Press, 1993)
-*Apocalypse: On the Psychology of Fundamentalism in America* by Charles B. Strozier (Beacon Press, 1994).
-*Naming the Antichrist: The History of an American Obsession* by Robert Fuller (Oxford University Press, 1995)
-*Millennium Rage: Survivalists, White Supremacists, and the Doomsday Prophecy* by Philip Lamy (Plenum, 1996)
-*Selling Fear: Conspiracy Theories and End-Times Paranoia* by Gregory S. Camp (Baker Books, 1997)
-*Millennium, Messiahs, and Mayhem: Contemporary Apocalyptic Movements*, Thomas Robbins and Susan J. Palmer, editors (Routledge, 1997)

one of the great contemporary scholars of religion has an excellent book on the history of the Devil:
-*The Origin of Satan* by Elaine Pagels (Vintage, 1996)

-I'm using the term "Marianist Catholics" as several others have to describe a far right, ultra conservative and mystically oriented wing of Catholic activism.

-the infamous Father Charles Edward Coughlin (1891-1979), a Roman Catholic priest, rabid anti-Semite, and borderline fascist, was one of the first political radio personalities to reach a mass audience (an estimated forty million plus) in the 1930s. He was in many ways a precursor of the contemporary right wing talk-radio stars.

-Adam Weishaupt, a Bavarian law professor and philosopher, drawing on Masonic, Gnostic and 18th Century rationalist and revolutionary ideas, founded a secret society, the Illuminati, in 1776 with a mission to establish a New World Order, i.e. the abolition of monarchy and organized religion.

-Thomas Pynchon's 1966 novel *The Crying of Lot 49* makes oblique reference to the Illuminati.

- *The Illuminatus! Trilogy*, three very popular and influential novels by Robert Shea and Robert Anton Wilson published in 1975, romp through a wide range of conspiracy theories, especially focusing on the authors' own fanciful take on the Illuminati. Many readers took much of this material way too seriously for their own mental health.

-Perhaps the first anti-Freemason paranoid conspiracy tome, John Robison's *Proofs of a Conspiracy Against All the Religions and Governments of Europe, carried on in the secret meetings of Free Masons, Illuminati, and Reading Societies, collected from good authorities*, is available in a modern reprint (Kessinger Publishing, 2003).

a few of the colorful late 19th/early 20th Century esotericists I mention:
-Aleister Crowley (1875-1947), the "bad boy" of British esotericism was a writer, poet, mountaineer, and junkie and was feared by many as a dark magician.
-Dion Fortune (1890-1946) was an influential occultist, novelist and author of a few well-known esoteric tomes: *The Cosmic Doctrine, The Mystical Qabalah*, and *Psychic Self Defence*.
-The very wild and fascinating Madame Blavatsky (1831-1891) was the founder of Theosophy and the very influential Theosophy Society.

-*Perpetual Peace and Other Essays* by the great German philosopher Immanuel Kant (1724-1804) includes some of the first ideas about transnational institutions to regulate world peace.

Just a few of the countless far right conspiracy-obsessed authors and their texts from the 20s to the 70s:
-Nesta Webster (1876-1960), a British aristocratic anti-Semite and fascist sympathizer who promoted conspiracy theories about the Illuminati's supposed links to communism, wrote books such as *World Revolution: The Plot Against Civilization* (1921) and: *Secret Societies and Subversive Movements* (1924).
-Father Denis Fahey (1883-1954) was a far right anti-Semitic Irish Catholic priest who wrote a number of books, including *The Mystical Body of Christ in the Modern World (1935); The Mystical Body of Christ and the Reorganization of Society* (1939); and *Grand Orient Freemasonry unmasked as the secret power behind communism* (1950).
-Gertrude Coogan's *Money Creators* (1935) was a rant about the covert control of the money supply by "alien outsiders" (i.e. Jews).
-Elizabeth Dilling (1894-1966), a rabid American anti-communist and anti-Semite was charged with sedition in 1944. She accused a wide range of famous people of being communist sympathizers, including Gandhi, Eleanor Roosevelt, and Freud in her four books, including *The Red Network, A Who's Who And Handbook Of Radicalism For Patriots* and *The Roosevelt Red Record and Its Background* in the 1930s, and *The Plot Against Christianity* in 1964.
-William G. Carr (1895-1959), a Canadian naval officer who wrote a number of histories of submarine warfare was also the leader of the anti-Communist National Federation of Christian Laymen of Toronto and one of the most influential far right conspiracy theorists with such works as: *Pawns in the Game* and *Red Fog over America* (both around 1955).
-Kenneth Goff, who claimed to be a Communist who turned against the "reds" was another influential 50s commie conspiracy-obsessed character, with his self-published pamphlets *Reds Promote Racial War* (1958) and *One World a Red World* (1952).
-with the still active Phyllis Schlafly, who emerged as an advocate of Goldwater-style con-

servatism in the 60s and is mostly known for her anti-feminism, we get a bit closer to the conservative mainstream, but her intense anti-communism brought her close at times to far right conspiracy thinking.

-Gary Allen, a contributing editor to the John Birch Society's American Opinion magazine who wrote speeches for former Gov. George Wallace during his presidential campaigns was a very influential organizer on the far right, whose most famous book was: *None Dare Call it Conspiracy* (1971).

-Hal Lindsey, an Evangelical "Christian Zionist" (like John Hagee), penned one of the most influential apocalyptic, "end times"-obsessed books of all time. His 1970 *The Late, Great Planet Earth* has sold more than 35 million copies in 54 languages.

- John F. Walvoord (1910-2002), President of the Dallas Theological Seminary from 1952 to 1986 was a major figure among "end times" believers and wrote some 20 books. His 1974 (and subsequent revised editions) *Armageddon, Oil, and the Middle East Crisis* was a major bestseller.

-The John Birch Society, founded by Robert W. Welch Jr. in 1958, was the most widely known extreme anti-Communist, anti-internationalist group in the 1960s, but seems almost tame today compared to the far more rabid sectors of the far right that have subsequently emerged.

-The Liberty Lobby (1955-2001), founded by Willis Carto, was a very far right conservative organization, influential at one point, but it became seriously tarred when the depth of Carto's anti-Semitism and racism was exposed, and it was ultimately denounced almost across the political spectrum.

-The "Christian Identity" movement is a term (coined by one Howard Rand, an American follower of a racist British Victorian theology of "British Israelism") that covers a range of very radical groups that hew to a convoluted racist theology that postulates that only white people have souls. Some groups associated with the movement committed robberies and murders in the 1980s (e.g. The Order). Significant figures in the formation of the movement include Wesley Swift (1913-1970), retired Col. William Potter Gale (1917-1988), a former aide to General Douglas MacArthur who became a leading figure in the paramilitary movements of the 1970s and 80s (including the Posse Comitatus) and helped found the militia movement; and Aryan Nations founder Richard Butler.

-The 1925 Scopes "Monkey" Trial was a famous Tennessee case that tested a law that made it illegal for any state-funded school in Tennessee "to teach any theory that denies the story of the Divine Creation of man as taught in the Bible." The history of the case is a complicated one because some local business leaders actually engineered the trial hoping the resulting publicity would help the town's economy. Three-time presidential candidate William Jennings Bryan was the main prosecutor, the world renowned Clarence Darrow was the defense lawyer, and the acerbic journalist H.L. Mencken covered it. The trial led to a 1955 play, a star-studded 1960 film, and TV movies in1965, 1988 and 1999, all titled *Inherit the Wind*.

-Moral Rearmament, a nondenominational religious revivalistic movement founded by U.S. churchman Frank N.D. Buchman (1878-1961), was globally influential in the late 30s through the 1960s. While not overtly a far right movement, it represented one of the first large scale involvements of Evangelical Christians in modern political affairs, and was accused of naiveté regarding the Nazis in the late 1930s.

-Rousas John Rushdoony (1916-2001), an Armenian-American Calvinist theologian is widely seen as a key figure in birthing the modern Christian right with his writings on Christian Reconstructionism, theonomy, and Dominionism. For an in-depth look at this complex figure who combined extreme theocratic and libertarian elements in his ideology, see: "The Libertarian Theocrats: The Long, Strange History of R.J. Rushdoony" by Michael J. McVicar, in The Public Eye Magazine, Fall 2007, Vol. 22, # 3 (www.publiceye.org/magazine/v22n3/libertarian.html).

- "Dominionism" or "Dominion Theology" is an ideology shared by a range of religious groups who believe that society should be governed by Biblical not secular law and who share a post-millennial interpretation of the End Times that requires that the Kingdom of God has to be established on Earth by true Christians before Christ can return. Overt Dominionists are a small minority among contemporary Evangelicals, but the ideology has had a far-reaching impact on the Christian right.

-regarding "spiritual warfare," *The Concise Dictionary of Christian Theology* by Millard Erickson defines it as: "The Christian's struggle against otherworldly forces." A whole subculture of mostly Pentecostal leaders and congregations who view themselves as "spiritual warriors" has arisen in recent years. Many of these people see secular political leaders and ideologies they dislike as influenced by Satan or demonic forces.
-on 2008 Republican Vice Presidential candidate Sarah Palin's affiliations with that movement," see - "Palin's Faith Linked to Form of Pentecostalism Known as Spiritual Warfare" by Laurie Goodstein in the NY Times, October 25, 2008

-David Noebel, the director of Summit Ministries in Manitou Springs, Colorado has written extensively since the 1960s on religion and popular culture and the evils of secular humanism. He really has a Beatles phobia, which is evident from the titles of just a few of this prolific author's many books:
-*Communism, hypnotism and the Beatles: An analysis of the Communist use of music, the Communist master music plan*, 1965
-*Rhythm, riots, and revolution: An analysis of the Communist use of music, the Communist master music plan*, 1966
-*The Beatles: A Study in Drugs, Sex, & Revolution*, 1969
-*The Marxist Minstrels: A Handbook on Communist Subversion of Music*, 1974
-*The Homosexual Revolution*, 1977
-*The Legacy of John Lennon: Charming or Harming a Generation?*, 1982

-The Covenant, the Sword and the Arm of the Lord (CSA), founded by Texas minister James Ellison in 1970, was a militia-style organization based in Arkansas, Missouri and Oklahoma

that was loosely affiliated with other white supremacist organizations such as the Aryan Nations, The Order, and the Militia of Montana. Between 1976 and 1985 the CSA was involved in weapons dealing, counterfeiting, arson, robbery, and murder. It was one of many militias that supported the American Christian Patriot Movement. It refused to recognize any form of government above the county level and wanted to achieve religious and racial purification of the U.S. On April 21, 1985, the FBI, ATF, and other law enforcement agencies raided the CSA's compound and seized weapons, ammo, explosives, gold, and thirty gallons of potassium cyanide (which the CSA intended to use to poison the water supply of several cities).
-for coverage of the CSA from the 80s, see: "Twisted 15-Year Path of CSA Winds to End as Leaders Convicted" by Michael Haddigan in the Arkansas Gazette, September 8, 1985

A few books on far-right armed groups:
-*Religion and the Racist Right: The Origins of the Christian Identity Movement* by Michael Barkun (University of North Carolina Press, 1997)
-*The Terrorist Next Door: The Militia Movement and the Radical Right* by Daniel Levitas (Thomas Dunne Books/St. Martin's Press, 2002)
-*Rural Radicals: From Bacon's Rebellion to the Oklahoma City Bombing* by Catherine Stock (Penguin Books, 1996)

-The Posse Comitatus, yet another armed group composed mostly of "Christian Identity" followers and some former Klan members, was active through the mid 90s. They only recognized county level government and therefore refused to pay taxes or even on occasion apply for drivers' licenses. In 1983, Posse member Gordon Kahl murdered two Federal marshals in North Dakota and became a fugitive and later died in a shootout with Arkansas cops in which a local sheriff was also killed. Kahl became a martyr to far right extremists all over the country. In 1987, retired colonel William Potter Gale, one of the founders of the Posse movement that I mentioned in an earlier note, and four others were convicted of threatening to kill IRS agents and a Nevada state judge.

-The Minuteman Project is a highly controversial anti illegal immigration group started in 2005 to monitor the U.S.-Mexico border. It describes itself as "a citizens' Neighborhood Watch on our border."

for an account of attacks on Forest Service employees by far-right local activists in northern Nevada, see:
- "Nature's Guardians Still Face Disrespect" by Jeff Ruch in the NY Times, (Op-Ed) December 22, 1999
- "Citizen Flora: The rise, fall, and resurrection of a Forest Service whistleblower" by Todd Wilkinson in the September/October 2003 issue of Orion magazine

-The World Social Forum (WSF) is a large annual meeting of groups from around the world that oppose the current forms of economic globalization. First held in Porto Allegre, Brazil, in 2001, the WSF usually meets each January because that's when its arch-nemesis, the World Economic Forum, gathers in Davos, Switzerland.

-Via Campesina (www.viacampesina.org/) is, in its own words, "an international movement which coordinates peasant organizations of small and middle-scale producers, agricultural workers, rural women, and indigenous communities from Asia, Africa, America, and Europe." The coalition of over 100 groups advocates human scale, family-farm-based sustainable agriculture and "food security" and "food sovereignty." Founded in 1992 by Rafael Alegria, its most famous member is the activist French farmer José Bové. Originally headquartered in Tegucigalpa, Honduras, its main office is now in Jakarta, Indonesia.

-The Slow Food movement (www.slowfood.com/), initially founded by Carlo Petrini in Italy in 1989 to combat fast food, seeks to resist the globalization and homogenization of agriculture and to preserve traditional cultural cuisines and the diverse, plants, seeds, farm animals, and regional styles of farming associated with them. The movement has grown globally to include more than 80,000 members in 122 countries. In 2004 Slow Food opened a University of Gastronomic Sciences in Northern Italy. The movement's goals have expanded to include: creating seed banks to preserve heirloom varieties of food crops in cooperation with local farmers; educating consumers about the risks of fast food, agribusiness, monoculture, and factory farms; defending family farms and organic farming; encouraging "fair trade" initiatives; and resisting genetic engineering of foods and the use of pesticides.

Princeton biology professor Lee Silver pushes his techno-utopian ideas in:
-*Remaking Eden: How Genetic Engineering and Cloning Will Transform the American Family* (Weidenfeld & Nicholson, 1998)
-*Challenging Nature: The Clash of Science and Spirituality at the New Frontiers of Life* (Ecco, 2006)

some of the main figures who tout an age of robots superior to humans:
-Marvin Minsky, the co-founder of the MIT Artificial Intelligence Laboratory and an author of books including *The Emotion Machine* (Simon & Shuster, 2006)
-Hans Moravec of the Robotics Institute at Carnegie Mellon, author of *Robot: Mere Machine to Transcendent Mind* (Oxford University Press, 2000)

-Extropians believe that science and technological breakthroughs (especially in biomedicine, life extension, genetics, robotics and nanotech) will someday soon give people the chance to live indefinitely. The main figure in launching the concept in 1988 was Max More, an academic and cryonics entrepreneur, who co-founded "Extropy: The Journal of Transhumanist Thought" and the Extropy Institute, which produced the first conferences on "transhumanism," but closed its doors in 2006.

-Vernor Vinge, a retired mathematics professor and computer scientist, is a science fiction author most famous for a highly influential 1993 essay "The Coming Technological Singularity" that makes the bold claim that exponential growth in technology will soon lead to a new, unknowable post-human era.

Ray Kurzweil, the inventor/futurist/techno-utopian, is the author of several very popular

books, including:
-*The Age of Intelligent Machines* (1990)
-*The Age of Spiritual Machines: When Computers Exceed Human Intelligence* (1999)
-*Fantastic Voyage: Live Long Enough to Live Forever* (2004)
-*The Singularity Is Near: When Humans Transcend Biology* (2005)

-the Luddites were early 1800s British textile workers who sabotaged new mechanized looms which threatened their livelihood. The term Luddite has by extension come to describe anyone in strong opposition to the impacts of technology. The movement was crushed by the British army in 1812 and many Luddites were executed.

-the word "saboteur" is thought by some to have originated during the early Industrial Revolution in Lyons' sewing factories in France when, it is said, in acts akin to those of the British Luddites, the workers would intentionally "clog" the looms with their wooden clogs ("*sabots*" in French). Others dispute that this ever happened and therefore reject that etymology and instead trace the origin of the term to a 1910 French railroad strike.

-William Blake's cursing of the "Satanic Mills" is in his preface to his *Milton: a Poem* (1804). The "Satanic mills" in question are thought by many to refer to the early industrial revolution and its destruction of nature. The Albion Flour Mills, one of the first big factories in London, built in 1769 (powered by steam engines) that burned down (perhaps arson) in1791, were referred to as Satanic by the locals...and the mills were very close to Blake's house. Here's the poem:

And did those feet in ancient time,
Walk upon England's mountains green
And was the holy Lamb of God,
On England's pleasant pastures seen
And did the Countenance Divine,
Shine forth upon our clouded hills?
And was Jerusalem builded here,
Among these dark Satanic Mills?

Bring me my Bow of burning gold;
Bring me my Arrows of desire:
Bring me my Spear: O clouds unfold:
Bring me my Chariot of fire!
I will not cease from Mental Fight,
Nor shall my sword sleep in my hand,
Till we have built Jerusalem,
In England's green and pleasant Land.

I mention some films that offer cautionary tales about technology:
-*THX 1138* (1971), George Lucas's first feature, portrays a dystopian future society in which the state uses constant surveillance, android police and mandatory use of drugs to suppress

emotions and sexual desire.

-*Farenheit 451* is François Truffaut's film adaptation of a 1953 science fiction novel by Ray Bradbury that describes a society in which books are banned and burned when found.

-*2001: A Space Oddysey* (1968), Stanley Kubrick's epic co-written by Arthur C. Clark, famously included a homicidal computer, HAL, who resorts to murder because he is "terrified" of being disconnected.

I list a number of science fiction writers and works that present at times dystopian pictures of technology's impacts on humanity:

-Aldous Huxley's prophetic 1932 *Brave New World* describes a world in which genetics are destiny and mood altering drugs and entertainment keep the population happily, permanently distracted.

-George Orwell *1984* is of course the great classic about propaganda and government control of all information.

-Mary Shelley's *Frankenstein; or, The Modern Prometheus*, written when she was 18 and 19 (!) and first published anonymously in 1818, is the classic foundational cautionary tale about the dangers of uncontrolled scientific hubris.

-John Brunner's *The Sheep Look Up* (1972) painted a dire but prophetic picture of the deterioration of the environment. It's perhaps the classic eco-dystopian novel.

-Philip K. Dick (1928-1982) was such a prolific writer and complex figure, with as many spiritual obsessions as socio-political ones, that it would be unfair to pigeonhole him as a dystopian writer, but he is nothing if not paranoid about government's and large corporations' uses of technologies and propaganda.

-Norman Spinrad is also far too prolific a writer and one who covers many themes, so he too can't be easily categorized, but a profound cynicism about the use of technologies by those in power does permeate quite a few of his main books.

- "Cyberpunk"-a term used to describe a number of sci-fi writers in the 1980s, such as William Gibson, Bruce Sterling, John Shirley, Rudy Rucker, Pat Cadigan, and Lewis Shiner, later became used more broadly to describe a larger aesthetic sensibility. Cyberpunk is ambivalent about technology: its "film noir"-style stories are invariably set in post-industrial dystopias where mega-corporations use technologies to pursue their nefarious ends, but the heroic protagonists find ways to use very "cool" technologies for their own ends as well.

Another older tradition in sci-fi is composed of writers who are far more sanguine about technology and progress. They include:

-Isaac Asimov (1920-1992): the incredibly prolific rationalist/humanist known mostly for the *Foundation* series is basically a great believer in progress and the human capacity to build rational systems.

-Jules Verne (1828-1905): the French writer who was the greatest pioneer of science-fiction as a genre was not only prophetic about coming technologies (he wrote about submarines, planes and space travel before any of them existed) but did more than perhaps anyone else to excite people about the promise of technology.

-H.G. Wells (1866-1946), the other "father of sci-fi" (along with Verne), while he did pen the occasional dystopian story, is mostly remembered as a utopian rationalist. His *The Shape of Things to Come* (1933), made into the 1936 film, *Things to Come*, anticipated the coming

World War, but posited that the ultimate resolution of humanity's warlike impulses lay with a world government run by scientists.

I mention a couple of notable scientists known to have used LSD:
-Kary Mullis who shared the 1993 Nobel Prize in Chemistry for his development of the Polymerase Chain Reaction, a now key technique in biochemistry and molecular biology, is a colorful, controversial and at times wacky character.
-Francis Crick (1916-2004), the English molecular biologist, physicist and neuroscientist, co-discoverer of the structure of DNA in 1953 and co-winner of the1962 Nobel Prize in Medicine, was known to have experimented with LSD, but his use of the drug came long after his work on DNA.

-Here are a few excerpted lines from the "Moloch" section of the late, great Allen Ginsberg's (1926-1997) famous epic 1955 poem *Howl* that capture his critique of the soullessness of modernity. His vision of Moloch was apparently inspired by a peyote-induced vision and by parts of Fritz Lang's classic silent film, *Metropolis*.

"What sphinx of cement and aluminum bashed open their skulls and ate up their brains and imagination?

Moloch! Solitude! Filth! Ugliness! Ashcans and unobtainable dollars! Children screaming under the stairways! Boys sobbing in armies! Old men weeping in the parks!

Moloch! Moloch! Nightmare of Moloch! Moloch the loveless! Mental Moloch! Moloch the heavy judger of men!

Moloch the incomprehensible prison! Moloch the crossbone soulless jailhouse and Congress of sorrows! Moloch whose buildings are judgement! Moloch the vast stone of war! Moloch the stunned governments!

Moloch whose mind is pure machinery! Moloch whose blood is running money! Moloch whose fingers are ten armies! Moloch whose breast is a cannibal dynamo! Moloch whose ear is a smoking tomb!

Moloch whose eyes are a thousand blind windows! Moloch whose skyscrapers stand in the long streets like endless Jehovas! Moloch whose factories dream and choke in the fog! Moloch whose smokestacks and antennae crown the cities!

Moloch whose love is endless oil and stone! Moloch whose soul is electricity and banks! Moloch whose poverty is the specter of genius! Moloch whose fate is a cloud of sexless hydrogen! Moloch whose name is the Mind!

(...)

Moloch! Moloch! Robot apartments! invisible suburbs! skeleton treasuries! blind capitals! demonic industries! spectral nations! invincible madhouses! granite cocks! monstrous bombs!

-Mondo 2000 (originally High Frontiers, then Reality Hackers) was a super-hip, Berkeley, California-based, early cyberculture/cyberpunk magazine in the 1980s and 1990s, founded by R.U. Sirius (Ken Goffman) and Queen Mu (Allyson Kennedy). The later, far more mainstream Wired was a watered-down, tamer version of Mondo.

-I mention the Beatles' classic 1967 album, *Sergeant Pepper's Lonely Hearts Club Band* because it was seen at the time as a state-of-the-art use of new recording technologies that permitted far more complex layers of sound, thus representing the embrace and pioneering use of sophisticated new technologies by certain sectors of the counterculture.
The Rolling Stones' album, *Their Satanic Majesties Request* (very unfairly maligned by some critics as an inferior imitation of Sergeant Pepper's) that same year, also went down this high tech production route. Those two albums along with Pink Floyd's early work probably represent a high-water mark for a psychedelic techno-utopian aesthetic as expressed through rock music.

-Terence McKenna (1946-2000), a writer, philosopher, ethnobotanist and incredibly gifted speaker, was the most significant, interesting, creative and provocative figure in the psychedelic counterculture in the 1980s and 1990s and in the revival of interest in the use of psychoactive plants by shamans. Terence had complex ideas about the possibilities of predicting "ingressions of novelty" in human affairs and speculated about some sort of major shift/transcendental end point in the year 2012.

-Arthur Clarke's 1953 sci-fi novel *Childhood's End* recounts humanity's transformation into a higher, non-corporeal form of existence (merger with "the Overmind"). This theme recurs in many forms, both in secular and religious forms: Teilhard de Chardin's Omega Point mentioned earlier, Vernor Vinge's and the extropians' much anticipated technological singularity, and in several Gnostic sects, as well as in the belief in the Rapture and End Times so important to many Evangelical Christians.

- Gnosticism is a broad term that describes a range of Neo-Platonic mystical traditions that were especially active in what is now Egypt and Syria in the first few centuries BCE, though there are still Gnostic practitioners of many stripes today. But I am using the adjective "Gnostic" as shorthand to describe an attitude of disdain for the flesh and a desire to evolve into pure mind. The word has come to be used that way because some (not all) Gnostic sects espoused that sort of mind-body dualism.

- José Arguelles, the creator of the "Harmonic Convergence" events held all over the world in 1987 (see his book: *The Mayan Factor: Path Beyond Technology,* Inner Traditions/Bear & Company, 1987) is another major figure in this current new age obsession/fad with deciphering the ancient Maya calendar to predict major coming events (that always involve some epochal collective shift to "new-age" spiritual realizations of one type or another).

-Edgar Cayce (1877-1945) is probably the most famous psychic in U.S. history. He would go into trance and answer his clients' questions, mostly about health, but he also made a wide range of predictions about coming historical developments that have been an object of fascination for many people. Cayce's ideas exerted a significant influence on the New Age Movement.

Here are sources for a few of the more widely known Native (North) American prophecies:

-Hopi Prophecy: see "Thomas Banacyca Talks about the Hopi Prophecy" at: www.welcomehome.org/rainbow/prophecy/bayanaca.html

-*Black Elk Speaks*, by John G. Neihardt (Washington Square Press, 1972, originally published in 1932), a translation of the oral history that the Oglala Sioux medicine man Black Elk shared with Neihardt in 1931.

-for some Iroquois Prophecies: wovoca.com/prophecy-iroquois-index.htm

Also, an upcoming book (not out yet as I was finishing this text) looks like it could potentially offer a serious survey of the topic:

-*Coming Down from Above: Prophecy, Resistance, and Renewal in Native American Religions* (Civilization of the American Indian Series) by Lee Irwin (University of Oklahoma Press (due out December 31, 2008)

-Nostradamus: I am not at all a complete skeptic about the "paranormal" or the possibility of precognition in some instances, but so much nonsense has been written about Michel de Nostredame (1503-1566) and his supposed predictions of world events in *Les Prophéties* (1555), that I would just like to point out that almost none of the wild claims made by generations of enthusiasts are based on accurate translations and that his actual words are vague enough to be able to accommodate nearly any interpretation. There has been a very sizeable body of solid scholarly work in France that convincingly rebuts nearly all the silly claims about Nostradamus' quatrains made over the years.

-The annual Burning Man festival in the Nevada desert that began as a small artists' bonfire party on a San Francisco beach in the 1980s, has become a giant avant-garde arts and radical self-expression extravaganza that is also a major focal point of contemporary psychedelic culture.

-The Millerites were the followers of William Miller who convinced his flock that the Second Advent of Jesus Christ was coming around1843 and to prepare themselves. It was a fairly large group with a national and even international following. Some Millerites abandoned all their earthly goods and waited on hillsides. A few predicted dates came and went and then after a lot of Biblical nitpicking and interpretation the movement settled on October 22nd 1844 as the big day. When nothing happened, the reaction came to be called "the Great Disappointment." Some clung to their beliefs and created a range of theological rationalizations. The majority joined other denominations and got on with their lives.

- Daniel Pinchbeck's two books are: *Breaking Open the Head: A Psychedelic Journey into the Heart of Contemporary Shamanism*, (Broadway Books, 2002); and *2012: The Return of Quetzalcoatl*, (Tarcher, 2006)

- Art Bell's late night radio show, Coast to Coast AM, which often dealt with paranormal, "fringe" topics, was wildly popular and was on over 500 stations nationwide until his recent retirement.

-Whitley Streiber's 1987 book, *Communion*, which Strieber maintained was based on his real life experiences, was a major marker in the eruption of interest in alien abductions in the 1980s and 1990s. It sold well upwards of 2 million copies.

-To get information on accessing data on past Roper Polls, contact the Roper Center for Public Opinion Research at: www.ropercenter.uconn.edu/
-For a detailed analysis of the 2 Roper polls on UFOs (1991 and 1998) by a pro-UFO but coherent source, see the National Institute for Discovery Science's site: nidsci.org/news/roper_surveys.html
-on the 2002 Roper poll on UFOs done for cable TV's Sci-Fi Network, see:
"Roper Poll Commissioned by SCI FI Channel Finds 2.9 Million Americans Report Symptoms Associated With UFO Abductions; 18-24 Year Olds More Likely to Have Had Symptoms" on Business Wire, Nov 20, 2002 (www.businesswire.com/portal/site/home/)

-*The Day the Earth Stood Still*, a 1951 film notable for being one of the few pro-peace, somewhat lefty sci-fi films during the McCarthy era and for its cool use of the theremin in its soundtrack, tells the story of an Intergalactic cop (Michael Rennie) with a really awesome robot (Gort) who comes to warn (and threaten) earthlings to play nice with nukes or face annihilation.

-Kenneth Arnold (1915-1984) was a pilot who made the first widely reported UFO sighting in the U.S., of nine saucer shaped objects flying near Mount Rainier in Washington State on June 24, 1947. The new term "flying saucer" caught on in the press, and hundreds of sightings around the country followed Arnold's sighting.

-C. G. Jung's discussion of UFOs is in his: *Flying Saucers: A Modern Myth of Things Seen in the Skies* (Harcourt, 1959)

-Jim Schnabel's take on the resemblance between current reported alien encounters and older visions of demons and angels is in: *Dark White: Aliens, Abductions and the UFO Obsession* by Jim Schnabel (Hamish Hamilton/Penguin,1994)

-Carl Sagan (1934-1996) the renowned astronomer, writer and popularizer of science who pioneered the Search for Extra-Terrestrial Intelligence (SETI), was also a leading (though usually moderate and thoughtful) skeptic about UFOs. He was the co-author of: *UFO's: A Scientific Debate* (Cornell University Press, 1972)

-John Mack (1929-2004), a psychiatrist and professor at Harvard's School of Medicine as well as a Pulitzer Prize-winning biographer, became the most prestigious academic researcher to take the alien encounter/abduction phenomenon seriously, causing great controversy at Harvard. His main book on the subject is: *Abduction: Human Encounters with Aliens* by John E. Mack (Scribner, 1994)

-Jacques F. Vallée, a French-born entrepreneur, computer scientist and former astronomer (and the model for the character played by François Truffaut in Steven Spielberg's *Close Encounters of the Third Kind*) who helped map Mars for NASA and helped create ARPANET, the antecedent to the Internet, is one of the most fascinating and complex investigators, writers and thinkers on the UFO phenomenon. Initially a believer in the extraterrestrial origin of UFOs, he became convinced something far weirder and more mysterious and multi-layered was going on, and alienated many of the true believers in the UFO community (see: "Five Arguments Against the Extraterrestrial Origin of Unidentified Flying Objects" in the Journal of Scientific Exploration, 1990) leading Vallée to call himself "a heretic among heretics." He wrote a number of books on the topic, including one that prophetically warned of the risks inherent in authoritarian UFO-based cults, *Messengers of Deception: UFO Contacts and Cults* (Ronin Publishing, 1979).

-Budd Hopkins, a well-known artist, became one of the main advocates for the literal veracity of UFO abduction narratives in the 1980s. His main book on the topic is: *Missing Time* (Berkley, 1983)

-There's background about Colonel H. G. Shaw's 1897 reported encounter with aliens as reported in the Stockton Daily Mail of that era at:
www.virtuallystrange.net/ufo/updates/2004/mar/m19-001.shtml

-Jerome Clark, one of the most serious and widely respected UFO researchers who ultimately became an open minded agnostic about the phenomenon, has written perhaps the most comprehensive survey of the whole topic in: *The UFO Encyclopedia: The Phenomenon From The Beginning* (2-Volume Set) (Omnigraphics Books, 1998).

-There's been a lot written about Barney and Betty Hill's experience, which occurred in 1961 but didn't become news till later. There was even a TV movie. For coverage from the time, see: "Testament for Believers" in Time Magazine, November 18, 1966.

- Dr. Michael Persinger theories on abduction experiences and mystical states' links to electromagnetic patterns in the brain are discussed in:
"The UFO Experience: A Normal Correlate of Human Brain Function," by Michael Persinger, pp 262-302 in *UFOs and Abductions: Challenging the Borders of Knowledge*, David M. Jacobs, editor (University Press of Kansas, 2000)

-*Guns, Germs and Steel: The Fates of Human Societies* by Jared Diamond (Norton, 1996).

CONCLUSION

I said at the onset that I was going to try to convince you, esteemed reader, that we Americans were collectively far less mentally balanced, far druggier, far kinkier and more hypocritical in our sex lives, more corrupt and unhinged in our relationship to money, and far zanier in our core beliefs than we generally assume, and that the overt and unspoken assumptions about these spheres of life that are dominant in our media at best sugarcoat the painful truth or are simply delusional. How convincing I have been is obviously for you to decide.

To recap, in the first chapter I marshaled evidence that I think establishes quite solidly that: close to or maybe even more than half our population will at some point suffer from at least one relatively serious bout of mental health problems; fairly substantial segments of our population are deeply troubled at any moment, and their numbers seem to be increasing rapidly. The fact that bigger and bigger swaths of the population, including more and more young children and adolescents, are being given powerful psychotropic medications is not in dispute. A reasonable, impartial outside observer could easily come to the conclusion that ours is an extremely mentally unhealthy society. It's in fact hard to imagine what else that observer could conclude.

As to drug use, the evidence, especially that drawn from the government's own most serious and rigorous long-term studies of the matter, seems incontrovertible: a majority, most likely a sizeable majority, of Americans has at least dabbled in illegal drug use, and while that use fluctuates a bit over the years, it seems to be a permanent feature of the nation's collective behavior, especially as a right of passage for the young. The use of over-consumed or illicitly diverted, synthetic prescription drugs (far more powerful than most conventional "street" drugs) now represents a far more serious health hazard than previous generations of illegal drugs. Given the fact that it's far more common to have tried an illegal drug at some point than not to have, our drug laws are astonishingly hypocritical.

Sex is a more difficult landscape to reach definitive conclusions about. It's nearly impossible to get impeccably honest answers from participants in surveys or polls on sex-related topics. Also it's been a domain of life that has undergone profound transformations in just a few decades. The social norms and institutions that surround it are in rapid flux, and the Internet is bringing radical changes to erotic behavior in ways we don't yet have a firm grasp of. What is pretty clear is that, even though we can't be totally confident about any of the statistical sources, behaviors such as marital infidelity and prostitution and viewing pornography are more widespread than is usually acknowledged; that lifelong monogamy, still held up as a sort of de facto ideal, is an exceedingly rare phenomenon; and that the population of aficionados of the wide array of "kinks" that emerge from the exuberantly creative human erotic imagination is also most likely much bigger than usually recognized.

In the chapter on money, I argue, mostly with anecdotal evidence and with some statistical support at times, that money by its very nature engenders corruption, and that corruption, far from an aberration, is in fact a foundational norm, a pillar of our economic structures at every level from the local to the international. No surprise then that our relationships to money are so problematic and lead so many of us into irrational behaviors from gambling to compulsive shopping as well as into widespread petty theft and cheating on our taxes. This may be the domain of life in which we are most insecure and about which honest discussion is most absent because it goes to the heart of the built-in inequalities and inconsistencies in our social order.

Finally I examined some aspects of the American belief landscape and found that extremely un-mainstream ideas and a range of apocalyptic prophecies and conspiracy theories are far, far more prevalent than is usually recognized, and that most likely a majority of us holds ideas at the core of our worldviews that the "dominant discourse" of the sophisticated elites would view as extremely marginal or as outright lunacy.

"So," I hear the reader who has slogged through all this (and if you are such a reader, I offer you my profound gratitude) say, "what's the point? What good does it do to have such a pessimistic outlook, even if much of what you say is true?" My reply to this excellent question is that it's much harder to transform a situation for the good if one doesn't have a realistic assessment of the facts on the ground. Pretending things are rosier than they are might actually serve to perpetuate the underlying problems, because how can you confront something if you haven't admitted it exists or if you've radically underestimated its scope? As we've seen so tragically in Iraq, going into a complex situation without a solid understanding of its social dynamics and history guarantees failure.

In the U.S., many on the right view any analyses of our society that high-light unflattering truths as close to treasonous, so politicians are forced to frame any timid looks at deep social problems by endlessly reiterating the mantra that we are the greatest nation on Earth and can solve our challenges if we just elect them and roll up our sleeves a bit. This prevents any honest, sustained look at the deeply systemic problems we face, from the global envi-ronmental catastrophe underway to crises in our health care to wisely nego-tiating the inevitable erosion of our imperial dominance. These all defy easy solutions. If we were going to begin even partially addressing these existen-tial threats in any serious fashion, they would all require truly radical changes in our lives, institutions, and our very guiding paradigms. Perhaps most dif-ficult for Americans whose worldview is so rooted in the myth of limitless-ness, we would have to face the implacable reality of limits: to ecosystems, population, consumption patterns, our political and economic power, and our capacity to dominate nature. As long as we don't face all these things squarely, we have absolutely no hope of tackling them.

If we admitted how widespread mental illness was in our society, we might become far more focused on finding humane treatments, and we might, more importantly, begin to try to understand why our society gener-ates so much of it. Might there be, besides the physiological and genetic components of such illness, deep civilizational factors at play? Might our: lifestyles, dwellings, transportation systems, diets, schools, cultural and rela-tional attitudes, environmental toxins, and the severance of our ties to human-scale communities and to the natural world (what Richard Louv has coined "nature deficit disorder") be contributing factors to this epidemic? We might begin to take a hard look at our society, one in which in 50 years the prison population has quintupled, violent crime quadrupled, teen suicide tripled, and divorce rates doubled, one in which people work longer hours and commute further and which does far worse by nearly all measures of public health than nearly any other "developed" country. We might ask ourselves why Americans, not long ago the world's tallest people on average (considered to be one of the best indicators of a population's health and vigor) are now fatter and shorter on average than nearly all Europeans-a pretty sure sign of neglected and badly fed children.

If we owned up to the fact that nearly all societies have consumed drugs and that a totally drug-free society is a ridiculously impossible goal, we could take a calm, reasoned look at our drug policies and adopt far more enlightened, less hypocritical approaches. We could decriminalize the least harmful as quite a few European countries have done, and use "harm reduction" rather than punitive suppression as our main guiding principle, and we could begin to draw down from the insane, un-winnable, unbelievably destructive and expensive "war on drugs," which has most likely ruined far more lives than even the worst drugs have and which squanders so much energy and so many resources that we badly need to deploy in other far more important arenas.

As to sex, unlike the situation with drugs, which has been static and unproductively stuck for so long because no major political figures have been willing to tackle it honestly and courageously, mores and attitudes are changing so fast that it's the culture itself that is proving to be the main, seemingly unstoppable force for increased tolerance and broad-mindedness. That said, we are still extremely squeamish about studying the whole galaxy of sexual predilections, and very, very confused about sex roles. More honesty and realism about topics such as the widening ways in which people form "families," the rarity of monogamy in nature, and the extent of prostitution certainly couldn't do any harm and might lead to better ways to address a wide range of sex-related conundrums.

On the subject of money, I realize that my views are quite radical and out of fashion, and I don't expect much can be done. I can bemoan money's toxicity as much as I want, but it's so fundamental to economic life one has to accept its inevitability and permanence. At the very least though, if we could wrap our brains around the fact that corruption is endemic and central in any system in which power and wealth are intertwined instead of buying into the childish illusion that "the system" is mostly honest with an occasional bad apple, we could more seriously revisit the ideal of real checks and balances in all our institutions and strive for much higher levels of permanent vigilance and transparency in our markets and political bodies. This is the toughest arena, of course, because it's where the most powerful vested interests have already rigged the game, so profound, authentic change only occurs in this sphere during those rare historical periods when dramatic crises shake loose the hold of an old order, and even then, most segments of that ruling elite usually re-assert themselves in slightly new configurations rather quickly.

Finally, the only domain that actually scared me was the wild and wooly realm of the nation's belief systems. I had some sense going in that many people have very offbeat worldviews, but the extent of it and the statistics spooked me. As I mentioned I have quite a few very offbeat ideological and spiritual/philosophical inclinations of my own, and I'm distrustful of much "mainstream" ideology, but I still view the best current scientific understanding (and yes, what constitutes the "best" science is in itself contentious) and reasoned deduction based on available facts as common reference points that can keep us all tethered to terra firma, whatever our other perspectives may be. I figure we can all be as zany as we want to be in our homes and specialized circles, but that rational norms of evidence for tangible phenomena have to be one of the core foundations for trying to settle most of our affairs in the commons.

I'm not at all saying that science offers any solid basis for morality, ethics and guiding principles: those are evolving human constructs we have to negotiate socially and about which there will always be strong disagreements, and religious, spiritual and various philosophical perspectives definitely all figure prominently in shaping our deepest values. But it's impossible to have those debates if our fundamental perceptions of reality and our interpretation of facts on the ground are so radically at odds. Without some sort of common language and universally agreed upon norms of evidence, there can't even be productive dialogue. C.P. Snow wrote famously of the divide between "two cultures" in the intelligentsia in the middle of the 20th Century, the scientific and that of the Humanities, but that is a puny intellectual divide compared to the ones we currently face.

Realizing just how widespread extremely paranoid, unsophisticated utopian belief constellations are at the moment terrified me a bit. Given how unstable a period this is, as climatic destabilization and other factors continue to unravel ecosystems and send floods of migrants on the move, as key raw materials become increasingly scarce, as one global empire declines and another emerges (always a period of instability and almost always of eventual war), and as nuclear weapons continue to proliferate, the fact that so many of us harbor such bizarre and unmoored beliefs adds to my already considerable apprehensions. The overall picture of the nation's ideological landscape scared me enough to make me wonder whether it was wise trying to bring it to people's attention, as perhaps this was one domain in which preserving the illusion of a sane, normal center might be the wisest course, one fig leaf not worth peering behind.

In the end, though, I keep, ultimately, coming down on the side of trying to clear away the fog of illusions to face the facts, no matter how depressing or frightening. Ignorance and delusion may work for a while. They may keep individuals happier than they might otherwise be and some societies persevering a bit beyond their shelf-lives during some historical periods, but they tend not to be very helpful when those inevitable crises re-introduce us to the nastiest Goddess of them all, Reality. She's a mysterious, tricky deity and very hard to define or decipher, but it's best to worship at her altar as often as possible, because she really doesn't like to be ignored, and her wrath is so…real.

Notes:

Richard Louv discusses "nature deficit disorder" in:
-*Last Child in the Woods* (Algonquin Books, 2005)

on the respective heights of people in the U.S. and Europe:
-"Underperformance in Affluence:The Remarkable Relative Decline in U.S. Heights in the Second Half of the 20th Century" by John Komlos and Benjamin E. Lauderdale in Social Science Quarterly, 2007, vol. 88, issue 2, pages 283-305

-C.P. Snow (1905-1980) was an English physicist, novelist and government official best known for " The Two Cultures," a 1959 lecture in which he decried the cultural separation between scientists and "literary intellectuals."

❋ ❋ ❋ ❋ ❋

Author Bio

J. P. Harpignies, a writer/editor and environmental activist, is an associate producer of the annual Bioneers conference, a former program director at the New York Open Center, the author of two previous books, *Political Ecosystems* (Spuyten Duyvil, 2004) and *Double Helix Hubris* (Cool Grove Press, 1997), editor of the collection *Visionary Plant Consciousness* (Park Street Press, 2007), and associate editor of the Bioneers books *Ecological Medicine and Nature's Operating Instructions* (both Sierra Club Books, 2004). J.P. was also, until recently a long-time instructor of taijiquan in Brooklyn, NY and co-founded the Eco-Metropolis conference in New York City.

Coolgrovepress with Ruthless Reality Institute, Brooklyn, New York